MOBILITY
OF
FARM FAMILIES

Author and publishers are grateful to the Dartington Hall Trustees for having commissioned this study and for a grant towards the cost of publication.

MOBILITY
OF
FARM FAMILIES

A STUDY OF OCCUPATIONAL
AND RESIDENTIAL MOBILITY
IN AN UPLAND AREA OF ENGLAND

by

J. S. NALSON

Professor of Sociology,
University of New England, Australia

MANCHESTER UNIVERSITY PRESS
UNIVERSITY OF WESTERN AUSTRALIA PRESS

© Manchester University Press, 1968

Published by the University of Manchester at
THE UNIVERSITY PRESS
316–324, Oxford Road
Manchester, 13

in association with

University of Western Australia Press
Nedlands
Western Australia

distributed in the U.S.A. by

The Humanities Press, Inc.
303 Park Avenue South
New York, 10010, N.Y.

GB SBN 7190 0299 O

Made and Printed in Great Britain by Butler & Tanner Ltd., Frome and London

CONTENTS

CONTENTS

CONTENTS

LIST OF TABLES

PREFACE

IN this study some facts are presented about the occupational and residential mobility of a defined population of farm people. Some of the social and economic influences on that mobility are discussed and the findings are related to other evidence on the mobility of farmers, and to those farming problems where mobility is considered to be important.

The study relates to conditions in an upland district in which the population has been declining for over one hundred years, and whose farmers are at an economic disadvantage compared with many others producing the same products. By describing the mobility of farmers in such an area, it is hoped to mirror what may be happening in similar areas, and what might happen over a larger sector of the farming industry in Britain, if economic and political conditions become less favourable for agriculture.

The area of study has not been named for two reasons. One is because I hope to preserve the anonymity of the people who generously provided information about themselves and their relatives. The other is because I do not consider that the exact location of the study is important. The important need was to study intensively the mobility of a defined population of farm people. The particular area chosen provided a suitable population but a similar study could have been made elsewhere.

The initial stimulus to undertake this work came from a consideration of the economic problems of agriculture, but the extent of mobility and of the structural farming changes associated with it clearly do not depend upon economic influences alone. Consequently, sociology and social anthropology have been freely drawn upon in formulating methods of study, in developing ideas as to the nature of mobility, and in drawing conclusions. I offer no excuses for stepping outside the bounds of one discipline for I feel that only by so doing have I been able to demonstrate and explain the patterns of mobility and the structural changes occurring in the farming area studied.

The argument for an intensive study of the mobility of farm people is presented in the first chapter. In this, reference is made to other studies bearing upon the mobility of farmers, but further discussion of such studies is deferred until the penultimate chapter in which the findings of my study are related to those of other studies and to farming problems with which mobility is associated. In the final chapter, suggestions are made for the amelioration of these problems by subsidizing mobility.

Chapter XI draws together in simplified form the findings of this study. The detailed study is presented in chapters II to X.

In chapter II the area of study and the farms are described. Reference is also made to the economic and social circumstances in the past, under the influence of which the present type of farming and pattern of settlement has evolved.

The demography of the farm people is presented in chapter III. Interrelationships are examined between the stages in the family developmental cycle, household size, the farm resources available to the family and work off the farm by family members.

The broad pattern of mobility in the area is presented in chapter IV. Mobility in relation to land, locality and occupation is considered for and between the different generations of farm people.

In chapters V to VIII the different types and degrees of mobility of farmers are considered for the various socio-economic groupings, and comparisons are made between the mobility of the farmers and that of their children.

Demographic influences on mobility are discussed in chapter IX and in chapter X the influence of the home environment on children is indicated, together with the influence of the work environment and the outside world.

Because of the complexity of the subject, some repetition of detail occurs, particularly in the mobility chapters. This repetition is the result of a deliberate policy designed to maintain the continuity of the discussion at different stages of the analysis, and to avoid complicated cross-references to previous or subsequent chapters.

A view of the study relative to other work on the subject may be obtained by reading chapters I, XI, XII and XIII, whilst a detailed account of the study itself can be obtained from chapters II to X.

The research on which this book is based was undertaken during the period 1959–62. The original manuscript was completed in 1963 whilst I was at the University of Western Australia. Since 1963, minor modifications and additions have been made to the text but no attempt has been made to update references or to assess changes which may have occurred in the area of study since 1962.

ACKNOWLEDGMENTS

MANY people have been of assistance to me in the research on which this book is based. The people in the area of study received me into their homes, discussed their lives and problems with me and provided personal details about themselves, members of their families and their relations. Various officials in organizations associated with the area gave me access to records and provided other information. My colleagues in agricultural economics discussed the study with me at all stages. I am especially indebted to those at Manchester, and particularly to M. Marks and W. T. Fletcher. Professor Gluckman and members of his staff allowed me to attend lecture courses and seminars from which I gained valuable knowledge of social anthropological methods. Dr. Alcorn, Dr. Stein, J. Grange and other members of the 'Leigh Seminar' gave advice and facilities and provided a forum for the discussion of my work. P. O'Keefe of the *Irish Farmer* and members of the Agricultural Research Institute and Agricultural Department in Dublin gave me an appreciation of the wider implications of my study. Dr. Sheppard and other members of the Social Survey gave advice and information, as did Mrs. Dennis of the Agricultural Land Service. W. M. Williams of Keele University permitted me to comment on parts of the manuscript of his book *Ashworthy* and Mr. T. W. Freeman of Manchester University gave me access to unpublished field data on Ireland. Clerical staff of the Agricultural Economics Department at Manchester prepared interview schedules, typed drafts and carried out statistical calculations; A. and R. Batsleer, N. Wilde and A. Martin typed and checked drafts and C. Solomon typed the final manuscript. All these people gave freely of their time but I could not have carried out this study without the especial co-operation of one body of people and three individuals.

The Dartington Hall Trustees had foresight of the need for a new approach to problems in agricultural economics and they provided generous financial assistance for me to make a sociological study of some problem in agricultural economics.

W. J. Thomas, Professor of Agricultural Economics at Manchester University, impressed upon me the need for a study of the mobility of farm people. He provided facilities for me to carry out the work, supervised it at all stages and was a stimulating mentor.

Professor W. Watson, Department of Sociology, University of Virginia, and formerly Senior Lecturer in Sociology at Manchester University and Director of the Leigh Social Research Unit, took a personal interest in an agricultural economist knowing no sociology and, quite voluntarily, undertook the task of enlightening me. He gave me an appreciation of the intricacies of social relations; he showed me the importance of process theory when handling the time dimension of studies involving people; he provided a theory of social mobility which was the basis for my approach to the particular mobility of farm people and throughout the study he stimulated, guided and reassured me. My work would have been infinitely harder and the results immeasurably poorer without the benefit of his illuminating lectures, deep sociological knowledge and insight, and personal friendship.

My wife helped me in many ways. Her sound common sense kept my feet on the ground and she cheerfully endured the endless discussion of my work. She was a constant support through all the frustrations, disappointments and monotony which constitute a large part of a research programme and she shared the elations of discovery.

To all I am most grateful.

J. S. NALSON

CHAPTER I

APPROACHES TO THE MOBILITY OF FARM PEOPLE

THE original stimulus to undertake the study on which this book is based came from a desire to understand why farmers, when faced by adverse economic conditions, frequently did not respond by migration out of farming. This still remains a major objective of the book, but it also provides an intensive analysis of social mobility in a specific industry—farming.

From an initial concern with providing a sociological explanation for income disparity between agriculture and other occupations, the focus of my interest and analysis shifted towards a more general examination of the phenomena of social mobility in farming. Consequently, whilst providing for agricultural economists' explanations of the mobility, or immobility, of farm people, the study also questions the validity, or adequacy, of established sociological analyses of rural communities and rural social mobility. The study thus falls squarely between the two stools of agricultural economics and of rural sociology and, therefore, may not satisfy those sitting firmly on either one or the other stool. My reading of the literature and examination and analysis of the empirical data for this study, and those of other people, has convinced me, however, of the necessity to straddle, if not to sit upon, both stools at once.

Economists have frequently neglected social phenomena in seeking explanations of economic activity, whilst sociologists have often ignored, or discounted, economic activity when studying social phenomena. This study draws on both disciplines in seeking to explain an activity of importance to both. The first part of this chapter considers the agricultural economic approach to the mobility of farm people; the sociological approach is discussed in the second part and finally the argument for a joint approach is presented.

THE AGRICULTURAL ECONOMIC APPROACH

In most countries changing from a predominantly agricultural society to a predominantly industrial society, incomes in agriculture have lagged behind those in industry. The extent of the income disparity has varied for different countries with changes in the rate and stage of their economic growth, but it has been negligible only when economic circumstances have been exceptionally favourable for agriculture, or when Governments have supported agricultural prices or incomes.

Bellerby[1] estimates that the 'incentive income ratio' between agriculture and non-farm enterprise can be very low in periods of depression and, even in prosperous periods, it can still be less than unity. For example, he estimates the ratio for Britain to have been 48·3 per cent in the period of depression from 1923 to 1929; 77·3 per cent in 1870 at the highest point of the 'Golden Age of British Agriculture', and 81·1 per cent in 1933, when government support was being given to agriculture.

Schultz[2] shows that there has been a wide variation in the extent of the disparity in different countries, and Kuznets[3] concludes that there is no consistent relationship between rates of growth in income per head and the inequalities of income which arise between people employed in different sectors of the economy.

Lewis[4] indicates that, even in an underdeveloped economy, earnings in subsistence agriculture may be substantially less than wages in its industry. Campbell,[5] however, is of the opinion that the association of increased income per capita with a decline in the proportion of people engaged in agriculture (as demonstrated by Clark[6] for many countries) cannot be unreservedly taken as a reason for the encouragement of accelerated transfers of population from agriculture to industry in the underdeveloped countries of the world. Campbell's view is supported by Schultz[7] who shows that, in most of the underdeveloped countries, the marginal productivity of labour in agriculture is in equilibrium with the marginal productivity of labour in other occupations.

There seems little doubt, however, that, for most countries in an advanced state of economic growth, income-disparity exists between agriculture and other occupations. This disparity is particularly

[1] J. R. Bellerby: *Agriculture and Industry Relative Income*, 1956, p. 56.

[2] T. W. Schultz: *The Economic Organization of Agriculture*, 1953, pp. 288–93.

[3] Simon Kuznets: 'Quantitative aspects of the economic growth of nations. Industrial distribution of national product and labour force', *Economic Development and Cultural Change*, Vol. 5, No. 4, July 1957, Supplement, p. 55.

[4] W. A. Lewis: 'Economic development with unlimited supplies of labour', *Manchester School of Economic and Social Studies*, Vol. XXII, No. 2, May 1954, p. 150.

[5] K. O. Campbell: 'Rural population movements in relation to economic development', *Tenth International Conference of Agricultural Economists*, Proceedings, London, 1960, p. 318.

[6] Colin Clark: *The Conditions of Economic Progress*, 1940, Chs. 9 and 10.

[7] T. W. Schultz: 'The role of government in promoting economic growth', *The State of the Social Sciences*, 1956, p. 375.

acute for those farmers operating with poor, or inadequate, resources of land or capital. Not only are they at a disadvantage compared with people in industry, but, by reason of their poor command of resources, they are also at a disadvantage compared with other farmers. The usual explanation of the income-disparity between people in agriculture and people in industrial employment can be summarized as follows:

During periods of economic growth, technological advance in agriculture results in increased output of food products per acre and per animal. Consumers spend more on food as their incomes rise, but low-income elasticity of demand for food ensures that the increased expenditure is not proportionate to the increase in incomes. Furthermore, part of the increased expenditure on food is a payment for processing, rather than for an increased quantity. Prices of farm products, therefore, tend to fall in relation to the prices of other commodities. Faced with lower returns, farmers attempt to maintain their incomes by increasing output, or by reducing unit costs. They do this by adopting further innovations which increase outputs or total costs, or which use more capital.

When industry is prosperous, the 'supply price' of new entrants to farming from industry tends to fall. The competition for farms between these new entrants and farmers' sons forces up rents and prices of land to levels higher than those warranted by the gross returns being obtained for farm products. Although some out-movement of labour occurs, particularly of hired labour when replaced by equipment representing capital investment, farmers and their families do not leave agriculture at a rate commensurate with the increased productive potential of farming. The result is a persistent disparity between incomes from farming and from other occupations.

In times of depression, lack of other available opportunities slows down the out-movement of labour. There may even be a reversal of the movement, as relatives and others return to the land in search of work or subsistence. This again leads to increases in output, as the swollen agricultural population attempts to maintain its income. Such increases during times of decreasing demand further reduce incomes in farming.

The remedy usually recommended for the state of affairs described above is to take measures to reduce the number of people sharing the proceeds from agriculture and to increase the business size of those who remain, so that they will be in a better position to make adjustments to changing economic circumstances affecting agriculture.[1]

---

[1] It is not the purpose of this study to discuss in detail the factors involved in the creation of income-disparity in agriculture, other than those related to the mobility

Experience in the U.S.A. has cast doubts on the efficacy of a reduction in the labour force as a means of correcting income disparity between farmers and others. There, the problem was still acute in 1959, despite a 25 per cent reduction in labour over the previous thirteen years. Johnson[1] considers that, under conditions of falling prices, capital losses on stocks have been very important in reducing incomes of farmers in relation to other occupations. He also considers that difficulty in liquidating capital investments prevents farmers from reducing their output, but that, despite labour losses, further increases in production are encouraged by the use of non-labour resources, of improved economic organization, and of new technology.

Heady[2] has emphasized that, in the short run, the removal of surplus farm population might well increase output to the detriment of the farmers who remain.

Campbell[3] points out that population-egress is often faster from areas where per capita earnings from farming are relatively high than it is from poorer areas. He considers that the fertility-differential between rural and urban areas is one factor helping to keep up numbers in agriculture, despite migration. Galbraith[4] argues that the higher birthrate in poor farming areas, by maintaining a sufficient supply of people for the farms, helps to perpetuate problems there, despite migration of a proportion of the population.

Whilst a net migration of farm population may not solve the problem of income-disparity, it should reduce its size. Furthermore, for political purposes, or from welfare considerations, most coun-

---

of farm people. Bellerby, *op. cit.*, discusses the price and income elasticities of demand for food, supply price for enterprise in agriculture, and factors of mobility. Bellerby and Allen discuss farmers' supply responses to falls in demand in J. R. Bellerby: 'Some causes of the disparity between farm and non-farm income per head'. *The Farm Economist*, Vol. VII, No. 8, 1954, p. 325, and G. R. Allen: 'Some causes of the disparity between farm and non-farm income per head—a comment', *The Farm Economist*, Vol. VII, Nos. 9 and 10, 1954, p. 383.

The influence of technological advance is treated by Schultz, *The Economic Organization of Agriculture*.

A useful statement of the argument is that by T. C. Warley: 'On keeping up with the non-farming Joneses', *Farm Management Notes*, Nos. 23 and 24, 1960.

[1] Glen Johnson: 'Some basic problems for economists and statisticians arising from U.S. agricultural policies', *Paper to Manchester Statistical Society*, 11 November 1959.

[2] E. O. Heady: 'Progress in adjusting agriculture to economic change', *Journal of Farm Economics*, Vol. XXXIX, No. 5, December 1957, pp. 1339–43.

[3] Campbell, *op. cit.*, p. 314.

[4] J. K. Galbraith: 'Inequality in Agriculture. Problem and Programme', First Morrison Mem. Lecture, 1956.

tries with advanced economies maintain farm incomes at levels higher than they would otherwise be. If there were a smaller farming population, the burden of food surpluses or Exchequer support would be less. Thomas[1] maintains that support to agriculture in the United Kingdom should not be given to preserve the *status quo* but should be distributed in such a manner as to reduce the problem by encouraging migration and amalgamation. The need to change British policy in this direction becomes increasingly important if Britain is to meet the challenge of the European Economic Community, where mobility of labour between countries and industries is an integral part of the policies agreed upon by the member nations.

In 1956, 27 per cent of the active population in the E.E.C. countries were engaged in agriculture, and 71 per cent of the farms were less than 25 acres in size. This compares with 5 per cent and 39 per cent respectively in Britain.[2] Maris[3] estimates that by 1972 a reduction of 30 to 50 per cent in the number of farms under 25 acres could occur within the Community, with a consequent reduction of 25 per cent in the number of people engaged in agriculture.

In the Netherlands, where rapid industrialization has taken place since 1945, the number of farm workers between 1947 and 1957 dropped by 35 per cent, that of farmers' sons working at home by 20 per cent, and that of farmers by 5 per cent. Concurrent with these reductions in the number of persons engaged in agriculture, infiltration of industry into rural areas occurred. As a result of these developments, the proportion of the total population living in 'decidedly rural municipalities' fell from 30 per cent in 1947 to 25 per cent in 1957; the proportion living in 'urbanized rural districts' rose from 16 per cent to 21 per cent; whilst the proportion living in towns remained the same.[4]

In England and Wales, over the same period, there was a 20 per cent decline in workers engaged in agriculture.[5] Figures comparable to the Dutch ones are not available, but evidence from an increase in the proportion of partners and non-hired family workers suggests

---

[1] W. J. Thomas: 'Post-War agricultural policy in the United Kingdom', *Paper to Manchester Statistical Society*, 10 December 1958.

[2] A. Maris: 'The efflux of labour from agriculture in Europe', *Rural Migration*, 1959, Table I, p. 56.

[3] *Ibid.*, p. 51.

[4] A. Maris and M. A. J. van de Sandt: 'Trends in the changing occupational structure of rural areas with special reference to manpower on farms', *Changing Patterns of Rural Organizations*, 1961, p. 506.

[5] Source: 'Agricultural Statistics' quoted by G. P. Hirsch: 'Manpower of British farms', *Changing Patterns of Rural Organization*, 1961, Table 5a, p. 533. Excludes farmers and wives.

that most of the decrease has probably been in farm workers.[1] Over the period 1950–5, the number of holdings in England and Wales dropped by less than 1 per cent, which does not suggest any appreciable change in the number of farmers.[2] Certainly, in the hundred years from 1851 to 1951, when the proportion of people engaged in agriculture fell from 22 per cent to 5 per cent, most of the absolute decrease in numbers was of farm workers. Over that period, in Great Britain, the number of farm workers fell by 63 per cent and that of family workers declined by 20 per cent; but the number of farmers remained almost the same.[3]

If movement of employed labour out of British agriculture continues at the rate of recent years; if out-movement of family workers does not increase; and if the number of farmers does not decline, there are likely to be two major consequences.

First, Britain is likely to lose much of its advantage over E.E.C. countries in farm-size structure, assuming that the projected reduction in persons engaged in agriculture in those countries does occur. A 50 per cent reduction in their holdings under 25 acres would bring down to 55 per cent the proportion of their holdings in that category.[4] If, at the same time, the industrialization of rural areas there is increased (as has been the policy in the Netherlands), the proportion of part-time farmers is likely to increase in addition to the absolute losses to industry of members of full-time farming families.[5] Britton[6] considers that the Community will encourage movement out of the smallest farms in the poorest areas, by establishing industry there. He also thinks that educational measures will be taken in those areas to discourage a proportion of school-leavers from entering agriculture. Lijfering[7] shows that, in the Netherlands, industrial-

---

[1] Hirsch, *ibid.*, Table 10, p. 536. Between 1945–6 and 1958, the proportion of regular adult male workers in England and Wales classified as 'partners' increased from 3·0 per cent to 5·5 per cent and those classified as 'non-hired family' increased from 7·0 per cent to 12·0 per cent.

[2] Natural Resources (Technical) Sub-Committee: *Scale of Enterprise in Farming*, 1961, Table 11, p. 9.

[3] J. R. Bellerby: 'The distribution of manpower in agriculture and industry 1851–1951', *The Farm Economist*, Vol. IX, No. 1, 1958. Calculated from Table 1, p. 3.

[4] On the assumption that, if the reduction in number of holdings occurs, it will be amongst those under 25 acres rather than amongst the larger ones.

[5] J. H. W. Lijfering: 'Changes in rural occupational structure and labour organization', *Changing Patterns of Rural Organization*, 1961, p. 494. Lijfering shows that commuting of farm people has increased where industrialization has occurred.

[6] D. K. Britton: 'Agriculture in the European Economic Community', *Journal of Agricultural Economics*, Vol. XIII, No. 2, 1958, p. 160.

[7] Lijfering, *op. cit.*, p. 494.

ization of rural areas has been successful in encouraging farmers and their families to leave farming.

Second, in the past, British farmers have been able to adjust to changing economic circumstances by dispensing with some employed labour, or by not replacing that which has left for industrial work. This will become increasingly difficult as the farm labour force becomes closer in structure to the family-farming pattern of the Continent. Already 50 per cent of British farmers do not employ any labour and another 32 per cent employ either one full-time man only or no regular full-time worker.[1] So, already, the opportunity for reducing the employed labour force lies mainly with the farmers who hold farms of 100 acres or more, and who employ more than one man. But these represent only 13 per cent of all farmers.[2] Unless future reductions in the farm labour force come more from the ranks of the farmers and their families than they have in the past, farm incomes will fall, or further Exchequer support will be necessary to maintain them.

An alternative approach to the problem of how to adapt British agriculture to meet the challenge of the European Community would be to encourage more part-time farming. This has increased in the United States, for two reasons: one, farmers have sought means of supplementing their decreased farming incomes and, two, highly paid industrial workers have taken farms for recreation and a home.[3] There is evidence that this is occurring in Europe too. Kuhnen,[4] reporting a 'representative enquiry' in Western Germany for 1956, states that, on every 100 farms, 42 of the farmers were drawing non-agricultural income, and 57 had other family members doing so.

Some information on the incidence of part-time farming in Britain is available from the National Farm Survey,[5] and more recent studies have indicated its importance in certain areas and for particular sizes of farm business.[6] It is not known, however, if part-time

---

[1] Hirsch, *op. cit.*, Table 6, p. 534.

[2] Calculated from Tables 6 and 3, Hirsch, *op. cit.*, pp. 533, 534.

[3] J. A. Beegle and D. Halstead: *Michigan's Changing Population*, 1957, p. 30; and R. E. Galloway: *Part-Time Farming in Eastern Kentucky*, June 1956, p. 3.

[4] F. Kuhnen: 'Die Vertreitung Nicht landwirtschaftlicher Einkünfte bei landbewirtschaftenden Familien in der Bundesrepublick Deutschland', *Changing Patterns of Rural Organization*, 1961, pp. 330, 441.

[5] *National Farm Survey of England and Wales*, Summary Report, 1946, pp. 6-14 and appendix IV.

[6] J. B. Butler: Part 2 of *The Small Farms of Industrial Yorkshire*, October 1958; J. Ashton and B. E. Cracknell: 'Agricultural holdings and farm business structure in England and Wales', *Journal Agricultural Economics Society*, July 1961, Vol. XIV, No. 4, pp. 472–98; W. J. Thomas and W. Richardson:

farming is increasing or not, or what part it plays in the mobility of people into, and out of, full-time farming. This raises a number of questions. How many part-time farmers are on the first rung up of the agricultural ladder and how many are on the last one down? Are there differences in the proportion of part-time and full-time farmers' sons taking up farming as a career? What kind of persons become part-time farmers, and why have other farmers with equally small businesses not taken up work off their farms?

Much more detailed knowledge of mobility and its determinants than we have at present would be required to design a policy for agriculture which would encourage a greater degree of partial or complete occupational mobility out of farming.

Agricultural economists have discussed mobility as one of the factors involved in studies of income disparity, problem areas or farms, and recruitment to agriculture. In their approach to mobility there is a tendency to impute psychological motivation when farmers do not react according to classical economic theory. Because farmers patently do not 'freely seek their own best material advantage and move from one occupation to another according to their earning capacity', it is sometimes assumed that they deliberately choose to remain poor. This type of thinking is illustrated by the concluding paragraph of the report on scale of enterprise in British farming:

> The solution of the problem of non-viable holdings presents many social and economic difficulties, especially as many are *content* to farm at a level of profit which gives them a total return less than that of a farm labourer, *knowing too* that their economic position is liable to worsen still further. While little little harm is being done to the nation's resources, there is little point in inducing them to give up farming, but they cannot reasonably expect to receive any special long-term financial support from the rest of the community.[1]

Farmers on small farms who earn less than wages may be accustomed to their situation, and even resigned to it, but to say they are content, knowing things will become worse, displays a lack of understanding of the environment in which many of them live and have been brought up. Moreover, such a statement is no help in solving the problem, and it ignores our responsibilities towards these people.

A faint air of reproach appears to be a common reaction of agricultural economists to 'small farmers' or 'inefficient farmers'. Many pronouncements seem to imply that such farmers are 'small' or

---

unpublished material on a problem farming area in N.W. England, Manchester University, Dept. of Agricultural Economics, 1961.
  [1] *Scale of Enterprise in Farming, op. cit.*, p. 70 (Italics are the author's).

'inefficient' from personal choice and that all would be well if they would only act like 'economic men'. Thus, in *The Problems of the Small Farm Business*,[1] stress is laid on 'the problem farmer rather than the problem farm'. The reports from the Provincial Agricultural Economists give 'lack of ambition', 'personal failings' and 'values put on leisure and independence' as reasons for low income. Bellerby,[2] in discussing mobility into and out of farming, considers that the 'psychic' attractions of farming are important in encouraging people into the industry and that 'inertia' is one factor preventing them from leaving.

These psychological correlates may be quite sound, although there is little empirical data in Britain to support them, but it does not help very much to enumerate them, or even to ascertain the frequency of their occurrence. Attitudes may only be outward manifestations of underlying social causes. Man is born with certain tendencies and abilities, the realization of which depends largely on the environment to which he is exposed. Consequently, examination of the social environment in which mobility of farm people occurs is more likely to provide useful data for planning future changes than is the organization of large-scale surveys[3] into the 'motivations' of farmers.

THE SOCIOLOGICAL APPROACH

Sociological material on the mobility of farm people in Britain is available from a number of sources. Some agricultural economists, notably Ashby and his co-workers, have investigated certain aspects of the social environment affecting the mobility of farmers. Social historians and demographers have studied population movement out of rural areas. Studies of rural communities by social anthropologists provide further incidental data, as do studies of social mobility carried out by sociologists. All these sources, however, suffer from deficiencies, in that mobility of farm people is often only one factor studied as part of some other work, or, where mobility is the main theme, the study is descriptive, rather than analytical.[4]

[1] Min. of Agriculture, Fisheries and Food: *The Problem of the Small Farm Business*, 1956 (limited circulation).

[2] J. R. Bellerby: *Agriculture and Industry Relative Income*, p. 80.

[3] Such as suggested in the discussion on E. W. Carpenter's paper 'The Small Farmer', *Journal of Agricultural Economics*, Vol. XIII, No. 1, June 1958, p. 28f.

[4] The section which follows is not intended to be a comprehensive survey of the literature. Rather it is designed as a critical appraisal of the main sources of information about mobility of farm people in Britain, with emphasis placed on the inadequacy of the material. The findings of the present study are often supported

Ashby and his co-workers have carried out a number of investigations into some aspects of the social environment affecting the mobility of farmers.[1] These investigations provide useful data on such correlates as age and size of farms, but in general they have insufficient cross-tabulations relating particular mobility groups to specific social or economic factors. The surveys of social origins of farmers in Wales[2] and in Oxfordshire and Warwickshire[3] both indicate that about 70 per cent of the farmers are themselves sons of farmers.

Ashby and Ashton also agree that, in the main, recruits to farming come in at the bottom of the farming ladder, and that, on average, they begin farming later in life than do the sons of farmers. This pattern is confirmed by a national survey,[4] a regional survey,[5] and by Ashby's analysis, from census data, of ages of farmers at recruitment and 'wastage' of farmers and relatives at different ages.[6]

It is important to note that certain categories of farmers were specifically excluded from both the national survey and the Welsh survey[7] and that a higher proportion of farms of over 100 acres was

---

on particular points by information in the studies cited. These will be referred to again in Chapter XII when relating this study to mobility in agriculture generally.

[1] A. W. Ashby, and J. Morgan Jones: 'The social origin of Welsh farmers', *Welsh Journal of Agriculture*, Vol. 2, 1926, pp. 12–35; A. W. Ashby, and J. Llefelys Davies: 'The agricultural ladder and the age of farmers', *Welsh Journal of Agriculture*, Vol. 6, 1930, pp. 5–19; J. Ashton: *The Social Origin of Farmers*, Agricultural Research Institute, Oxford, 1950, unpublished B.Litt. thesis; A. W. Ashby: 'The farmer in business', *Journal Proc. Agricultural Economics Society*, Vol. X, No. 2, February 1953, pp. 91–126.

[2] Ashby and Morgan Jones, *op. cit.*

[3] Ashton, *op. cit.*

[4] D. Chapman and others: *Agricultural Information and the Farmer*, The Social Survey, C.O.I., May 1944. This indicates 81 per cent of farmers as sons of farmers and a higher proportion of sons of non-farmers on the smaller holdings.

[5] *An Economic Survey of Agriculture in the Eastern Counties of England 1932*. University of Cambridge, Farm Economics Branch Report No. 22, p. 60. This shows that occupants of large farms were, on average, eight years younger at commencement than were those of small farms.

[6] Ashby and Davies, *op. cit.*, and Ashby, 'The farmer in business', *op. cit.*

[7] The Welsh survey was of 'persons who gain a livelihood by farming land large or small'. Others—miners, tradesmen etc. also farming—were excluded. The sample was not a random one but was carried out by 'local correspondents' who were 'recommended to take a whole parish and endeavour to record details for every farm, leaving out only farmers whose origins could not be ascertained'. There is no indication of refusal rate, or of the numbers of farmers whose origins could not be ascertained. The national survey was 'basically a random sample of holdings over 20 acres . . . within the main areas of arable, dairying and mixed farming; sheep farming was specifically excluded'.

shown in Ashton's survey, than occurred amongst all farms in the two counties surveyed.[1] The effect of these exclusions and differences is to underestimate the inter- and intragenerational mobility of part-time farmers. This is particularly serious if a farming ladder is assumed to exist, for (on such an assumption) part-time farmers could become full-time farmers, or sons of part-time farmers could move in the next generation to full-time farming status. But none of the surveys provides information on progression or regression between part-time farms, small farms and larger farms. Ashton shows that rather less than a third of farmers' sons of working age were not employed in agriculture, and the survey of farmers by Chapman[2] indicates that for farmers aged 55 and over, two-thirds of their sons were in agriculture. No information is available as to which sons left the industry, and which remained.

Interpretations of the available information vary. Thus, Ashton[3] considers that his data indicates a high degree of immobility, whereas Ashby states that the most important conclusion from his work is that the farming class is a fluid one, allowing entry from other occupations.[4] Bellerby[5] considers that 'established farmers are as wedded to their careers now as in the past' but that 'occupational mobility has greatly increased in recent years, and personal immobility and inertia probably affect farmers' sons much less than more senior groups'. There is no evidence to support Bellerby's second statement which tends to contradict his first one. Whether Ashton's or Ashby's interpretation is the more accurate depends on the degree of occupational mobility of farmers in Britain, compared with that in other countries, and of farmers compared with other occupational groups.

Comparisons between countries are difficult to make. Birth surpluses vary from one country to another and Britain has a lower proportion of its population engaged in agriculture than has any other country. In those countries in which birth surpluses are high, industrial activity is increasing rapidly and the proportion of the population engaged in agriculture is still considerable, we would expect to find a greater movement of sons out of farming than in Britain. This expectation is confirmed by the figures for the Netherlands quoted earlier in this chapter.[6] Also, in a country which has been

[1] There is no indication in Ashton's thesis of the way in which the sample of farmers was drawn.
[2] Ashton, *op. cit.*, p. 175; Chapman and others, *op. cit.*, p. 51.
[3] Ashton, *op. cit.*, p. 168.   [4] Ashby and Morgan Jones, *op. cit.*, p. 35.
[5] Bellerby, *Agricultural and Industry Relative Income*, p. 80f.
[6] See page 5 above.

developed on an agricultural basis and has then changed progressively to an industrial economy (as has occurred in the United States), we would again expect to find that fewer farmers' sons would remain in agriculture. This is confirmed by figures for parts of the U.S.A. and for the country as a whole. Anderson[1] shows that 31 per cent and 47 per cent of farmers' sons in two New York State counties followed their fathers' occupations, and Lipset and Bendix[2] quote figures of 30 per cent and 38 per cent for sons of people in farm employment throughout the U.S.A. Compared with the U.S.A., Lipset and Bendix quote the proportions of farmers' sons following their fathers' occupations, as 35 per cent for Sweden, 50 per cent for Japan and Switzerland, 50 per cent to 70 per cent for Western Germany and 70 per cent for France. The data for all countries quoted were derived in rather a different way from those of both Ashton's survey and the Social Survey (Chapman) in Britain, but, even used as a rough comparison, the figures suggest that the degree of mobility of farmers' sons out of farming is lower in Britain than in a number of other countries.

Many studies of social mobility are concerned with inter- and intragenerational mobility of people between social-class or status categories, in which some occupations are given a high rating, and some are given a low rating. In these studies, farmers are frequently considered as one occupational group and are placed in a single status category.[3] This makes for ease of classification, but is a misleading simplification, since farming differs from many other occupations in that it comprises a wide range of economic and status levels. Often there is insufficient attention paid to this wide range either in studies of whole populations, or in those more limited studies which consider what proportion of farmers or their sons had farmers for fathers. A dustman's son who becomes a doctor is a clear example of a jump from the lowest status category to the highest. In most social mobility studies, however, the son of a roadman-cum-farmer who becomes a farmer of 1,000 acres of land cannot be distinguished from a son who takes over from his father a 100-acre family farm.

That intergenerational mobility does occur within the occupation of farming is evident from Ashton's study.[4] He shows that farmers occupy small farms for shorter periods of time than they occupy

[1] W. A. Anderson: *The Transmission of Farming as an Occupation*, October 1941, p. 1.
[2] S. M. Lipset, and R. Bendix: *Social Mobility in Industrial Society*, 1959, pp. 19–21.
[3] See for example: D. V. Glass (editor): *Social Mobility in Britain*, 1954, Table 2, p. 34.   [4] Ashton, *op. cit.*, p. 153 and p. 122.

larger farms, and that less than 30 per cent of the farmers surveyed had followed their parents on the same farm. He makes little comment on this latter fact, which appears to me to be one of the most important revealed by his study. It is important, because it runs counter to the image of farming as a stable occupation, changing little from one generation to another, with sons following fathers in an unbroken line. The strength of this image can be gauged from the descriptions by social anthropologists of farming society in Britain. In these studies, considerable emphasis is placed on generational continuity (based usually on the genealogies of a few prominent farming families).[1] That the image is not confined to social anthropologists is obvious from a statement made by the Natural Resources Technical Sub-Committee[2] (which had access to Ashton's study): 'three quarters of the farmers in England and Wales are farmers' sons and the *majority* of these succeeded their fathers on the *same* farm' (author's italics).

Williams has recently retracted his statement about family continuity on farms in Gosforth, as a result of his analysis of the movements of farmers between farms over a period of 100 years in a Devon parish.[3] Although Williams shows clearly the extent of the farm-to-farm movement in Ashworthy, the nature of his study precludes any attempt to analyse the relation between particular movements, occupational mobility, and other possible social and economic correlates for a defined current population of farmers.

Lipset and Bendix[4] consider that 25 per cent to 30 per cent mobility between generations across 'high and low occupation prestige lines'[5] is evidence of a high degree of mobility, whether this mobility relates to non-farm populations only or to populations made up of both urban and rural occupations. Lipset and Bendix present figures showing this percentage as a common level of mobility for the United States, Germany, France, Sweden, Switzerland, Denmark, Great Britain and Japan.

If movement into and out of farming is considered to be as definite a social change as that from 'working class' to 'middle class',[6] then it is clear that the reported proportion of farmers who

---

[1] See C. D. Arensberg: *The Irish Countryman*, 1955; A. D. Rees: *Life in a Welsh Countryside*, 1951; W. M. Williams: *The Sociology of an English Village, Gosforth*, 1956.

[2] *Scale of Enterprise in Farming, op. cit.*, p. 60.

[3] W. M. Williams: *A West Country Village: Ashworthy, Family Kinship and Land*, 1963.   [4] Lipset and Bendix, *op. cit.*, p. 25.

[5] By this they mean from 'working class' to 'middle class' and vice versa.

[6] Nowadays, this may not have the economic implications it had in the past; but the social changes involved will still be considerable.

are not themselves sons of farmers (that is, 25 per cent to 30 per cent) represents the same degree of mobility as for other occupational groupings. The same is true of the proportion of sons of farmers who are not engaged in agriculture. This movement into and out of farming does not take into account the other changes, in both economic and social status, that occur within the farming occupation itself.

Whilst this similarity between farming and other occupations is no consolation to farmers with low incomes, or to economists who would like to see more of them leave the land, at least it indicates that the so-called 'lack of occupational mobility' is not a phenomenon peculiar to the agricultural industry. What this comparison does suggest, however, is that, if the pressures keeping people in agriculture are no greater than those keeping other people within certain occupational groupings, extraordinary measures are likely to be needed where it is considered desirable to speed up the process of movement of people away from agriculture.

One movement which is peculiar to rural areas and occupations is the differential mobility of women. This has been extensively studied by demographers and others, but most of their investigations have been parts of large-scale studies of movement amongst rural populations generally. These studies have relied to a large extent on census material, and they have established the ages at which women leave the country areas, the degree of movement, and the changes in sex distribution of the population for different areas and time-periods. The process has been shown to be related to occupational opportunities for women in the towns, but little intensive work has been done to show the effects of this movement of women on the various occupations in rural areas and particularly the effects on farming.[1]

Some figures in Ashton's study suggest one effect of a greater spatial and occupational mobility of women from rural areas. These show that fewer farmers' *wives* came of farming parents than did farmers themselves.[2] Ashton concludes that the figures indicate a considerable degree of intermarriage amongst farmers. From the sociological aspect the striking feature is that, in an area of relatively large farms, so many farmers' sons married outside farming. Interesting cross-tabulations could have been made between the occupational background of the farmers' wife, the size of his farm and the

[1] The whole subject is dealt with by J. Saville: *Rural Depopulation in England and Wales 1851 to 1951*, 1957. Saville considers that studies at the parish level are required to determine net migration and to elucidate further the causes of movement.   [2] Ashton, *op. cit.*, p. 171.

off-farm employment of the farmer or his children. Ashton, however, does not present any further analysis on this point.

Littlejohn[1] has suggested both cultural and economic reasons for the movement of women out of rural areas and has related this movement to the marriage patterns and opportunities for males in different occupations. Thus, he indicates that young farmers from the large farms of the region he studied were spatially mobile in their day-to-day occupational and social activities and that their socio-economic status was high. Consequently they had a wide spatial and social range over which they had opportunities for meeting potential marriage partners. By contrast, shepherds frequently lived in isolated locations and occupied a low socio-economic status relative to people in the local urban areas and even relative to those in the less isolated rural areas. Furthermore, the requirements of their job—weekend work and attendance to sheep at all hours in some seasons—restricted their spatial mobility and social interaction compared with other workers in the same income bracket. Rejection of rural living and work by working-class young women thus left shepherds with restricted local marriage opportunities.

Littlejohn[2] indicates contrasts between rural boys and girls in their attitudes to social mobility and cultural aspirations, with the girls seeing themselves as part of a wider society compared with the local orientation of the boys. Frankenberg[3] observes the reverse phenomenon in a village where the men move out to work and the women remain at home. Unfortunately his study does not include the type of demographic data which would enable interrelationships to be studied between cultural orientation, male and female occupations prior to marriage and the sex and marital structure of the community.

Neither Littlejohn nor Frankenberg is concerned specifically with the mobility of farming people, but Watson's study of the Mambwe in Northern Rhodesia[4] is more closely related to the problem of mobility, even though it is concerned with adjustments occurring in a subsistence agricultural economy. Watson shows that amongst these people wage labour at a distance, undertaken by over a third of the adult male population, is compatible with and complementary to the maintenance of a subsistence farming economy in the tribal area. He attributes this to the communal methods of working land, the interchangeability between men and women of certain essential

[1] J. Littlejohn: *Westrigg*, 1963, Chs. 1 and 8.
[2] Littlejohn, *op. cit.*, Ch. 7, pp. 133 and 134.
[3] R. Frankenberg: *Village on the Border*, 1957.
[4] W. Watson: *Tribal Cohesion in a Money Economy*, 1958.

farming tasks, the patrilineal society, the linking of rights to the use of land with village membership and the concentration of local political power amongst the older men of the villages. Watson's study is important relevant to the examination of mobility in European farming for a number of reasons. Firstly, it indicates the necessity in mobility studies of enumerating demographic factors and particularly the importance of taking a genealogical view of the population to be studied. Secondly, it shows the interrelationship and complementarity which can occur between industrial employment and agricultural activity for a rural-based population. Thirdly, some of the data presented again suggest interrelationships between the availability, at a distance, of work for one sex and the local sex ratios and marriage patterns. Thus, in the English studies referred to previously, there was a high masculinity ratio, and male celibacy was considerable in areas where migration of women to work and social opportunities had occurred. By contrast, amongst the Mambwe, it is the males who migrate, ostensibly only on a temporary basis, but the enumerated population of residents plus associated absent workers and wives shows a low masculinity ratio and considerable polygyny amongst the older men, despite an excess of males over females in the under-14 age groups.[1]

Watson's study also points up another facet of mobility of rural people which has not been considered in the other studies quoted. This is the alternation between rural and urban occupations by the same individuals. Under the urban work conditions existing in Africa, it was not possible for the Mambwe to work in industrial occupations and still live with their tribe. In the past, however, when work had been available nearer to the tribal areas than it was in the 1950's, some of the men had worked away in the 'slack' months of their home farming season, returning home to undertake the major tasks of crop cultivation. In the 1950's, workers tended to stay away for two or three years at a time, making a number of trips away interspersed with years spent at home. The wages earned away helped to sustain a higher standard of life than would have been possible from subsistence agriculture alone, which itself provided unemployment insurance and old age security. Furthermore, employment away provided money and 'know-how' to enable ambitious men in the community to bid for leadership or independent headship of a new village founded by them.

There are parallels between the Mambwe labour situation and

[1] Masculinity ratio 80 per cent, 28 per cent of married men polygynists, 162 males and 141 females in 0–14 years age group. Calculated or taken from Watson, *op. cit.*, Table V, p. 45, and Table VI, p. 54.

the casual labour practices current in Britain before widespread mechanization of agriculture occurred. In those parts of Britain easily and cheaply accessible from Ireland, the casual work of corn and potato harvesting was frequently undertaken by itinerant Irishmen who returned to their peasant holdings in Ireland for the winter and spring. This practice either was not current in the areas studied by Arensberg or he failed to appreciate the significance of this temporary, but regular, alternation between peasant proprietorship and wage labour.

The study by Butler and unpublished data from the University of Manchester[1] indicate the importance of dual occupations in areas where small farms occur in close proximity to industrial employment.

These studies show over 50 per cent of the holdings in the hill border areas of Yorkshire, Lancashire, Cheshire, Staffordshire and Derbyshire operated either as part-time holdings or with a substantial part of family earnings coming from work off the farm. They also indicate greater total family incomes from part-time than from full-time holdings and a greater turnover of part-time holdings from one occupier to another. The studies, however, tend to keep separate the 'social' and the 'economic' aspects considered[2] and, consequently, fail to provide adequate explanations of the reasons behind the situations described, or of the process of spatial and occupational mobility occurring amongst the population of farmers studied.

From the viewpoint of a student of mobility in farming, all the studies considered in this part, with the exception of Watson's study of the Mambwe, cling too closely to the orientation and methodologies of the respective disciplines of their authors. This statement is not primarily a criticism of the works, or of the authors, but rather of the inadequacy of the material to meet my objective of explaining the process of mobility of farm people. In the next section, I discuss these inadequacies and present the argument for an interdisciplinary approach.

[1] Butler: *Small Farms of Industrial Yorkshire*; G. W. Furness: *The Economics of Small Farms in the North West of England* (unpublished M.Sc. thesis), 1959; unpublished material, Dept. of Agricultural Economics, University of Manchester, 1961.

[2] *Small Farms of Industrial Yorkshire* for example has four parts, I. Introduction and Historical Background; II. Social; III. Economic; and IV. Conclusions, without cross classifying or cross-reference material linking the first three parts.

THE NEED FOR AN INTEGRATED APPROACH

Agricultural economists have advocated mobility as a means of adjusting income disparity between agriculture and other occupations and as a means of increasing the efficiency of agricultural production. Because the concept of 'economic man' assumes that men can, and do, transfer between locations and occupations in seeking their own best advantage, agricultural economists have been puzzled when they have observed that farming people frequently have not responded to adverse economic circumstances by leaving for other occupations. 'The economic incentives to move are present so there must be something wrong with the *individuals* who remain.' This has led agricultural economists to postulate, but not prove, that psychological motivations are the root of the trouble—'lack of ambition', 'the best leave', 'happy where they are', 'economic motivation absent'. In studying mobility, moreover, they have failed to examine the effects of the farming social environment and particularly its interrelationships with the industrial environment by which, in Britain and other highly industrialized countries, it is surrounded and interpenetrated.

Sociologists and anthropologists have been concerned with mobility in agriculture, either as one of the phenomena observed in studies of rural communities, or as the rural element in general studies of social mobility.

In social mobility studies, farmers have been considered as a social category distinguished, by a particular occupation, from 'shopkeepers', 'mechanics' or 'doctors'. Their relative position in the status hierarchy of different studies has varied, however, according to the stereotype accepted as typical of 'farmer' as an occupation.[1] Thus, the status position has been low where 'farmer' has been equated with 'peasant' but high where he has been seen with well-filled waistcoat and polished leggings, or, in more up-to-date form, as driving a tax-deductible Jaguar and smoking a big cigar. In part, this is a function of the attempts in social mobility studies to categorize people by one simple occupational description. The same errors of oversimplification are likely to occur from the use of such classifications as 'manager' or 'shop proprietor'. Because of the range in occupations considered, differentiation between farmers on the basis of their economic status has not been common in social

---

[1] This can be seen from a comparison of social mobility studies undertaken in different countries and at different time periods: cf. Lipset and Bendix, *Social Mobility in Industrial Society*; Glass, *Social Mobility in Britain*; and L. Broom, F. L. Jones and J. Zubrzycki, *Five Measures of Social Rank in Australia*, 1966.

mobility studies. An interesting recent exception is the study by Broom, Jones and Zubrzycki which distinguishes between graziers and wheat farmers on the one hand and other farmers (fruit, vegetable, sugar cane, poultry, mixed, dairying, etc.) on the other. This distinction does take some account of economic status but could also have been influenced by circumstances whereby the 'poor dairy cocky' is a figure of fun in urban Australian society whereas wheat farmers are considered the richest of the 'dirty boot' farmers and the families of old-established graziers have in the past wielded considerable political power and been accorded high social prestige. This study, like the others, however, is too general for any conclusions to be drawn from it as to the mode or determinants of mobility within the occupation of farming or between it and other occupations.

Until recently, studies of British rural communities have had a strong *Gemeinschaft* orientation with emphasis placed on internal solidarity, kinship ties, generational continuity in the ownership of land and the importance of tradition and face-to-face relationships. Studies such as those of Williams, Butler, Littlejohn and Frankenburg already cited have indicated that considerable occupational and spatial mobility has occurred, and is occurring, in rural areas and that in some rural communities there is a strong dependence on urban areas for economic opportunities, social interaction and cultural values. Even in the face of this evidence, however, Frankenburg (whose own study showed a village in transition with a large number of its work force employed outside), can still postulate a dichotomy between 'rural' and 'urban' when setting up a model from which to examine communities in Britain.[1] One reason for this is possibly because the studies of rural communities which he considers were either 30 years old or were concerned with areas which were relatively isolated from the effects of industrialization. In addition, limitations in the methodologies of some of the studies have resulted in great emphasis being placed on the immobile members of the communities and their way of life, with insufficient weight being given to the mobile siblings of immobile farmers, to the occupationally mobile families within the communities and to the transient families or individuals. A study of a community at one point in time becomes a study of a residual population, unless adequate genealogical data is collected for all—or a sample of all—the members of that community.

The examination of changes in ownership and tenancy over a period of 100 years which Williams has made for Ashworthy has pointed up for him the spatial and occupational mobility of the people associated with those farms. The economic, demographic and

[1] R. Frankenburg: *Communities in Britain*, 1966.

occupational mobility data which he collected about farmers is not in a suitable form for cross-classification analysis, however, nor is it sufficiently detailed. Williams appreciates many of the sociological variables involved, but the importance of the mobility of some people to the perpetuation of a stable sector of the rural community —the major farming families—does not emerge from the other studies of rural communities in Britain.

Social historians have adequately documented the decline in rural population with the rise in industrialization and much has been written in nostalgic vein deploring the 'drift from the land' and the disappearance of many rural occupations. Demographers have indicated the higher fertility of rural families, the high masculinity ratios in rural areas and the tendencies towards late age of marriage and male celibacy. Little attempt has been made, however, to assess the interrelationships between demographic and economic trends, occupational changes and the apparent stability of the major rural occupation of farming.

There are marked contradictions between an anthropological image of rural society as stable with a high degree of generational continuity and the demographic facts of population decline, differential migration of women and male celibacy. Furthermore, the economic image of farmers as relatively immobile does not tie in with historical evidence of movements from farm to farm and decline in the number of holdings; with social mobility studies which suggest that intergenerational movements into and out of farming may be no less than interclass movement between generations for other occupational groupings or with sociological studies indicating the marked dependence of some rural communities upon occupational opportunities located in urban areas.

Faced with a mass of contradictory evidence from other studies which have not been centrally focused upon mobility of farm people, the obvious solution is to carry out an investigation designed specifically to *describe* the many facets of the mobility of farm people and to *explain* the apparent contradictions by means of a detailed study of the *process* of mobility within and between farming generations.[1] Such a study needs to be descriptive of the mobility of a defined population, and of such a nature as to make it possible to attempt an analysis of causal agents. This can be done by confining the study

---

[1] I realize that the results of an intensive small-scale survey such as is presented in subsequent chapters will need confirming by further, more extensive investigations. But I consider the intensive study is necessary first in order to obtain some understanding of how the whole process of mobility of farm people operates, within and between generations, and also to obtain insights into causes.

to a limited area, so that community and family influences can be observed using a combination of sociological and social-anthropological techniques. It is important that the whole family unit should be considered, in order to compare the mobility of all family members, whether male or female. In addition to confining the study to a limited area, it is desirable that there should be a gradation of farmers within that area from those working small farms part-time up to at least those with full-time farms where the whole family is dependent on the farm. Also, if the area chosen is a problem one for farming, the study should contribute information of use in helping to alleviate the difficulties of farmers in such areas. At the same time, it may also indicate how conditions may develop elsewhere in the future should the terms of trade, or political considerations, react unfavourably upon agriculture.

The study reported in subsequent chapters is an attempt to meet these requirements. The concepts of mobility and its determinants on which it is based can be summarized as follows:

Mobility of farm people is complex. It involves movements of people in time and space within and between occupations, farms and social milieux. It occurs within and between generations of people and results in exchange, gain or relinquishment of land; rise or fall in social status and increase or decrease in economic well-being.

The determinants of the mobility of farm people can be broadly classified as demographic influences, the home environment and the world outside the home.

Demographic influences are those factors, such as sex, age and position in the family, over which the individual has no control, together with those associated with birth, marriage and death, such as age at marriage, age at death and size of family, which the individual can influence initially, but cannot alter once they have occurred.

The influences of the home environment are those resulting from the memberships of a family and of a kinship-network within which the occupation of farming, or other occupations, affect the standard of life, way of living, attitudes and values of the members.

The influences of the world outside the home are those which cannot be directly controlled or affected by the members of a farm family. They comprise such factors as general economic conditions, work-environment other than that of the home farm, cultural and value orientations at micro- and macro-societal levels and the activities of government and other bureaucratic agencies.

Because mobility is a process occurring over time, it needs to be considered in relation to various time-scales, of which three can conveniently be used. These are the life cycle of the individual, the developmental cycle of the farm family and the cycle of generations.

In looking at mobility on these scales, the locations, occupations and social positions of an individual may be compared at different points in time, and those of different individuals (or groups of individuals) may be compared at the same point in time or at different points in time. Comparisons can be made between farmers, farmers and their wives, farmers and wives and their parents, farmers and wives and their children, and between farmers' sons and daughters. Consequently, a pattern of mobility over time can be synthesized for a defined population by studying the past mobility and the current state of mobility for people who at one point in time (the time at which a survey takes place) are at different points on the three time-scales considered.

Consideration of the above concepts indicates that, in examining the mobility of farm people, we are dealing with a 'feed-back' system rather than with a simple cause-effect relationship. Thus, the present socio-economic status of the farmers living in any defined area is partially a result of the different types of mobility which they, or their parents, have undergone in the past; moreover, their present status is likely to influence the future mobility of their children. In other words, something which is an effect of previous causes can be the cause of subsequent effects. Furthermore, a particular mobility state in an individual, or shared by a sub-group within a community, may generate subsequent demographic, economic or social causes of future mobility states or patterns.

The complexity of the phenomena to be studied has led me to adopt, in subsequent chapters, an interdisciplinary approach which combines historical perspective with an analysis dependent upon viewpoints and methodology drawn from both sociology and agricultural economics.

CHAPTER II

THE AREA OF STUDY AND ITS
FARMING ECONOMY

THE area chosen for study is a problem one for farming. The effects of high altitude and exposed situation combine in a harsh climate, with a short growing season subject to violent fluctuations in temperature and precipitation. Annual rainfall is 40 inches or more, snow falls on about 40 days each year, and, at the nearest weather station, August was the only month in which a frost has not been recorded.

In general, the soils at the lower altitudes (from 700 ft. to 1,100 ft.) are the deeper and more fertile clays and loams, with the less fertile millstone grit, shale or peat soils at altitudes from 1,100 ft. to 1,600 ft.

The slope of the land is no impediment to cultivation, except on the escarpments separating the high moorland plateau from the broad valleys, but drainage is poor on the peat, shale and clay soils. This results in poor permanent pastures, often with rushes, on much of the shale and clay soil and in water-logged rough grazings on the peat.[1] Even at the peak of the wartime ploughing-up policy in 1943–5, tillage as a percentage of cultivated land was only 6·9 per cent and temporary pasture 1·8 per cent. Ten years later, despite increases in the price of feeding stuffs, a national campaign for better grassland and ploughing-up grants, tillage area had fallen to 1·4 per cent and temporary pasture to 1·3 per cent of cultivated land.

On many farms at higher altitudes, the only fields with productive grasses are the meadows near the farm buildings. Conditions of access, soil-type, and drainage are partly responsible for this, for many of the farmhouses and buildings are built on the dry ridges, and therefore are likely to be surrounded by the drier land. Tradition cannot be discounted, however, particularly amongst those farmers with experience limited to a radius of a mile or so from their farms. To them, there is pasture-land and meadow-land; the former is where the cows go between milkings in the summer, and the other

---

[1] Most generalizations in the text are based on the analysis of information obtained from the sample farms which comprise just less than half the farm businesses in the area (see Appendix 1). Tests of significance or relationships quoted, or of tables on which statements in the text are based, are presented in Appendix 6.

provides hay and aftermath grazing. The former receives virtually no fertilization apart from what the cows put there. The latter is limed and dunged annually and might even occasionally receive further 'management' (bag fertilizer), although this type of farmer usually considers that 'artificials take all the goodness out of the land'.

Exposure and altitude are closely linked and three-quarters of the survey farms situated at over 1,100 ft. are in an exposed situation. The degree of exposure within altitude levels varies considerably, and a farm 200 ft. below and to the leeward of a 1,300 ft. rocky outcrop can be much more sheltered from wind and weather than one situated at the same altitude on an exposed upland flat. Consequently, farm reputations within very limited areas vary widely in the estimation of the local people.

Despite the high altitude and exposure of many of the farms, access to them from the farm gate is very good, 73 per cent being classified as having easy access. This is partly due to the operation of the Marginal Grants Scheme under which a subsidy was given for the provision of farm roads. The majority of roads have been improved within the last few years, and many farmers spoke appreciatively of the scheme—'the best subsidy there has ever been'.[1] It was also apparent that some of the stimulus towards improvements to farm roads had come through local contractors (living and farming in the area) persuading their neighbours, who were often relatives, to take advantage of the grant for their mutual benefit. A high proportion of the farms at the highest altitudes have easy access, because many of them are situated on or very near a public road.

With a general picture of the soils and topography in mind, we can examine the type of farming which has developed under these unfavourable natural conditions.

In a rational settlement of people on virgin country, the type of farming, size of farms, and intensity of their operation, bear some relationship to the productive potential of the land, and to the economic circumstances affecting agriculture. For example, in New Zealand, which has natural advantages favouring the growth of grass, there are dairy farming areas, fat lamb farming areas, and first-class, second-class and third-class hill country devoted to sheep farming. As the productivity of the land decreases, the type of farming changes, the farm sizes increase, and the intensity of their operation decreases.

---

[1] This is indeed praise in an area where memories of official interference in their affairs were very bitter, and anything stemming from what was still termed 'the War Ag.' was looked on with considerable suspicion.

Galbraith[1] has pointed out that original settlement plans may not stand the test of time if the land-potential and long-term economic prospects for agriculture are assessed on too optimistic a basis at the time of settlement. Nevertheless, the competitive power of the products which the resources of the newer-developed countries are best suited to produce indicates the economic advantages of a settlement and type-of-farming pattern which is closely related to the productive potential of the land.

In Britain the farming pattern we see now is the result of a continued process of adaptation applied to a limited area of land. Through the centuries, individuals, governments and various power or pressure groups have attempted to mould ways of life and productive resources in agriculture to fit in with changing social, economic and political circumstances. The larger the area of land controlled by an individual, and the more flexible its productive potential, the greater the chances of changing its agricultural uses to suit the individual—assuming he has the requisite skill, knowledge or capital.[2] Where land use is inflexible and farms are small, individual occupiers will not be very successful in altering land uses to meet changing circumstances and the farm families will suffer, unless they adapt themselves in other ways not dependent on the land.[3] This is clearly evident in the area of study.

A farming development based on land potential would probably have resulted in large farms extensively operated on the poor soils at the high altitudes, with smaller farms more intensively operated in the sheltered valleys. The actual position in the study area is the reverse of this. Between the altitude levels of 700 ft. and 1,100 ft., 53 per cent of the farms have a size of business of 15 'cow equivalents' or over,[4] whereas only 23 per cent of the farms are as large as

[1] Galbraith: 'Inequality in agriculture. Problem and programme', *op. cit.*

[2] Examples are: the success of the Enclosures for the landowners and large farmers; the swing to dairying on large downland farms prior to 1939, and their recent changes to sheep production from grassland; the ease with which production patterns may be adjusted on mainly arable farms. M. Marks has demonstrated the latter in comparisons with other types of farms (unpublished MS., Dept. of Agricultural Economics, Manchester University, 1961).

[3] For example, the failure of a tillage and temporary pasture system in the area of study, even under coercion; see above, page 23. The disastrous effects of attempting to increase the intensity of cropping with potatoes in Ireland is another example which also illustrates a non-agricultural adjustment by the farming people, i.e. migration from a country with little industrial development to the centres of industry in Britain and the U.S.A.

[4] The total acreage of the farm was not considered a good measure of either size of land resources, or of size of business. Areas of 'rough grazing' varied widely from farm to farm, but of more importance was the interpretation placed

Table 1: Size of farm business (in cow equivalents—C.E.)
and altitude

Altitude	Under 15 C.E.	15–29 C.E.	30 C.E. and over	Total
1,100 ft. and below	45	30	20	95
Over 1,100 ft.	59	14	4	77
Total	104	44	24	172

this at altitudes between 1,100 ft. and 1,600 ft. (Table 1). Further-more, the intensity of operation on the larger farms is greater than that on the smaller ones (Table 2). This is partly due to the general low level of intensity on cattle-rearing farms, most of which are small businesses on small farms at the higher altitudes. Most of the farms, however, are dairy farms and many of these are also small in size.

Table 2: Intensity of operation,* type of farm and size of business

	Low	Medium	High	Total
Total no. of farms	59	38	75	172
Type of farming:				
Mainly dairying	24	25	56	105
Dairying plus another enterprise	6	8	16	30
Cattle rearing	29	5	3	37
Size of business in cow equivalents:				
Under 15 C.E.	49	24	31	104
15–29 C.E.	10	8	26	44
30 C.E. and over	0	6	18	24

* Measured in acres of mowing grass per cow equivalent.

Even if cattle-rearing farms are excluded, the intensity of operation increases as the size of farms increases (Table 3).

Some adjustment of farming type to environment is evident: a greater proportion of the dairy farms at higher altitudes and on the poorer soils have another important enterprise in addition to dairy-ing compared with those at lower altitudes on the better soils

on the term by different farmers. Size of business was therefore measured in relation to adult livestock carried, stated as 'cow equivalents'. Intensity of opera-tion was taken as quantity of mowing grass per unit of cattle livestock carried. The reasons for using these measures and the methods of calculation are set out in Appendix 2.

(Table 4). This adjustment is rather more common on the larger farms than on the smaller ones.

Table 3: Intensity of operation and size of business: dairy farms only

	Low	Medium	High	Total
Under 15 C.E.	21	19	29	69
15–29 C.E.	9	8	25	42
30 C.E. and over	0	6	18	24
Total	30	33	72	135

Table 4: Type of farming, altitude and soil type

Type of farming	Altitude		Soil		
	1,100 ft. and below	Over 1,100 ft.	Good	Poor	Total
Mainly dairying	69	36	64	41	105
Dairying plus another important enterprise	17	13	14	16	30
Non-dairying	9	28	10	27	37
Total	95	77	88	84	172

Where other enterprises are important, these are usually sheep or poultry. No farm was encountered producing crops for sale, and only four farmers stated that pigs were produced for sale. Only thirteen survey-farms have more than 100 laying birds, although most have some poultry which play an important part in the internal economy and nutrition of the farm families. Where hen numbers are not very high, the egg money is usually the perquisite of the farmer's wife. It provides some regular money for housekeeping, and the hen food will be charged in with the total feed bill and paid out of the farm account.[1] On the isolated farms, where butchers do not call, meat is not a daily item on the menu. Eggs, together with cheese, provide a valuable source of protein to supplement a basic diet mainly dependent on bread, butter, syrup and sweet tea.

[1] Figures to support this impression were not collected as the whole matter was a most delicate one. Where details were sought, the interview-situation rapidly deteriorated, and the topic had to be dropped to safeguard the rest of the interview.

Sheep in small numbers—up to ten ewes—are run on some of the farms. However, only nine survey-farms have thirty ewes or more; of these, two have over 100 ewes. Six of these nine farms have a lot of rough grazing on their farms, or have access to moorland. In general, however, the extensive area of moorland which occurs in some parts is not available for either sheep or cattle grazing, because of estate policy in the past and because the shooting rights over the land were retained after the sale of the estate in 1951. This is unfortunate for the farmers, particularly where farms are small and the grazing season is short, for availability of 'keep' from the moors in autumn would be of considerable assistance in supplementing aftermath pasture, thus delaying the need to feed out the limited supplies of hard-won hay. In an area where the stone fences adjoining open country are not mountain-sheep proof, and often not cattle-proof either, stock inevitably do obtain some moorland grazing at the expense of friction between farmers and landowners. The difficulty of confining sheep within a man's own farm is probably another important factor limiting their numbers, for the opinion was expressed frequently that 'sheep and good neighbours do not go together'.

The pattern of farming described would not have arisen under conditions where the major determinants were agricultural ones. For almost two hundred years, however, agricultural production in Britain had been influenced by the industrialization of the economy and by the parallel growth of population. These two influences have had profound effects on the farming practised in the area of study.

For centuries, lead and copper were mined in some of the survey parishes and in adjacent parishes. The miners settled in the villages near the mines, which in some places formed separate distinct communities. Some miners squatted on land not in agricultural use, built houses on it and enclosed small areas. Such communities were on the poorest soils, in places situated either round the mines, or on the edge of moorland adjacent to tracks leading from the mines or villages.

From the seventeenth century onwards, trade developed in salt, lime and textiles, and coal of poor quality was mined locally for burning the limestone found in adjacent parishes. Like the base metals, the coal occurred in the least-populated parts of the area, and again the miners built homes near their work and enclosed land around them. Quarrying for stone developed later and was stimulated by the growth of industry in towns within a ten-mile radius. These nearby towns were linked to other more distant industrial centres by trade routes crossing the area. 'Out-work' was brought in by the pack-horse trade which passed through the area and this stimulated the development of cottage industries such as weaving, button-making and nail-making. As a result, by 1831 the land least suited to agriculture had a population with a variety of trades not directly linked to agriculture, although the more sheltered lower parishes continued to have a population dependent predominantly on farming.

A gazetteer published in 1834 includes button-makers, weavers and flax spinners amongst the 'principal inhabitants' of two of the parishes at the highest altitudes but mentions only three 'farmers' in one of these parishes which today has over twenty full-time farmers. All the lower parishes have village craftsmen and traders listed with farmers as 'principal inhabitants', but no occupation not dependent on agriculture is mentioned.

In all the parishes of the area for which the gazetteer gives information (except the two parishes at the high altitudes, mentioned above), the number of farmers listed is higher than the estimated number of full-time farmers for the same parishes in 1960.[1]

The banner of one of the local friendly societies provides graphic evidence of the importance of industrial employment in the past. The society is over one hundred years old and its present banner is a replica of the original. The scene depicted is almost entirely an industrial one. A blacksmith and a mason are shaking hands, in the background a factory chimney is smoking, while in the foreground lie a number of cog wheels. The only concession to agriculture is a bee-hive, and even this could represent 'industry'. Little now remains of the past industrial activity—a deserted flax mill, some scattered refuse from old coal workings, and a yellow ochre settling tank. Today, many of the office-bearers in the society belong to the old-established farming families, as do the majority of the ordinary members.

In the past, the industrial settlements and their population provided a local market for the dairy and livestock produce from the full-time farms in the agricultural parishes and also for any surplus

[1] There have been slight boundary changes in five of the parishes concerned and a major change in one parish. Excluding the latter parish, there were 133 'farmers' listed in 1834 as against an estimated number of 107 full-time farmers in 1960. The difference between these is close to the estimated increase in the full-time farmers in the highest parish, but mobility of farmers from low to high altitude parishes should not be imputed from this. The basis of classification of farmers included in the 1834 list is not known. It is possible that small full-time farmers were included in the lower parishes because they would be on the rent rolls, but similar ones in the high parishes who had squatted on waste land were not counted as 'farmers'. Examination of census enumeration-schedules would probably settle this point, but time was not available to do this in the present study.

production from the part-time subsistence holdings associated with the extractive and cottage industries.

As the pack-horse tracks were made into turnpike roads, trade in agricultural produce developed with the nearby towns. Thus, a locational advantage at a time when demand was increasing made dairying and livestock farming profitable, even though the natural features of the area were not very suitable for these types of farming.

Railways came late to the area and as a result the sale of liquid milk was not common up to the present century. Dairy farms produced store cattle and farmhouse cheese and butter and later supplied milk to cheese factories which were established in the area during the last quarter of the nineteenth century and the first part of the twentieth.

Recent work[1] suggests that, although farmers in corn-growing districts suffered from periods of agricultural depression in the nineteenth century, those farmers producing livestock products fared much better. The size of the farmhouses built on the more fertile farms in the area suggests that this general prosperity of livestock farmers was evident there too. A number of new houses were built about one hundred years ago. Without exception these are larger and more imposing than the older homes which remain alongside, or have been incorporated in them. There is similar visual evidence of prosperity in the farm buildings built during the same period.

Whilst full-time farmers prospered during the second half of the nineteenth century, the position of part-time farmers was changing for the worse. Cottage industries were declining under competition from factory-produced goods, and the poor-quality coal produced in the area lost its locational advantage once large-scale quarrying and lime burning began, using coal transported by railway and canal. In addition, as early as 1834, mining for metals had ceased at the two principal mines in the area.

Population statistics show that the better farming parts of the area increased in population until 1851, and did not lose much until after 1891. Those parts where cottage and extractive industries were common had already declined appreciably in population by 1851, and by 1891 had been reduced to almost half their 1831 figure (Table 5).

Since 1891 the population in each of the parishes has continued to decline, but not at any greater rate in the poorer farming parishes

---

[1] T. W. Fletcher: 'The Great Depression of English Agriculture, 1873–1896', *The Economic History Review*, Second Series, Vol. XIII, No. 3, 1961, pp. 417–32; and 'Lancashire livestock farming during the Great Depression', *Agricultural History Review*, Vol. IX, Part 1, 1961.

than in those where the better farms were situated. Figures are not available to indicate what proportion of the decline was of the non-farming, part-time farming or full-time farming population in the different parishes. The frequent occurrence of derelict holdings in all

Table 5: Population changes, property rateable values and part-time farming

Parishes*	Populations as percentage of 1831 populations				1951 population as percentage of 1931 population	Average rateable value of farmhouses in 1960	Part-time farming as percentage of all farmers surveyed, 1960
	1951	1931	1891	1851			
A	31	38	44	85	82	£6·1	50·0
B	32	34	55	71	94	£7·2	57·9
C	37	45	56	91	82	£7·6	40·7
D	40	50	52	84	81	£7·2	34·6
E	53	64	72	103	83	£8·3	30·0
F	57	73	88	96	78	£9·5	15·4
G	76	90	99	108	84	£10·7⎱	15·0
H	103	109	119	131	95	£10·2⎰	
All parishes	49	57	67	93	85	£8·1	34·3

* With the exception of parish C, the listing of parishes in ascending order of their 1951 population as a percentage of the 1831 population is roughly in descending order of their altitude levels and/or farm sizes. Parish C is surrounded by the others and at a lower altitude than D or F, but with rather more small farms than F.

stages of decay in the poorer parts of the area suggests that at least some of the reduction in population was made up of people who had been farming there. In the better farming districts there is no similar visual evidence of farming depopulation.

In the first quarter of the present century, the area lost its locational advantage for dairy products, but cheap concentrated feeding-stuffs, improvements in transport, and a demand for liquid milk enabled most of its farmers to remain in dairying. The full-time farmers either supplied the cheese factories, or transported milk to the railways which, while not running through the area, surround it on three sides. The part-time farmers on the small farms at the higher altitudes used to travel to work in the quarries, on the roads, in cheese factories located in the area, or in other factories in the surrounding countryside. Some of them took their milk to the railway station on their way to work. Others produced butter and eggs for sale in the local markets. Not being dependent on farming alone for a living, they maintained a system which would not have shown an adequate profit for a full-time farmer on a small farm.

The area was brought almost completely into the liquid milk market with the advent of milk collection by lorry, after the setting up of the Milk Marketing Board in 1933. The district by then was well served with roads and there was a guaranteed market for milk produced by all those who could comply with the minimal standards for cleanliness of production, and who could get their milk to a hard road.

Up to 1939, most of the farmers remained in dairying because of favourable ratios between the prices of milk and purchased feed, low rents, and the lack of profitable alternative uses for their land. Then, during the war, feeding-stuffs were rationed, and production of home-grown feed was not very successful.[1] Afterwards the ratio of the price of milk to the price of feed narrowed and other costs increased, but few farmers attempted to increase their returns by producing a higher quality of milk or by improving their grassland. Resentment arising from the compulsory powers exercised by the Agricultural Executive Committee made farmers suspicious of advice or innovations stemming from official quarters—to the extent that in 1955 only 15 per cent of the herds in the area were T.T. or attested, and most of the land was back in permanent pasture.

In addition to the adverse changes in prices and costs, very large changes from tenancy to owner-occupation occurred from 1950 onwards, due to the sale of a proportion of the main estate in the area. About 60 per cent of the farms surveyed had been tenanted in 1950, but only 31 per cent of them were tenanted in 1960. At that date, relatively more of the farms with a small size of business were wholly owned compared with the medium and large-sized farms, a situation arising from the high proportion of small farms included in the estate sale (Table 6).

Many of the farmers bought their farms as sitting tenants, at what appeared to be a very reasonable figure. Where the land and buildings were in good order, and either up to T.T. and attested standard or easily made so, the farmer probably benefited. But often, two or three years after the sale, the farmer found that he had merely bought the partially improved value of the farm. This was particularly so with the small farms at high altitudes. The cost of repairs necessary to bring these properties up to the new standards required

[1] See the reference on page 23 above to the tillage and pasture areas.

for milk production was often prohibitive, particularly if money had to be spent both on making the houses reasonably habitable and on buying attested cows. Rather than meet these costs,[1] particularly when they had to meet mortgage charges which were often

Table 6: Ownership of Farm and Size of Business

Ownership	Under 15 C.E.	15–29 C.E.	30 C.E. and over	Total
Tenanted	27	19	8	54
Part-tenanted, part-owned	9	8	6	23
Wholly owned	68	17	10	95
Total	104	44	24	172

greater than the original rent, some farmers went out of milk production. Most of these, but not all, were part-time farmers.

Of the farmers included in the survey thirteen of the thirty-seven on cattle-rearing farms had changed over from milk production early in 1960, when compulsory attestation came into effect and when clean milk regulations were strictly enforced. Other farmers were under a time limit to alter their buildings, water supply, and other facilities if they wanted to continue to sell milk. The marginal producers had put off changing to attestation until they were forced to do so or go out of business. This forced choice involved them in selling stock nobody wanted and in buying replacement stock locally,[2] in competition with other farmers similarly placed.

The final straw for some was the attitude of the newly set up Planning Authority which, quite within its rights, insisted on building alterations being carried out, either in local materials, or in such a manner as to blend with the countryside. Aesthetically, such standards were often higher, and consequently more costly, than those which the farmers who had to make the changes had in mind. It is not surprising, therefore, that a number of farmers went out of milk production, and some got into financial difficulties. There was evidence of mental strain, some farmers' wives were suffering from mental disorders and I frequently encountered bitterness against 'Them' (i.e. the authorities).

In this area for two centuries it has been a normal practice on the

[1] Or because they had not the resources to meet them.

[2] Few of the smallest producers had either the means of transport or the market confidence to venture beyond the local town.

part of some of the farming population to supplement farm incomes with industrial earnings. It is to be expected therefore that the social and spatial distribution of the farming people in the present will reflect that of the past. The parishes at the highest altitudes where the cottage and extractive industries were common in the past are the ones with the highest proportion of part-time farmers in the present. The full-time farmers with the larger farms are where they have always been—on the best land at the lower altitudes. The economic and social subtleties involved in the interrelationships between farming, other employment, and area of residence would be missed, however, if we were merely to consider the farmers as 'full-time' or 'part-time' farmers at 'low' or 'high' altitudes.

Four very distinct types of farm families can be distinguished. First there are the full-time farmers dependent wholly on their farm for earned income, and who have no family member working off the farm. These are at the top of the farming social scale, for there is no 'squirearchy'. Individual members vary widely in their economic status and this, together with the length of their family association with the area, determines their ranking within their class. Although more of them are farming at lower altitudes, the number of them at the higher altitudes is quite appreciable (Table 7a), and almost half of them are operating a small size of business (Table 7b). For convenience, in future chapters these full-time farmers will be referred

Table 7: Type of farmer, altitude of farm
and size of business

| | Type of farmer | | | | |
	Full-time, no family member working off	Full-time, some family member working off	Dual-business	At least farmer or wife working off	Total
a. Altitude of farm					
900 ft and below	21	3	4	4	32
901–1,100 ft.	33	14	8	8	63
1,101–1,300 ft.	19	7	3	15	44
Over 1,300 ft.	14	2	1	16	33
Total	87	26	16	43	172
b. Size of business					
Under 15 C.E.	41	17	7	39	104
15 C.E. and over	46	9	9	4	68
Total	87	26	16	43	172

to either as *small business* farmers (those with a size of business of less than 15 cow-equivalents), or as *larger business* farmers (those with a size of business of 15 cow-equivalents and over) whenever it is necessary to distinguish between them and other types of farmers in the area.

At the other end of the farming social scale are the farmers who have a full-time job off the farm. Rather more than a third of these have other family members who also work off the farm. In subsequent chapters these farmers will be termed *other-work* farmers. With only a few exceptions, the other-work farmers have a small size of business, and almost three-quarters of them live at the higher altitudes. Few of them work in the parishes where they live, and only two included in the survey work for other farmers. Most travel to quarries, roadwork, or factories in nearby parishes or in the town. The situation of their farms gives them an advantage over small farmers on better land, since often the farms at the higher altitudes are adjacent to the main roads passing through the area, and are thus conveniently situated for travel to work by the occupiers. This is particularly important in winter, for the main roads are kept free of snow when subsidiary ones, or long farm tracks, are impassable.

Many of the other-work farmers consider themselves workers first, and farmers second. The conversation in their homes is not confined to farming topics: indeed farming is often not discussed at all. They tend to compare their situation with that of other workers rather than with the farmers on larger farms, whose ways of life are considered remote: "some of 'em down there are a bit too toffee-nosed, you know, and not like us up here."

The third type of farming family has the farmer and his wife working full-time at home, but has other family members working off the property, usually as a matter of necessity, because farm sizes and family needs are not well equated. Unlike the other-work farmers, these farmers feel the status implications involved in partially moving away from full-time farming. These farmers will be referred to subsequently as *family-earning* farmers, to distinguish them from full-time farmers whose families do not work off the farm and from the other-work farmers.

The farmers who obtain the best of two worlds are those who are self-employed in two occupations, of which one is farming. These farmers will be referred to subsequently as *dual-business* farmers. None of these has family members working for anyone else, all are relatively prosperous, and most enjoy a high status in the community. Included amongst them are the surviving rural craftsmen, now become builders—whether originating as masons, wheelwrights

Table 8: Farm and non-farm earnings for a random sample of farms in the area of study and adjacent parishes, 1955

Area of farms	No. of farms	Persons in full-time employment per family	Time spent on work outside farm %	Average earnings from farming		Average earnings from non-farm work		Total earned income (average)		
				per farm £	per full-time person £	per farm £	per full-time person £	per farm £	per full-time person £	per person of working age £
Under 20 acres	7	1·3	62	222	458	353	441	575	447	268
20–50 acres	20	1·6	25	326	267	146	361	472	291	197
50–100 acres	10	1·8	11	415	257	126	628	540	298	200
Over 100 acres	6	1·8	4	759	430	25	375	784	428	248
All farms	43	1·6	23	390	308	158	422	548	334	216

or joiners; the rural traders—publicans, cattle-dealers and corn merchants, and the agricultural contractors who have taken over from the carters and the blacksmiths of the past. Like the rural crafts-men of the past, the dual-business farmers are bound by social and economic ties to the full-time farmers and identify themselves with them.

No particulars of income were obtained from any of the farmers, but it is obvious from the spending habits and the material goods possessed by those with a job as well as a farm, that they are better off financially than are many of the full-time farmers. This impression is confirmed by evidence from economic surveys[1] of farms in the area and similar adjacent parishes. Over the ten years 1948–58 the average net farm incomes for farms of under 50 acres were less than agricultural wages, giving no return to management, or on capital invested. Average net farm incomes for farms of 50–100 acres never exceeded £600 and were less than £500 in seven of the ten years. But, for a group of farms specially surveyed in 1955, although net farm incomes were lowest on farms of under 20 acres, the average total earned incomes on these farms were only exceeded by those farms of 100 acres and over. The extra income going into the smallest farms from work off the farm by family members more than made up for the lower farm incomes compared with farms of 20 to 100 acres (Table 8). On the farms surveyed in 1955 the average farm income per 'full-time male equivalent' was £345. This compared with average earnings of £384 for farm workers at that time, and of £423 for the family members working full-time off the surveyed farms.

The above figures suggest that at the present time it would be financially more rewarding to engage in non-agricultural work from all except the largest farms in the area. Social position and advance-ment, however, still depend on a person having close associations with farming and on his accepting the values of the farming com-munity. This social aspect has probably always been evident, but the conflict between how you obtain your money, what you do with it, and in whose company you spend it, is becoming more intense as economic conditions make it increasingly difficult to obtain an adequate income exclusively from farming.

[1] G. W. Furness: *The Economics of Small Farms in the North West of England*, unpublished M.Sc. thesis, University of Leeds, 1959. Unpublished material, University of Manchester, Department of Agricultural Economics, 1961.

CHAPTER III

FARMS, FAMILIES AND OTHER WORK

WHEN agricultural economists examine the problems of family farming, they tend to set up stereotypes: 'the farmer and his wife', 'the farmer and his family', the 'family labour force plus employed labour'. Average figures of labour use obscure reality further, particularly when they are based on assessed hours of labour and not related to frequency distributions of the actual number of people working on particular farms.

The 'farmer and his wife' can be a useful concept when both are young and have no children, but, on a farm where the wife has to care for a number of children under school age, neither 'the farmer and his wife' nor the 'farm family labour force' are good descriptions of the family labour available for farm work.

The *family* in family farming is not a constant unit. At any one point in time a group of 'family farms' will have very disparate elements. One may consist of a bachelor living alone, another may be the 'ideal' of father, mother and working son, yet another may be a widowed mother with her single son. In course of time, a particular farm family will change in number, vigour and requirements. Frequently, the farm resources available will not change to the same extent as either the quantities and qualities of labour to exploit them, or the needs of the family. Herein lies the basic problem of family farming. To overcome it, farmers move from farm to farm, or acquire and give up land; they prevail on their single sons to remain at home, and they marry off their daughters; they change the intensity of operation of their farms, or go out to work; they quarrel with kin, whilst befriending neighbours.

Before looking at the mobility of farmers and their kin, we need to have a clear picture of the variation in structure of the families concerned, and we need to know the degree to which those structures harmonize or conflict with the farm sizes, types of farming and the opportunities for employment off the farm.

SEX AND AGE DISTRIBUTION OF FARM PEOPLE[1]

Of the 172 farmers[2] included in the survey, 27 are single and 145

[1] Some of the demographic features of the farm families surveyed are compared with figures from other surveys, and with national statistics, in Appendix 3.

[2] The term 'farmer' is applied to the person who was stated at the interview

are married. Four of the single farmers are women, and there are three widowers and four widows amongst the married farmers.

Nine per cent of the farmers are under 35 years of age, and 12 per cent are 65 or over, with the remainder more or less evenly distributed over the intermediate age ranges. More of the wives are under 35 than are their husbands, and fewer of them are over 65 (Table 9).

Table 9: Ages of farmers and wives compared

Age group	Wives	Husbands	Total
Under 35	30	14	44
35–44	33	40	73
45–54	31	32	63
55–64	33	35	68
65 and over	11	17	28
Total	138	138	276

The extent of the age difference between married pairs varies considerably. Twenty per cent of the wives are older than their husbands, whilst 19 per cent of the husbands are eight or more years older than their wives (Table 10).

Table 10: Age difference between farmers and wives*

Age difference	Percentage of marriages
Wives older than husbands	20
Husbands and wives same age	7
Husbands 1–3 years older than wives	31
Husbands 4–7 years older than wives	23
Husbands 8 years or more older than wives	19
Total	100

* Includes widows and widowers.

There are 633 family members[1] living on the farms. The farmers, their wives and unmarried children account for 89 per cent of these, the remaining 11 per cent being made up of married children and

---

to be the farmer. Where there are siblings in partnership, particulars about the 'farmer' refer to the eldest sibling.

[1] Exact information about non-family members living on farms was not obtained, but there are 27 workers employed on the farms, one housekeeper and one lodger. Of the 27 workers, fewer than 10 are living in the farmhouse with the family.

Table 11: Sex and age distribution of all family members living on the farms surveyed

Family member	Under 5 M	Under 5 F	5–14 M	5–14 F	15–20 M	15–20 F	21–25 M	21–25 F	26–30 M	26–30 F	31–35 M	31–35 F	36–44 M	36–44 F	45–54 M	45–54 F	55–64 M	55–64 F	65 and over M	65 and over F	Total M	Total F	Grouped totals	%
Single farmers									1		1		8	1	7	2	4	1	2	0	23	4	310	49
Married farmers									6		8		40	0	33	0	37	2	17	2	141	4	(310)	
Farmers' wives							—	6	—	8	—	16	—	33	—	31	—	33	—	11	—	138	(310)	
Children not working	22	24	51	48	0	2															73	74	252	40
Single children working					32	12	21	8	10	6	8		8								79	26	(252)	
Married children					1	0			1		1	3	2	0							4	3	21	3·3
Married child's spouse									1		1	1	1	3							3	4	(21)	
Grandchildren	1	2	1	1	1	1															3	4	(21)	
Siblings of husband or wife									3		1	1	1		3		1			0	9	1	27	4·2
Spouse of siblings											1	1	1				0	5	0	0	2	6	(27)	
Children of siblings	1	0	1	0	1			2				3		1							3	6	(27)	
Single farmers' parents																			3	3	3	3	23	3·5
Married farmers' parents																			0	5	0	5	(23)	
Wife's parents																			3	2	3	2	(23)	
Parents' siblings																			1	6	1	6	(23)	
Totals	24	26	53	49	33	14	23	14	23	14	18	25	61	38	43	34	42	43	27	29	347	286	633	
Percentage in each sex	48	52	52	48	M 67			F 33	M 51			F 49	62	38	56	44	49	51	49	51	M 51	F 45		

their families, siblings and their families, and parents and parents' siblings of the farmers or their wives (Table 11).

Altogether, there are 82 females for every 100 males, but there is considerable variation between age groups in the proportion of males and females. From 0–14 years of age, 26–35, and 55 and over, the sex proportions are approximately equal; but there are rather more males than females between the ages of 36 and 54, and twice as many males as females in the age range 15–25.[1] The differences are mainly due to the much greater numbers of single male children of working age, compared with single female children of working age and to the predominance of males amongst the single farmers. In addition, there are eight more females than males amongst the parents and parents' siblings living on the farms. Other variations in the proportion of males to females are accounted for by the generally younger ages of farmers' wives compared with their husbands.

The lower proportion of females in rural populations is a well-known phenomenon. Saville[2] has calculated that in England and Wales in 1951 there were 98·9 females to every 100 males in the rural districts, compared with 108·5 in the population as a whole. In 1951 the ratio was 100·5 for the rural district in which the surveyed parishes were situated, but for the eight upland parishes included in this survey it was 93·0, indicating a considerable difference between the upland and lowland parts of the district. For the sample farming population the ratio is 82·0. This much lower proportion is due partly to a statistical anomaly, and partly to different rates of occupational and marriage mobility for farmers' daughters compared with farmers' sons. The latter will form one of the themes of discussion in later chapters, but the statistical anomaly needs an explanation here.

The ratio of 82·0 applies to all the family members actually living on the farms at the time of the survey but excludes those sons and daughters who have left home. If we look at the distribution of males and females amongst *all* children who have been born and reared in the families of the people now farming, we would expect to find that there are approximately the same number of males as females. This is true for the children under 15 (77 compared with 75), but for those aged 15 and over there are rather more sons than daughters (136

[1] For reasons related to other analyses, some of the relatives of the farmers are classified slightly differently from others. This causes the ranges in some adjacent categories to overlap by one year.

[2] Saville, *Rural Depopulation*, p. 34; he discusses the phenomenon for different time periods and areas in Ch. I and III.

compared with 120). The difference is not statistically significant either when the total numbers are considered, or when only those under 30 and over the age of 30 are considered. A significant difference in the numbers of sons and daughters is apparent, however, when the children under 30 are divided into three further age categories, for there are less than half as many daughters as sons aged under 20, and only two-thirds as many sons as daughters aged 26–30 (Table 12).

Table 12: Ages and sex of farmers' children of working age

Age	Males	Females	Total
Under 21	43	19	62
21–25	28	24	52
26–30	21	31	52
Over 30	44	46	90
Total	136	120	256

Most of the excess of sons over daughters can be traced to the group of families who have children both under and over working age, and within this group mainly to 13 families in which the wife is still of child-bearing age (i.e. under 45). No causal relationships can be established by statistical means, but examination of the individual circumstances indicates some patterns which might help to explain the anomaly. For those families with more than three children, and where the youngest is under five, it is possible that the wife could still have one or more children. If a higher proportion of these were girls, this would help to redress the balance. Seven families of the 13 consist of only one girl, with two or three boys. In five of these, the girl is the youngest, and in one she is the eldest. For the five families, once a girl has been born after a run of boys, the parents may then have taken measures against having more children. Where the girl is the youngest the supposition could be that the parents have taken measures against more children, once they have an adequate 'work force' of boys.

I realize that these theories are highly speculative, based as they are on such a small number of families. They fit in, however, with farmers' needs for sons to help operate full-time farms and to supplement farm income by work off the farms on part-time ones. (Sons are more valuable than daughters for either purpose as they are available for a longer period than are daughters, who marry at earlier ages.) The idea of 'trying for a boy', or of being satisfied with one child if it was a boy but not if it was a girl, is supported by a comparison of the actual proportions of sons to daughters in the completed families (i.e. those in which the wife is over 45) with an expected distribution based on the size of the families and a postulated 50:50 chance of a boy or a girl at each birth.

If some farming parents limit their families once they have a male heir, continue to have children until they have a male heir, or only cease to have children once a girl has been born, we can expect:

i. More families with an only child a male than with an only child a female.

ii. More families with 'boys only' than with 'girls only'.

iii. More families with 'more girls than boys' than with 'more boys than girls'.

These expectations are confirmed by Table 13.

Table 13: Actual and expected* sex proportions in completed families

Sex distributions in completed families	O (actual no. of families)	E (expected no. families)	O−E	(O−E)²	(O−E)²/E
Only boy	11·0	6·5	4·5	20·25	3·1154
Only girl	2·0	6·5	−4·5	20·25	3·1154
Only boys	7·0	7·9204	−0·9204	0·8471	0·1070
Only girls	5·0	7·9204	−2·9204	8·5287	1·0768
More boys than girls	10·0	14·5116	−4·5116	20·3545	1·4026
Same number of boys and girls	21·0	17·1328	3·8672	14·9552	0·8729
More girls than boys	19·0	14·5116	4·4884	20·1457	1·3882
Total	75·0	74·9968	+12·8556 −12·8524	—	11·0783

χ^2 = 11·0783. Significant at 10 per cent level
v = 6   Significance point for 5 per cent at
           v = 6 is 12·59

* See Appendix 4 for calculation of 'expected' number of families.

The largest components of χ^2 in Table 13 are those relating to more families with an only boy than with an only girl. This would support an alternative theory that some parents who have failed to have a son may leave farming once their daughters marry.

Information is not available from the survey material to show conclusively whether the larger proportion of male to female births is either a chance occurrence peculiar to the sample, a function of family limitation operating in favour of boys, or due to the emigration of 'all girl' families. Evidence of intent would be required to support the thesis based on family limitation. This was not collected, nor was there any indirect evidence from conversations of a desire for boys rather than for girls. No demographic data was obtained

Table 14: Sex, age and marital status,
all farmers' children of working age

Age	Single	Married	Total
Under 26:			
Sons	71	0	71
Daughters	24	19	43
Total	95	19	114
26–30:			
Sons	12	9	21
Daughters	6	25	31
Total	18	34	52
Over 30:			
Sons	18	26	44
Daughters	9	37	46
Total	27	63	90
All ages:			
Sons	101	35	136
Daughters	39	81	120
Total	140	116	256

about families who had moved out of farming, so it was not possible to test whether in fact there was a greater emigration of 'all girl' families. This latter thesis does not seem to be supported by other observations, for amongst the farmers and wives whose parents were farmers the proportion of wives who have no brothers is not significantly different from the proportion of farmers who have no sisters.[1] Furthermore, in an 'all-daughter' family of a full-time farmer, a daughter will tend to take the place of a son and work on the farm.

[1] 21·6 per cent and 18·7 per cent respectively.

Often when such a daughter marries she does not leave home but her husband joins the family and operates the farm for the parents.

The absolute discrepancy in the *number* of farmers' daughters compared with farmers' sons does not greatly affect the analysis presented later, for the comparisons drawn in this and subsequent chapters are between the *proportions* of sons and daughters in different categories. The major difference between sons and daughters of working age is in the proportion who are married and single. Twenty-six per cent of the sons are married, compared with 59 per cent of the daughters. This difference is a significant one for all age categories (Table 14).

FAMILY COMPOSITION AND HOUSEHOLD SIZE

Two-thirds of the married households consist of elementary families (parents with unmarried children) and approximately one-eighth are either childless couples, couples whose children have left home, or widowers living alone. The remainder are composite households made up of elementary family units in some combination with parents, siblings, married children, grandchildren or other relatives.

Ten of the single farmers live alone, six live with one or both parents, seven with unmarried or widowed siblings, one with a married sibling, one with a parent and married sibling, one has a housekeeper, and one is an unmarried woman with young children.

Considering the people living on the farms in terms of households, rather than on the basis of their relationship to the farmers, there are 26 per cent one-generation, 62 per cent two-generation and 12 per cent three-generation households.

Others[1] who have studied rural communities in England and Wales have remarked on the relatively small number of three-generation households, and suggested that this was probably related to the absence of the custom (common in some peasant communities) whereby parents retired into a part of the house instead of to a separate dwelling.[2] They have not, however, examined the economic and housing circumstances of three-generation households. This has been done for the 21 three-generation households in this study. In two households there is the equivalent of a 'West Room'. One of these is of long standing, and is actually on the west gable end of the house. The parents of the wife retired to this when in their seventies,

[1] Williams, *The Sociology of an English Village;* Rees, *Life in a Welsh Countryside*, p. 70; Williams, *Ashworthy.*
[2] Exemplified by the 'West Room' of Ireland, see Arensberg, *The Irish Countryman.*

and the daughter and son-in-law took over the farm. Prior to this, the son-in-law went out to work, and he and his wife lived on an adjacent smallholding. In the same area as this particular household, one other farm with a West Room construction was observed, but the West Room part was occupied by people not related to those in the farmhouse, both sets of occupiers being tenants. The other example is of recent origin: a house has been split into two in order to accommodate the different generations. In 14 of the other 19 households, the houses are large enough to accommodate comfortably the three generations living in them.[1] In two, there are two houses on the farm property, as a result of amalgamation of the original farm prior to the marriage of the present farmer.

The economic bases of all the three-generation households are adequate by the standards current in the area. In 17 out of the 21 households, one or more of the oldest generation is of pension age and eligible to receive it.[2] Eleven of the households have a farm business size of under 15 cow equivalents, but in 10 of these one or more of the members of the household works off the farm full-time, and in nine of the 10 cases one or more is eligible for the old age pension. The household where no one is eligible for the old age pension has three members, including the farmer, who work off the farm. In the five households where the business size is between 15 and 30 cow equivalents, either at least one member is eligible for the old age pension, or some other member works off the farm. The size of business in the other five households is over 30 cow equivalents, and adequate to the needs of the three generations living in them.

In contrast to the situation for three-generation households, no house occupied by the 12 farmers living on their own would have been adequate in size for a three-generation household, without overcrowding, and six of them would have been inadequate for a two-generation household. Ten of the 12 farmers living alone have a size of business which is inadequate, without other work, even to support themselves. However, four of these have other employment and one has an old age pension but the other five are in a 'social problem category' which will be discussed later in this chapter.

A similar limitation in size of house and size of business is evident in the households of those 14 single farmers who live with their parents, their unmarried or widowed siblings or with non-relatives. Twelve of these have houses which would be inadequate for a three-

---

[1] Particulars of the number of bedrooms and public rooms were available from sale catalogues for rather over 40 per cent of the farms; for the others, size was assessed on the basis of observed outside and inside features.

[2] That is, either not nominally the farmer, or over 70 years of age.

generation family, and nine of them have sizes of business inadequate for the households as they are. Of these nine households, four obtain other income from work off the farm or from old age pensions, but five have either insufficient off-farm income, or none at all. Again, these present a special problem which will be discussed later.

In an area such as this, where farm resources are relatively poor, we might expect to find that the family living conditions[1] would deteriorate as the total number of people in the household increases. The relationship, however, is not such a simple one. In fact, greater proportions of the households at the two extremes of the size-range have poorer living conditions than have those in the middle of the range. Thus, 'poor' living conditions exist in a greater proportion of the households with only one or two members than in households with three or more members. Conversely, 'good' living conditions obtain in a lower proportion of households with five or more members, than in households of smaller size (Table 15). The households which have the highest proportion of 'poor' living conditions are those consisting either of one person only, or of seven or more people.

Table 15: Household size and living conditions

| Total family in household | Living conditions | | | Total |
	Poor	Medium	Good	
One or two	11	18	17	46
Three or four	4	33	46	83
Five or more	5	24	14	43
Total	20	75	77	172

The foregoing discussion on household size suggests that the majority of farm families have either adequate farm resources or

[1] Living conditions were assessed partly objectively and partly subjectively. The basis was:
i. Presence or absence of electricity, whether mains or generated on the farm;
ii. Evidence of overcrowding as indicated by the number of bedrooms in relation to the type and number of people in the household;
iii. An appraisement of furniture and fittings.
The assessment into three categories is an attempt to classify living conditions on the basis of the standards of living accepted in the area, and should not be taken as a comparison with urban or any other area. Mains water is completely absent from the area, many of the farms have no indoor or septic tank sanitation, and where electricity is generated on the farm, it is usually adequate for lighting, milking machinery, small domestic appliances and a television set, but not for cookers, refrigerators and all the equipment of modern urban living.

sufficient supplementary employment to provide them with reasonable living conditions, but that some households of all sizes have a poor balance between resources and number of family members. This imbalance is particularly marked amongst single people living alone and large households. The difficulties of some of the single people have already been mentioned. It is pertinent to note that all the households with seven or more members, and living under poor conditions, are elementary families who depend for a living almost entirely on their farm resources.

FARM AND HOUSEHOLD SIZE

When households of different size are examined on the basis of farm resources, as indicated by size of farm, a progressively greater proportion are found to be in the larger size categories as household size increases. Thus, only 9 per cent of the households with one or two family members live on farms of 120 acres and over, compared with 17 per cent of the 'three and four' households, and 26 per cent of the 'five and over' households. Despite this tendency, there is an obvious imbalance between farm size and household size, for 59 per cent of all households live on farms of under 60 acres.

In Chapter II, the acres of mowing grass on the farms and the cow equivalents kept were taken respectively as standards of productive land resources and of the use made of these resources by the farmer. When these standards are related to the number of people in the farm household, they provide measures of land resources and size of farm business per person in the household.[1] On this basis fewer households are in the low category, and more in the medium and high categories, than in a straight classification based on size of farm resources, irrespective of household size (Table 16). Even so, 45 per cent of the households are still classified as having low re-

---

[1] For 'acres of mowing grass per household member':

low	=	under 5·0 acres
medium	=	5·0 to 9·9 acres
high	=	10·0 acres and over.

For 'cow equivalents per household member':

low	=	under 3·5 C.E.
medium	=	3·5–6·9 C.E.
high	=	7·0 C.E. and over.

For example, for a household of six on a farm of over 120 acres (with 70 acres of mowing grass and 40 C.E.) they show figures of 11·7 acres of mowing grass and 6·7 C.E. per head. This compares with 8·0 acres of mowing grass and 7·5 C.E. per head for a household of two on a farm of less than 60 acres which has 16 acres of mowing grass and 15 cows.

Table 16: Comparison between different classifications
of farm size

| Size of farm classification | Acres of mowing grass | | Cow equivalents | | Total acres per farm |
	per farm	per household member	per farm	per household member	
Low	97	79	104	85	101
Medium	53	63	44	47	42
High	22	30	24	40	29
Total	172	172	172	172	172

sources, and less than half this proportion as having high resources.
Some farmers supplement dairying with other enterprises (mainly
poultry), and it might have been expected that a greater proportion
of those with low land resources per family member would have been
supplementing their business in this way. This is not so. Amongst
those farmers who are dairying, there is no significant variation,
amongst the farmers with low, medium or high resources, in the
proportions who have another important enterprise (Table 17). The
great majority of non-dairying farmers have low land resources and
low sizes of business per household member.

Table 17: Type of farming and land resources per person
in household

| Type of farming | Acres of mowing grass per household member | | | |
	Low	Medium	High	Total
Mainly dairying	36	47	22	105
Dairying plus another important enterprise	11	12	7	30
Not dairying	32	4	1	37
Total	79	63	30	172

RESOURCES PER FAMILY MEMBER AND EMPLOYMENT OFF THE FARM

It would appear from the above comparisons between household
size and farm resources that the economic circumstances of the
households living in the area cannot be adequately explained in
terms of farming factors alone. A clearer picture emerges, however,
when employment off the farm is examined. The availability of other
work in this area enables people to live on farms which would other-

E

wise be too small to support a family. Fifty-one per cent of the farmers with small sizes of business per family member either have another full-time job themselves, or have another business (such as building or agricultural contracting) (Table 18); in a few cases it is

Table 18: Size of business and off-farm employment of farmer or wife

| Farming employment | Cow equivalents per person in household | | | Total |
	Low	Medium	High	
Farming mainly	42	37	34	113
Dual business	5	5	6	16
Full-time work off by farmer or wife	38	5	0	43
Total	85	47	40	172

Table 19: Size of business and off-farm employment of other family members (i.e. excluding farmer and wife)

| | Cow equivalents per person in household | | | Total |
	Low	Medium	High	
No workers off	60	35	40	135
Some workers off	25	12	0	37
Total	85	47	40	172

the farmer's wife who works full-time off the farm. In addition, 29 per cent have other family members working off the farm (Table 19). In all, 62 per cent of the farming households with small sizes of business have someone working off the farm. This may be simply the farmer himself, his wife, some other member or members of his family, or it may be the farmer together with some other member or

Table 20: Size of business and off-farm employment of any family member, including farmer and wife

| | Cow equivalents per person in household | | Total |
	Low	Medium and high	
No workers off	32	71	103
One working off	34	13	47
Two or more working off	19	3	22
Total	85	87	172

members of his family (Table 20). The proportion of households with members working off the farm is significantly lower for those with a medium size of business than for those with a small size of business, and no farmer or other family member works off the farm from those households with a large size of business.

Size of household could be expected to influence both the need for off-farm employment and the availability of family labour for such work. In line with this expectation, a higher proportion of households with only one or two family members have no one working off the farm, compared with those having three or more members (Table 21).

Table 21: Size of household and off-farm employment
of any family member

| | Total family in household | | Total |
	One or two	Three or more	
No workers off	34	69	103
Some workers off	12	57	69
Total	46	126	172

Those farmers who work off their farms are not under the same pressure to maintain an intensive system of farming as are those who depend upon their farm for their whole livelihood. Thus we find that, compared with full-time farmers, a much higher proportion of the farmers who work off their farms are not dairying and the size of their businesses tends to be low (Table 22). To the individual

Table 22: Type of farming employment and size of business

| | Cow equivalents per household member | | Total |
	Low	Medium and high	
Dairying and dairying plus another important enterprise:			
Farming and dual business only	38	79	117
Full-time work off by farmer and wife	13	5	18
Not dairying:			
Farming and dual business only	9	3	12
Full-time work off by farmer and wife	25	0	25
Total	85	87	172

concerned this has the advantage that he need not work as hard or invest as much capital as would be necessary if he were to maintain a dairying business. The nation gains too, for a less intensive system should not require the same degree of Exchequer support in the form of direct or indirect subsidies.

THE FAMILY DEVELOPMENTAL CYCLE

The interrelationship between the demography of the farm people, the farm economy, and other employment, has so far been considered in terms of a slice through time, that is, at the point in time when the survey was undertaken. Such a view is unrealistic, unless examined in the context of a time scale, since a study of mobility is by its nature concerned with movements of people over time. Obviously, information of the type presented in this chapter cannot be obtained in practice by carrying out a series of stage-by-stage investigations into the developmental cycle of the families concerned. Some picture can be obtained, however, by examining groups of families within the present sample who are at different phases in the cycle.

Watson[1] suggests that there are four distinct phases in family development:

> *The phase of expansion*, which commences at marriage and ends when the youngest child achieves adult status, either by reaching the age of 21 or through marriage at an earlier age.
> *The phase of dispersion*, which commences when the first child achieves adult status and is free to leave home, and ends when all children have achieved adult status and left home.
> *The phase of independence*, which commences when the last child has left home and ends in retirement.
> *The phase of replacement*, which commences when the parents retire and ends when they are both dead.

The onset and duration of these phases is influenced by the age of the wife at marriage, the length of her fertile period, the family's health and expectation of life, and the age and conditions of retirement. Not all families exhibit all phases, and the onset and termination of one phase may overlap those of another.

Where family farming predominates[2] and small farm businesses

---

[1] W. Watson and M. Susser: *Sociology in Medicine*, 1963, Ch. 6: The cycle in family development, p. 195.
[2] 87 per cent of the farmers surveyed employ no labour other than members of their families. Most of the 13 per cent who do employ other labour are at a stage in their family developmental cycle which make it necessary to do so because insufficient labour is available from within their own family.

are supplemented by one or more members of the household working off the farm, the phases of family development outlined above will influence both the operation of the farm and the degree to which off-farm supplementation of income is possible. Thus, in the households of married farmers, the early stages of the phase of expansion place a strain upon family income and upon the labour-force available for earning that income. Children's needs make demands on the family income, and usually the farmer and his wife are the only family members in a position to earn that income, either by operating the farm or by working off it.

The duties of the farmer's wife are particularly arduous in the early stages of the phase of expansion, if there is a number of children in the family. In addition to caring for the children and carrying out her normal household tasks on the full-time farm she has to assist her husband with farm work whenever the farm operations require more than one person and, on the part-time farm, she has to carry out essential farm jobs while her husband is away at work. Under these circumstances it is not surprising that the children begin to help on the farm as soon as they are old enough to be useful.

The financial or work burden on parents lessens as children leave school and start to work on the farm, or at jobs away from it. But a surplus of family labour may then occur amongst those families with no tradition of working off the farm and whose farm businesses are not large enough to provide adequate full-time work for more than one or two people.

The onset of the phase of dispersion can have a number of effects on farm families. A parent is likely to prevail upon a son or daughter to remain at home, unmarried, and to assist, on those farms where either more than one person is needed for at least part of the farming year, or one parent has died whilst the other is relatively young. Under these circumstances, although legally free to leave home, children frequently remain, whether from a sense of filial duty or from an interest in the prospects of inheritance. By contrast, the departure of some children from home will be welcomed in those families where the farm-size is not large enough to offer adequate employment for all the children or to cater for the needs of a family of adults. On part-time farms where children have worked off, the onset of the phase of dispersion may not greatly affect the family. A child who reaches adult status and leaves home will no longer need to be fed and cared for, and this will compensate for the loss of part of its earnings which it may have contributed towards the family income.

The phase of independence will not occur in those families where one or more of the children remain at home until the death or retirement of their parents. Such a position may arise when one child remains unmarried with the parents, or when the youngest child of a late marriage reaches adult status only after the parents' retirement, or after one or other of them has died. It is unlikely that farm families remaining on farms will pass into the phase of independence if there is property considered to be worth inheriting; but, if all children leave home for better opportunities, some aged couples may be left alone on the farms. These people may have difficulty in supporting themselves or in effectively operating their farms.

The above discussion on the phases in family development suggests that, for this sample of farm people, three other phases are likely to be of importance when considering labour utilization on the farms, the size of farm and size of family, and the supplementation of farm income with earnings from other work. These other phases are:

a. *An early phase*, in which either all the children are under 15, or the farmer's wife (though young enough to bear children) has no family.
b. *A middle phase*, in which some of the children are of working age, live at home, and work on or off the farm.
c. *A late phase*, in which either children have all left home, or the wife is past the age of childbearing and has no children.

Phase *a*. covers the first part of the phase of expansion; phase *b*. covers the latter part of the phase of expansion and all the phase of dispersion; and phase *c*. is identical with the phase of independence.

These three phases, which I propose to use, are not so precise as the phases which Watson uses in describing the family developmental cycle. For example, some families may have children under 15 living at home and some children of working age not living at home. These families will be closer to my phase *a*. than to my phase *b*. from the point of view of availability of family labour for work on or off the farm.[1] Despite their lack of sociological precision, these three phases are useful when examining the effects of the family developmental cycle on economic conditions of family farms.

Phase *a*. will be a period where the vigour of the parents and the demands of the family (if there is a family) will be high, but where only the labour of the parents will be available.

Phase *b*. will still be a period of high family demand, but it will coincide with the availability of family labour for farm and off-farm employment, thus off-setting the reducing vigour of the parents.

[1] The six which occur in the sample are included in phase *a*. for analysis purposes.

Phase *c*. will be a period of lower family needs, coinciding with the decline in vigour of the parents.

The presence of other family members—unmarried siblings, parents or married children—during these phases will increase the total demands of the family, but may assist in meeting them by providing extra productive labour for utilization by the family, on or off the farm.

When the married households living on the sample farms are classified in terms of the above three phases, 55 are in the early phase, 67 in the middle phase, and 23 in the late phase. There are no families in the early phase with other members working off the property apart from the farmer or his wife, and there are only two other family members working off from families in the late phase. This follows from the definitions of the three phases, and from the composition of households indicated earlier.[1] Most of the other family members working off are from families in the middle phase, where children of working age are present.

In all three phases, there are households where the farmers or their wives work off the properties, with rather fewer doing so from households in the middle phase. Despite this, a greater proportion of these middle-phase households have a family member of some sort working off the property. This may be the farmer, one or more of his children, his wife, or another relative (Table 23). The absence of available 'other workers' in the early and late phases more than makes up for the rather greater proportion of farmers who work off from early-phase households.

Table 23: Phase in family developmental cycle and off-farm employment of any family member

Phase in family cycle	None working off	Some working off	Total
Early and Late	50	28	78
Middle	33	34	67
Total	83	62	145

There is little difference in size of household between those families in the early and middle phases, but, as would be expected from the

[1] Others available for work off the farm are siblings, parents or other relatives of the farmer and his wife. As none of these work off from families in the early phase and, by definition, this phase has no children of working age, there are no other people working off from the households in this phase, apart from the farmer or his wife.

definition of the phases, most of the late-phase households have only one or two family members. It has already been indicated that fewer households comprising one or two members have members working off, and that as size of farm business increases, the proportion of households with members working off decreases; also, that the size of household tends to increase with the size of business. To eliminate the effects of small household size, large size of business, and late phase in the developmental cycle on the number of households with people working off, we can examine the early and middle phases for households of three or more family members, on farms of under 30 cow equivalents in size. For these, a considerably greater portion of households in the middle phase of the family developmental cycle have some member working off, compared with households in the early phase (Table 24).

Table 24: Phase in family developmental cycle and off-farm employment of any family member, allowing for effect of household size, large size of business and 'late' stage*

Phase in family cycle	None working off	Some working off	Total
Early	23	17	40
Middle	13	32	45
Total	36	49	85

* Applies to households of three or more family members on farms of under 30 cow equivalents in size.

Considering all households in the middle phase of the developmental cycle, a greater proportion have two or more members working off amongst those with five or more family members, than amongst those with four or less.

The proportions in the different size-of-business categories do not

Table 25: Phase in family developmental cycle and size of business

Phase in family cycle	Under 15 C.E.	Over 15 C.E.	Total
Early and Middle	64	58	122
Late	19	4	23
Total	83	62	145

differ significantly between the households in the early and the middle phase of the developmental cycle, but a greater proportion of the late-phase households are in the small size-of-business categories (Table 25).

There are no significant associations between phases in the cycle of family development, and either type of farming or intensity of operation.

It would appear that going out to work is the main economic adjustment which farm families in this area make to meet the demands of the family developmental cycle and of their size of household. Family labour resources are available more in the middle phase than in either the early or the late phase; whereas needs are greatest in the early phase, and least in the late phase. Thus, when size of business is small and a family is in the early phase of the developmental cycle, there will be a tendency for the farmer to work off the property. Later on there is not the same necessity for the farmer to work off, once one or more of his children reach working age and take employment off the farm. On the larger properties one or more of the children usually stay at home and eventually take over the farms on the death or retirement of their parents. Consequently, many farmers from the large farms never enter the phase of independence whilst still operating a large size of business. Some die, some retire completely and a few retire to smaller farms. In contrast, on many of the smaller properties, all children leave home and their parents continue to live on their properties and farm them until they die. A random sample of farmers thus shows more of those in the late stage of the family developmental cycle on small farms than on large farms.

Some households are successful in making adjustments to their family circumstances but others are not so fortunate. It is pertinent therefore to look at the situation of those families with a small size of business in relation to their household size and phase in the family developmental cycle, who do *not* have any member working off the farm. There are 12 'early-phase' households with three or more family members, with no resident member in employment off the property, and with a small business size. Four of them have a 'dual business' which provides them with an adequate income from farm and non-farm sources. All except one of the other eight have eight or more cows (rather too many to milk by hand before going to work), and wives who either have a young family, or who have worked in urban jobs prior to marriage. Most of these farmers admitted that it was hard to make a living, but they were hoping to build up their stock numbers gradually, and eventually to obtain more land, or another farm. The one exception has a small mixed farm. He admitted that he could earn more by going out to work, but preferred to be independent, asserting that he could always earn a bit extra by doing jobs for neighbours. The standard of living of this family was not high, judged by the level of amenities and diet.

There are seven 'middle-phase' households with three or more family members, a small business size, and no family member in employment off the property. Most of these have a size of business which, although small, is adequate for their needs. One of them has a 'dual business' providing part-time employment for the farmer and a son. In all the others the parents are semi-retired, or close to retiring, and have one or more children remaining at home to run the farm for them. Three of the six farmed a larger property prior to the marriage of a child, split off one part for this child, and are themselves living on the other part. One of the others supplements dairying with a substantial pig enterprise, and the other two have a dozen cows to provide a living in each case for the farmer, his wife and one son.

A much greater proportion of the middle- and late-phase farmers than of the early-phase farmers occupy farms at altitudes between 901 and 1,100 feet (Table 26). This cannot be explained in terms either

Table 26: Phase in family developmental cycle and altitude of farm

Phase in family cycle	900 ft. and below	901– 1,100 ft.	1,101– 1,300 ft.	Over 1,300 ft.	Total
Early	14	12	17	12	55
Middle and Late	16	42	19	13	90
Total	30	54	36	25	145

of present or previous tenancy or of ownership or of size of farm, for this altitude range occupies an intermediate position in the trends relating these factors to altitude. It is possible, therefore, that the higher proportion of middle- and late-phase families at this altitude is some function of the mobility of the farm families.

The farmers at this altitude occupy an intermediate position on the scale of farming status, between the predominantly part-time farmers at the top of the hill, and the predominantly full-time farmers at the bottom. Although few of them go out to work themselves, a higher proportion of them have children who work off the farm, compared with the farmers either at the lower or the higher altitudes. It is possible that fewer of them are in the early phase of the family developmental cycle than are those at other altitudes, because they include both full-time farmers' sons who have moved uphill in search of a farm (but who have not subsequently been able to make a further move) and progressive farmers, originating higher up the hill, who have moved downhill for a better farm part-way through their careers. Not being able either to make further progress in their farming careers, or to provide adequate employment at home for all their children, these farmers have adjusted to their situation by allowing children to go out to work, while remaining in full-time farming themselves.

THE SINGLE FARMERS

Single farmers have been referred to at various points in this chapter. It is obviously not possible to classify them on the same basis as

Table 27: Marital status of farmer, size of household, size of farm, type of farmer, and living conditions

	Single	Married	Total
Household size:			
One or two	18	28	46
Three or four	8	75	83
Five or over	1	42	43
Total	27	145	172
Size of farm in acres of mowing grass:			
Under 20	20	77	97
20 and over	7	68	75
Total	27	145	172
Type of farmer:			
Farming mainly	22	91	113
Work off or dual business	5	54	59
Total	27	145	172
Living conditions:			
Poor	9	11	20
Medium	15	60	75
Good	3	74	77
Total	27	145	172

married farmers. From the point of view of family farming, however, they can be classified according to the types of family members of working age in the household. On this basis, in 12 out of 27 single farmers' households, there is only one adult family member (the farmer himself or herself) while in seven the farmer is living with his parents (with or without other family members) and in eight the farmer is living with one or more siblings.

In two of the cases where both parents are alive and living with the farmer, the father still has some control over the business, although nominally retired and receiving the old age pension. In the other two cases another brother is in partnership, the father apparently not taking managerial decisions. In the three households where only one parent is alive the management has both nominally and actually passed to the son.

The single farmers are concentrated on small farms, generally have small households, and are mainly dependent on their farm resources for a living (Table 27). Only one of those living alone has a farm larger than 20 acres of mowing grass. He is a younger son who has come from a better farming area in search of a cheap farm. A smaller proportion of the single farmers have good living conditions compared with the married farmers, and a third of them live under very poor conditions indeed (Table 27).

PROBLEM FAMILIES

Although the majority of farm families have achieved a balance between size of family, size of farm business, and work off the farm, there are a number of exceptions. Of the 42 farmers with a small size of business per household member, 23 are dependent wholly or mainly on their farm for a living. Nine others (although their farm resources are rather higher or they have some work off the farm) are obviously in poor financial circumstances, or are at a stage in life or health which will make it increasingly difficult for them to continue to make a living from their farm. There are thus 32 farm families whose economic circumstances are very poor. Four of the largest families are in this group, as are also 13 of the single farmers. The others comprise three barren couples and one whose children have left home, and five families in which it is likely that either the parents will remain alone after the children have left home, or a single child will remain after the death of the parents. Another six families who started farming within the last 15 years have children of school age and under, and are attempting to make a living from small-sized or poor farms.

These 32 families, representing 19 per cent of the total families in the survey, are not the only ones with problems, but they seem to be the least able to make favourable adjustments to the circumstances in which they find themselves. Through forced-choice family situations (for instance the early death of a parent) and occasionally because of low intelligence or irresponsibility, they are on farms too small to support them adequately. Many of them are not old enough for 'the pension' but are unable to take other employment or move away because they are too old, or too set in their ways by reason of their upbringing, or through subsequent misfortune. They have bought, or inherited, their farms, which are their major assets but which are only valuable if they farm them themselves, since such farms have a poor market value. By debt, by a sense of family duty, by pride or by sentiment, they are tied to holdings incapable of providing them with a decent living. Most of them can do little except hope that conditions will not become worse. Conditions are, however, worsening for them. Compulsory attestation and more stringent 'clean milk' regulations are forcing them either into further debt to make the necessary changes, or on to a still lower level of production from cattle rearing.

These people represent the human cost of measures designed to increase the efficiency of farming. Because of inadequate knowledge, confidence or money they are unable or unwilling to benefit from the subsidies which were designed to help 'marginal farms' but were not tailored to fit 'marginal farmers'.

CHAPTER IV

THE BROAD PATTERN OF MOBILITY

SUCCESSION TO FARMS

FARMS pass from one generation to another in a number of ways. Often, sons take over from parents but daughters, sons-in-law, and male or female relatives other than sons and daughters, may also succeed to farms. Not all farmers have 'available kin' capable or willing to follow them, and when these farmers die, or retire, their farms are taken by other people not related to them.

For this sample of farms, 28·5 per cent of all farmers are sons who have followed parents, 14·5 per cent are daughters or sons-in-law of the previous occupier, and 3·5 per cent and 1·5 per cent respectively are males or females following near relatives other than parents.[1] The other 52 per cent of farmers occupy holdings not previously tenanted or owned by their parents or near relatives, or those of their wives. Thus, although there is a bias towards descent in the direct male line, the pattern of succession to farms is very different from the usual concept of farming inheritance, with its emphasis on generational continuity and the maintenance of 'the name on the land'.[2]

On 25 per cent of all farms, either the farmer or his wife has lived there from childhood. Thus, in general, among those farmers currently succeeding parents, only one half have parents who were associated with the farms from the early stages of their married lives. This suggests that in the previous generation the proportion of farmers succeeding parents or relatives was also about one half.

The concept of a halving of family connections with farms in each generation is supported by the number of generations of association with their farms reported by the farmers. Ninety farmers have no family associations before their own occupation of the farm, 47 have associations extending to the parental generation and 35 have associations extending to the grandparental generation or beyond. Assuming an exact halving of association in successive generations, the

---

[1] 'Near relatives' refer to grandparents, uncles, aunts, or siblings of the farmer or farmer's wife. Although some of the previous occupiers of the holdings may have been more distantly related, these were not claimed as relatives in reply to the question: 'Was this person (the previous occupier) related to you or your wife in any way'?

[2] See Arensberg, *The Irish Countryman*, p. 57.

'expected' number of farmers in these categories would be 86, 43 and 43. The observed numbers do not differ significantly from the 'expected' ones. Further support comes from the fact that only 15 farmers can trace back family associations with their present farm for over one hundred years. For six of these (all small businesses) the association is likely to end with the current generation, for the farm families concerned are 'incomplete' ones[1] with little chance of a successor. Eight of the nine families likely to continue the association into the next generation have medium to large businesses. In three of these nine families, continuity has been maintained because the farmers have 'married into' farms previously occupied by their wives' parents.

Farms may pass from parents to children in three distinct ways. First, if a farm is tenanted, a child can succeed to the tenancy; second, where a farm is owned by the farmer, he may bequeath it entirely to one child; or, third, he may bequeath it to several of his children.

Succession to a tenancy is dependent on the policy, or whim, of a landlord. In the past, a high proportion of farms in the area were tenanted. Tenancy could be a factor leading to generational continuity of occupation amongst those families of whom the landlord approved, but it could lead to discontinuity of association with particular farms amongst other families. I was told that the gamekeeper had been a very influential person when tenants were being chosen for farms in those parts of the area where game was more important than quality of farming.

Where several children inherit a farm, this can lead to discontinuity of family association with it, if the farm size is inadequate to provide a living for all the inheritors, and it is sold to give them an equal share of the inheritance. Alternatively, one child may 'buy out' the others, but—in doing so—may place himself in financial difficulties which force him to leave the farm. Even where only one child inherits a property, he may not necessarily be able to remain on it: other children may inherit such shares in the livestock, dead stock, and working capital that he cannot operate the farm effectively.[2] The

---

[1] Single farmers, deserted parents and so on as described in Ch. III.

[2] An attempt was made to find out by direct enquiry if there is a predominant method of inheritance in the area. Most people were extremely reluctant to talk about their own experience, and adequate data for analysis could not be collected. Time was not available to examine wills (as Williams has done for Ashworthy). Impressions obtained were that partible inheritance was common for the larger farm businesses, but that—for many of the small farms—the child who remained at home with the parents inherited from them. William's method is very useful where the size of the inheritance is sufficiently large for a will to have been

high proportion of tenanted farms prior to 1951, together with partible inheritance, would obviously have had effects on the proportion of children following parents in this area,[1] compared with the situation in Ireland described by Arensberg. Unfortunately, because of all the changes from tenancy to owner occupation which have occurred in recent years, it has not been possible to estimate in this area, whether or not there is any difference in the proportions of tenanted and owner-occupied farms passing from parents to children.

MOVEMENT FROM FARM TO FARM

Some farmers stay on the same farm throughout their farming career, others move about from one farm to another. One farmer may move to a smaller farm towards the end of his career, so that his son can take over his previous holding. Another may add land to his farm during the early or middle stages of his career, and then retire to a part of the farm, handing over the other part to a son. A son may start farming on his own account away from the 'family' holding, and then move back home when his parents retire; or he may never return home, but move to another farm with which he again has no family connections. Another son may start to farm on a small 'family' holding, but later leave it for a larger 'non-family' farm.[2] Yet another farmer may be unsuccessful on a particular farm (which could be a family holding or not) and may move to a smaller property more suited to his managerial capabilities, or to his financial position.

The system whereby farmers gradually retire by moving to a smaller holding, and thus allow their children to take over the main holding, does not operate to any great extent in this area. Only four farmers had retired to a smaller holding in their old age to release a farm for a son or daughter; three of these farmers had retired to smaller farms acquired earlier in their careers. There were also three examples[3] of multiple holdings being split up, the father continuing

---

deposited. It may only give an idea of what happened amongst a relatively small section of a farming community, however, where small farm businesses predominate.

[1] And possibly in England and Wales generally, where (until very recently) two-thirds of the farms have been tenanted—the same proportion as that in the area of study prior to 1951.

[2] To avoid using the cumbersome terms 'family-connected farms' and 'non-family-connected farms' these are abbreviated to 'family' farms and 'non-family' farms. In the usual sense of 'family farm', (i.e. a farm operated mainly by family labour), practically all the farms surveyed were 'family farms'.

[3] Not included in Table 28 as the farmers concerned have only had the one farm.

on one part, and the son starting on the other. The farmers on these holdings had started their farming career on the one farm and had added to it, during the middle phase of their family developmental cycle, by acquiring an adjacent farm. This device is very useful in that it increases the farm resources available to the father at a stage in his family's developmental cycle when both family needs are greatest and family labour is available. Later, a child can marry and start farming without having to wait for the death or retirement of the parent. Where there is only one inheriting child, a multiple holding can in time provide for the developing needs of the child's own family after the death or total retirement of the father. The arrangement presumably is not common, because of the unlikelihood of an adjoining farm becoming vacant (by inheritance or otherwise) at the appropriate phase in the family developmental cycle. Also, where there is more than one inheriting child, complete partition will probably occur—hence, unless one or other of the children has no family, the process cannot be repeated in the following generation.

As distinct from the farmers who retired to a small holding, eight farmers 'retreated' from larger holdings. Three of these eight are other-work farmers who moved nearer to sources of non-farm employment for themselves or their children, and the other five are 'incomplete families' who moved to smaller holdings more suited to their capabilities.

Of all those farmers who began farming on a non-family farm,

Table 28: Farm-to-farm movement and family associations
with farms

Reason for movement	From family-connected to non-family-connected farm	From non-family connected to family-connected farm	Between family-connected farms	Between non-family-connected farms	Total
To bigger farm business	7	12	2	21	42
Retiring or retreating	6	0	5	1	12
Total	13	12	7	22	54*

* Two more than the number who had more than one farm because of the inclusion of two farmers who had moved from a non-family-connected farm, where they had commenced farming, to a family-connected farm, and who had later retired to a non-family-connected farm again.

only a small proportion returned to a family holding. The 12 who did return all moved from a small to a larger business, but over twice as many other farmers improved their economic position by moving from a smaller to a larger non-family holding, or by moving away from a small family holding to a larger non-family holding (Table 28).

Most of the opportunities for moving from a smaller to a larger business would appear to have arisen from differential movement amongst those seeking to better themselves, and from people ceasing to farm on leaving the district—since 42 farmers had moved to bigger businesses, but only 12 had retired or retreated to smaller farms.

Most of the farm-to-farm movement took place within the survey area. However, a quarter of all those moving to better themselves are incomers, for all incomers who have farmed previously came to the area in search of a larger farm. Eight of them came from within a 15-mile radius of their current farms, and three came from more than 20 miles away. These 11 farmers all moved uphill in relation to the situation of their previous property. The fact that, in total, almost twice as many farmers moved uphill as downhill for a farm is largely due to the influx of the farmers from outside the area. Excluding them, as many of the locals moved uphill to a farm as moved down-hill to one. A third of all farmers who have moved from farm to farm have not changed appreciably the altitude situation of their farms (Table 29). These farmers have all moved from one farm to another

Table 29: Altitude changes in movements from farm to farm

Altitude change	Locals	Incomers	Total
Little or no change	18	0	18
Moved uphill	11	11	22
Moved downhill	12	0	12
Total	41	11	52

within a limited local radius of under two and a half miles; so have 13 of the locals, who have moved uphill or downhill. The other 10 locals have moved within a five-mile radius in their search for a farm suited to their particular requirements.

The period of residence on current holdings reflects the turnover of farms in the area. The average period of occupation is 14 years, but there is an uneven distribution about this mean, with 64 per cent of the farmers having been in residence 15 years or less and 36 per cent for over 15 years. This scatter is related to the proportion of farmers who have moved from one farm to another in the past (Table 30) as well as to the faster turnover of the smaller farms at high

Table 30: Number of farms farmers had occupied

Present farm only	120 farmers
Present farm plus one other	40 farmers
Present farm plus two others	11 farmers
Present farm plus more than two others	1 farmer

altitudes. A higher proportion of these smaller farms have been occupied for shorter periods than have larger farms at lower altitudes, both by present and previous occupiers.

The average period of occupation for this area is similar to the 14·7 years quoted by Ashton[1] for a sample of farmers in Warwickshire and Oxfordshire, which, however, had a much higher proportion of 'larger-sized' farms, with a greater diversity of types of farming, than in this area. Both averages agree reasonably closely with that of 13·7 years quoted in the National Farm Survey[2] for England and Wales. All three surveys, although referring to widely differing populations at different times, show that the periods for which farms were occupied varied directly with their size, despite differences in the range of farm sizes in different places (Table 31).

Table 31: Farm sizes, this and other surveys

Farm sizes	Ashton's survey 1950	This survey 1960	National Farm Survey 1941–3
Under 100 acres (under 120 acres for present survey)	45%	83%	73%
100 acres and over (120 acres and over for present survey)	55%	17%	27%
Average length of occupancy	14·7 years	14·0 years	13·7 years

If, irrespective of location, size of farm influences period of occupation, Ashton's survey should have shown a longer average period of occupation than my survey does because his survey included a greater number of larger-sized farms. That the two averages do not differ appreciably suggests that other social and economic factors are

[1] Ashton, *Social Origin of Farmers*, p. 152.
[2] *National Farm Survey of England and Wales*, Table 15, p. 33.

involved which result in similar average periods of farm occupation in different areas.[1]

AMALGAMATION AND LOSS OF LAND

Moving from farm to farm is one way of adjusting the size of business in response to social, economic or demographic pressures. Another way is to increase or decrease the amount of land attached to a particular farm. Such transfer of land may not necessarily be permanent. With changes in needs or family fortunes, accommodation land, or parts of some holdings, may pass between farms, and into or out of the control of particular farmers or of particular groups of kin.

The exchange of land in this area appears to occur mainly when farmers die, retire or leave their farms. It does not involve much interchange of land between two farmers, both of whom continue to farm. This is evident from the fact that many more of the surveyed farmers have acquired additional land whilst occupying their current holdings (37 per cent) than have disposed of some of their land (9 per cent). Even this 9 per cent overstates the 'loss' of land for, out of 496 acres 'lost', 341 acres represent the transfer of parts of farms by fathers, who continued to farm, to sons who had not previously farmed.[2]

Examination of the sources of amalgamated land showed that the majority of the transactions (and the bulk of the acreage) involved the purchase or lease of accommodation land and the acquisition of the whole or part of other farms. These transactions almost invariably occurred on the death, retirement, or movement of the previous occupier of such land. The average acreage per transaction is largest for those transfers which occurred on the death, retirement, or movement of a farmer. It is smallest for those transfers where land was obtained from a neighbour who continued to farm (Table 32). The nature of the transfer is apparent, too, from the remarks of the farmers as to how they acquired their additional land. Often, single men or women were stated to have 'given up', retired or died; others were stated to have 'gone banked' (bankrupt), or left farming for another job.

---

[1] It might be argued that differences in ages of farmers would affect the average period of occupation, on the supposition that the sample with the higher proportion of younger men would have a lower average period of occupation. Even if this supposition were true, (and there are no data to prove it) any correction made for age would have the effect of bringing the two averages closer together, for the proportion of younger men is higher in my survey than in Ashton's (see Appendix 3, Table 2). [2] See above, page 64.

Frequently, a person would retire from farming, but would remain on his farm and lease the land to a neighbour—on either a normal tenancy, or a grazing[1] tenancy. If the retired farmer was not the owner of the land, such subletting required the consent of the landlord, or it had to be undertaken without his knowledge.[2] Arrangements of this kind need not be permanent—indeed, their lack of permanence is one of their attractions to the people concerned, for they enable retired farmers to obtain some income from their land

Table 32: Amalgamation of land

| | Type of transfer of amalgamated land | | | |
	Purchase or lease of accommodation land	Purchase or lease of some land from a farming neighbour	Take-over of whole or part of farm at the death, retirement or movement of a farmer	Total
Number of transactions	23	16	36	75*
Acreage involved	608 acres	275 acres	1,246 acres	2,129 acres
Acres amalgamated per transaction	26·4 acres	17·1 acres	34·6 acres	28·4 acres

* This is greater than the number of farmers who amalgamated land because some farmers added more than one area.

without relinquishing control over it; and they provide land for farmers who wish to expand their businesses without necessarily wanting permanent possession of particular pieces of land.[3] On the death of a retired tenant farmer, the owner may wish to rent the farm

[1] That is, the grazing rights to a piece of land for a period of time not longer than one grazing season. This arrangement is similar to that of conacre in Ireland, under which land is leased for periods of 11 months.

[2] It was not difficult to conceal a grazing tenancy from an absentee landlord who had insufficient local knowledge to know whether cattle grazing on a particular holding actually belonged to the legal tenant.

[3] Leasing for less than a year has been criticized strongly, on the grounds that— by giving no security of tenure—it leads to exploitation of land resources: lessees fail to maintain the fertility of the land, lessors fail to maintain permanent equipment, such as fences, ditches, and drains. In the absence of alternative systems which are socially and politically acceptable to the farmers concerned, the conacre type of lease, however, does serve as one way of redistributing land between those who do not want it and those who need it. Certainly, in the area of study, many lessees are making far better use of such land than some other

(complete with house) to another tenant. An owned farm may be inherited by kin of the deceased, who may want to farm it as a unit, add it to a farm of their own, use it as accommodation land, or lease it to others.

The divisions between the three types of amalgamated land should not be considered as rigid ones. A farm taken over on the death or retirement of a farmer, or a piece of land exchanged between practising farmers in one generation, could become a parcel of accommodation land in the next, or it could be absorbed into a particular farm. What happened to such land would depend on how near it was to the farm of the person taking it over, the disposition of his estate (or that of the former occupier), the interest in the particular piece of land taken by successors, or competing offers for it from others.

The system of land exchange which has been described has some disadvantages. Farmers wishing to expand their size of business by amalgamation can do so only if land becomes available at the appropriate times. Further, the chances are greater that *nearby* land will become available more frequently than land which is *contiguous* with their existing holdings. Consequently, after amalgamation, many farms will consist of two or more parcels of land at some distance from each other. Over a number of generations, considerable fragmentation of holdings may result, if land amalgamated in one generation becomes firmly associated with particular farms in the succeeding generation.[1] As it appears to operate in this area, the system does have some advantages over the tidy theoretical concept usually associated with 'land amalgamation'. It provides some scope for farmers to take in more land when they need it (for example, when family requirements are greatest) and ensures that the additional acreage does not necessarily remain permanently associated with any one farm. In addition, the transfers of land operate within the kinship and friendship networks and under the economic pressures felt by the people. It would be very difficult for any land commission to achieve such a result by means of an arbitrary redistribution of land based on theoretical concepts of 'viable' farming units. This does not mean that no further measures are required to ensure

---

farmers, through old age, incapacity or incompetence, are making of theirs. In Southern Ireland, the land laws prevent other types of tenancy; consequently up to 20 per cent of all land may be let on conacre in high emigration areas, where the proportion of 'incomplete' families is high. (P. F. Smith Louis: 'Studies in a declining population', *Rural Migration*, 1959, p. 75.)

[1] This could provide an explanation of the fragmentation of holdings which occurs in some areas where the strip-system of cultivation is not known to have existed.

a reasonable distribution of land in units adequately suited to the needs of either full-time or part-time farmers in the area. The study indicates, however, that any measures taken by Government would probably achieve their objects better and stand a greater chance of acceptance by the local population if they were designed to work within the system already operating, accelerating or modifying it when necessary. Other methods which did not take into account local demographic, social and economic circumstances would certainly be regarded with great suspicion and could meet with active opposition.

GEOGRAPHICAL MOVEMENT OF FARM PEOPLE

Birthplaces and mobility prior to marriage

Most of the farmers and their wives were born and brought up within 10 miles of where they are farming, and the majority of them lived in the country prior to marriage. Single farmers have been less mobile than the married ones. Three-quarters of the married farmers and two-thirds of their wives live within five miles of their birthplaces; three-quarters of the single farmers live within two and a half miles (Table 33). A third of the married farmers have come in from

Table 33: Distance from birthplace

Distance of present abode from birthplace	Single farmers	Married farmers	Farmers' wives
Nil	6	17	9
$\frac{1}{4}$–2$\frac{1}{2}$ miles	14	62	62
2$\frac{3}{4}$–5 miles	2	29	25
5$\frac{1}{4}$–10 miles	3	16	22
Over 10 miles	2	21	26
Total	27	145	144*

* Particulars not available for one farmer's wife.

other districts (urban and rural), or have moved residentially between the survey area and elsewhere. Again, single farmers have been less mobile than married ones, for 85 per cent of them have never lived outside their area of birth (Table 34). Movement to work[1] for married farmers and their wives shows a wider geographical spread

[1] This relates to all the period up to the time of the survey but excludes any war service. It includes both living away from home to be near sources of work and travelling to work whilst still living in the survey areas.

Table 34: Spatial mobility of farmers

Area movement	Single farmers	Married farmers	Total
Only within area or adjacent parishes	23	95	118
Between the area and other country or urban areas	2	18	20
Inward from other country or urban areas	2	32	34
Total	27	145	172

Table 35: Movement to work

Furthest place worked from present abode	Single farmers	Married farmers	Farmers' wives
2½ miles and under	17	59	58
2¾–5 miles	6	33	27
5¼–10 miles	2	28	28
Over 10 miles	2	25	31
Total	27	145	144

than residential movement. Most single farmers, however, have never worked very far from home (Table 35).

For men brought up in the district, the only likely sources of employment within a distance of two and a half miles were joinery, building construction, or work on the roads. The other two major sources of non-farm employment in the past were quarrying, and factory work in the nearest towns. These were more than two and a half miles from the nearest parts of the area, and well over five miles from the most distant. Farm work was sought mainly by the sons of small business, family-earning and other-work farmers. Most of these sons came from the poorer, higher land, where few farms were big enough to provide employment for non-family labour. Consequently they often had to move five miles or more to obtain farm employment. Employment in the vicinity of their homes was scarce for women who had been reared in the area but who could not be employed on their parents' farm; they had to seek work either on large farms some distance from home, or in the nearest town.

In almost three-quarters of the married couples both the farmer and his wife have lived in country areas prior to marriage, and also have parents who live, or used to live, in the country. In the other quarter, more wives than husbands have lived in urban areas prior to marriage. This is because some country-bred men married women brought up in the towns and some married country-bred women who had lived and worked in the towns prior to marriage. Although most of the combinations between urban- and country-living wives, husbands and parents are represented, the only other grouping of numerical importance is that where husbands, wives and parents on both sides have been urban-dwelling (Table 36).[1]

Table 36: Residence prior to marriage

	Home of husbands and wives before marriage								
	Husband: urban area				Husband: country area				
	Wife: country		Wife: urban		Wife: country		Wife: urban		Total
Home of husbands' parents at death, retirement etc.:	Home of wives' parents at death, retirement, etc.								
	Urban area	Country area	Urban area	Country area	Urban area	Country area	Urban area	Country area	
Urban area	0	3	8	1	0	3	2	0	17
Country area	0	2	3	0	2	103	7	10	127
Total	0	5	11	1	2	106	9	10	144

Movement of farmers uphill or downhill

A measure of the distance which farmers have moved from their birthplace or from the most recent abode of their parents does not give any indication of changes in their farming status. But we know that wide changes in type, quality and size of farms can occur over short distances due to the marked influence of altitude on the farming of the area.[2] A measure of the movement of farmers uphill or downhill compared with where their parents lived will give therefore some indication of changes in farming status which have occurred.[3]

[1] These figures are based on details for farmers and wives currently living in the area and give no indication of the proportions of country-dwelling people of either sex who married urban-dwelling partners. Nor do they indicate the proportion of mixed urban/rural marriage pairs, or urban/urban pairs who had farmed in the past, but were no longer doing so in the area at the time of the survey. Urban/rural marriages can be studied for the farm families by examining what happened to the children of the farmers (see *Spatial mobility of farmers' children* below, p. 78).   [2] See Ch. II, p. 24.

[3] A difference in altitude of 200 ft. or more between birthplace or where parents were living and the current situation of the farmers' holding was used to indicate

Most of the farmers and farmers' wives whose parents lived outside the survey parishes or the adjacent parishes have moved uphill, compared with where their parents were living (Table 37). In general,

Table 37: Change in altitude: abode of farmers and wives compared with that of respective parents[1]

| | Mobility uphill or downhill compared with parents' home | | | |
	Little or no change	Uphill	Downhill	Total
Single farmers				
Father lived:				
same area	21	1	2	24
elsewhere	0	3	0	3
Total	21	4	2	27
Married farmers				
Father lived:				
same area	73	22	17	112
elsewhere	2	30	1	33
Total	75	52	18	145
All farmers				
Father lived:				
same area	94	23	19	136
elsewhere	2	33	1	36
Total	96	56	20	172
Farmers' wives				
Father lived:				
same area	60	30	14	104
elsewhere	5	32	3	40
All farmers' wives	65	62	17	144*

* Particulars not available for one farmer's wife.

whether an appreciable movement uphill or downhill had occurred. A change of 200 ft. or more at high, medium or low altitudes is usually marked by considerable changes in the type, quality and size of the farms.

[1] For all farmers, the location of parents was taken to be where they were living currently (if not retired), prior to retirement (if retired or dead) or where

there is nothing very remarkable about this, for the towns and the better farming country are situated at lower altitudes. The absence of movement downward from outside locations indicates that people have not moved into the good farms in the lower parts of the area from the nearby limestone country, where there is a considerable acreage of land at high altitudes.

It is worth noting that in the whole of the hill-country of which the survey area forms a part, a sharp distinction is made between people from limestone country and those from gritstone, as well as between 'limestone land' and 'gritstone land'. Thus, one farmer said: "I don't really know what it is about them, maybe it's the water, but limestone folk are different from folk over here." In gritstone country, farmers would concede: 'limestone land is all right, but it burns up in summer'. The limestone farmers, on the other hand, considered that 'gritstone land may be all right in a dry summer, but a lot of it is either heather or rushes'.

In an occupation which is so largely learnt at home, it is not surprising that these distinctions should arise. The two types of country differ in their husbandry requirements, are sharply distinct in their physical characteristics and appearance, and the boundary between the two soil types is often that between different estates and different counties. Consequently, all the day-to-day knowledge of the land, landlords' policies, influential people, markets and stock, together with kinship bonds, tend to keep the people apart, except in 'fringe' areas.

Obviously, people have moved between the two areas; but, if the 'wave motion'[1] suggested by the spatial distribution of married daughters has been the general pattern, it may take two, three or more generations before the descendants of farming 'stock' in the heart of one area come to be farming in the heart of the other. By this time, although they may well have some distant cousins 'over there', they will certainly consider themselves in every way either gritstone farmers or limestone farmers.

Movements uphill or downhill, indicating changes in farming status, have occurred, in varying degrees, amongst those single farmers, married farmers, and farmers' wives who have parents living in the area. It is here that marriage plays an important part in mobility, for marriage may force a man to change his farming status in relation to that of his parents. His limited knowledge and contacts

---

they lived at death (if death had preceded retirement). Thus, for all those with farming parents, the comparison was between the current location of the farmer and that of the parents whilst still farming.   [1] See below, p. 79.

will tend to restrict him to his local area, but he may have to move uphill or downhill within it to find a farm. This movement may occur at the beginning of his farming career, or later when the pressures of expanding family needs force him to look for a larger farm or for supplementary employment. A single man, on the other hand, will not be under the same pressures. This is evident from a comparison of the altitude-situation of single and married farmers in relation to parents, for significantly fewer single farmers have changed their altitude-level (Table 37).

Table 38: Change in altitude compared with place of birth

	Mobility uphill or downhill compared with birthplace			
	Little or no change	*Uphill*	*Downhill*	*Total*
Single farmers Father lived:				
same area	17	6	1	24
elsewhere	0	3	0	3
Total	17	9	1	27
Married farmers Father lived:				
same area	58	37	17	112
elsewhere	2	28	3	33
Total	60	65	20	145
All farmers Father lived:				
same area	75	43	18	136
elsewhere	2	31	3	36
Total	77	74	21	172
Farmers' wives Father lived:				
same area	54	38	12	104
elsewhere	6	30	4	40
All farmers' wives	60	68	16	144*

* Particulars not available for one farmer's wife.

Rather fewer farmers' wives have parents living in the area than have their husbands; and proportionately more of the wives have moved uphill in relation to where their parents were living (Table 37). The shortage of women in the higher altitude parishes suggests that some of those farmers who were tied to a particular farm, or to a limited choice of farms at one altitude level, sought their wives amongst the daughters of non-farmers living in the villages at the lower altitudes.[1]

There is little difference in the movements uphill or downhill of farmers and wives in relation to where they were born (Table 38). This suggests that a greater movement uphill occurred amongst the farmers' parents than amongst their wives' parents—which would be consistent with a greater proportion of non-farmers amongst the wives' parents.

If we consider farmers and farmers' wives separately, about two-thirds of each group (with local parents) have moved neither uphill nor downhill. If we consider *married couples*, however, only one-third of all couples (with local parents) comprise a husband and wife who have remained at about the same altitude level as that at which their parents are now residing, or did reside. The greater part of the movement uphill or downhill for these 'all-local' married couples has consisted of one partner moving uphill or downhill to join the other partner, who has remained stationary. In addition, a few couples moved uphill together (Table 39). This gives a picture of movements

Table 39: Changes in altitude compared with where parents living: married pairs, where both husbands' and wives' parents living in the survey area

| | Farmers | | | |
	Little or no change	Uphill	Downhill	Total
Farmers' wives:				
Little or no change	34	10	12	56
Uphill	15	10	1	26
Downhill	9	1	3	13
Total	58	21	16	95

at marriage and movements to farms occurring within the same altitude boundaries, together with interchange across adjacent boundaries, but little movement of partners from extremes of altitude

[1] The lower proportion of farmers' wives with farming parents (indicated later in this chapter) further supports this supposition.

towards each other. In fact, 81 per cent of the married couples with local parents lived within two and a half miles of each other prior to marriage and, of these, rather more than a quarter lived on adjacent farms.[1]

Spatial mobility of farmers' children

The farmers' children of working age are not all farmers. Consequently, although the spatial mobility of some married children is associated with moving to a farm, much of the movement of children who have left home has been to a place where work could be obtained. For those sons who are farm workers this could be a larger farm on better land; or it could be a town or semi-urban district for both sons and daughters whose work is not connected with farming.

Rather less than a quarter of the unmarried children of working age are living away from home. Sons and daughters do not differ significantly in this respect although, for all unmarried children of working age, proportionately more daughters than sons are living outside their home area or are working at distances of over two and a half miles from home. The location of places of work for the two sexes has a bearing on this. Half the daughters have to live in or travel to areas away from their home district in order to find work; but three-quarters of the sons are employed at home or have found employment in their home area.

The geographical dispersion of both married sons and married daughters is wider than that of unmarried children. This is because the majority of unmarried children have remained at home, whilst the married sons have left home and settled mainly in the immediate vicinity of home, or completely out of the district, and the married daughters have left and settled at intermediate distances rather than locally (Table 40).

In respect of places of work, the wider area covered by unmarried daughters compared with unmarried sons is reflected in a similarly wider range of residence for the married daughters (Table 40). Since a greater proportion of sons than daughters take over family holdings and some sons move away from the immediate vicinity of their homes to farm other holdings, the result is a greater dispersion of married daughters compared with married sons. Daughters who marry farmers usually move from their own homes to those of their hus-

---

[1] All the above refers to people who remained in the area, and in farming. Details for the farmers and wives' contemporaries who left the area before, at, or after marriage were not obtained. Some measure of this movement in relation to altitude may be gauged from the details presented in the next section for children of farmers.

bands in those cases where the husbands succeed to their fathers'
farms. Where the husbands begin their farming careers on non-
family farms the daughters and their husbands move to such farms,
away from both their homes. Moreover, the wider dispersion of
places of work for daughters prior to marriage extends their marriage
range geographically. This range is still within the area considered
'local' by the inhabitants of the area, for 56 per cent and 60 per cent

Table 40: How near children live to their parents

	Single sons	Married sons	Single daughters	Married daughters
With parents	79	2	26	3
¼–2½ miles away	10	20	1	27
2¾–10 miles away	7	4	6	37
Over 10 miles away	5	9	4	14
Total	101	35	37	81

respectively of married daughters and married sons have spouses of
'local' origin.[1] It should be noted, however, that 69 per cent of the
working-age daughters are married, compared with only 27 per cent
of the sons. Of these married sons, 37 per cent have worked away
from their home area before marriage, whereas only 26 per cent of
unmarried sons are currently working outside their home area. This
suggests that for sons as well as daughters, a wider spatial mobility
increases their marriage range, and possibly their chances of marriage.

Movement of children uphill or downhill

For those married children who are farming on their own account,
or who have good prospects of doing so,[2] changes in the altitude
level at which they are living compared with where their parents are
living can be taken as indicative of changes in their farming status
compared with that of their parents.[3]

[1] Parents were asked the question: "in which town or parish was the home of
your daughters' husband (or son's wife)?" Which children had married a 'local'
spouse was determined from this—the survey area and the immediately adjacent
parishes being termed 'local', and all other areas 'non-local'.

[2] Good prospects of doing so, because they are working on the farm of their
parents, or their spouse's parents, and are thus likely to take over the farm when
the parents retire.

[3] In the same way that movements of the parents uphill or downhill during their
career could be taken as indicative of changes in their farming status, because of
the close association between altitude and quality and size of farms.

For all children, a movement downhill can be taken to indicate a movement towards a better climate and an improved standard of living, whether obtained from a better farm, from employment on a better farm, or from urban employment. Uphill movement is into a harsher climate but does not necessarily result in a lower standard of living, because it is much more common to supplement farming with other employment at the higher altitudes than it is at the lower ones. Nevertheless, an uphill movement will probably be a step down on the social scale. Children who have remained at the same altitude level as their parents may not necessarily have remained very close to home, because, as indicated previously, places can be five miles or more apart, yet be situated at the same altitude. Such children, however, will probably be living in a similar social environment to that in which they have been brought up, because of the close connection between altitude and social differentiation.[1]

Proportionately more married than unmarried children live at different altitude levels from their parents. This is because a high proportion of unmarried children have not left home. Those unmarried children who have left home, however, have mostly moved downhill. There is no significant difference between sons and daughters in this respect. This downhill movement of some unmarried children is not surprising, for urban sources of employment, as well as those farms sufficiently far from home to make 'living in' necessary, are at lower altitudes than are most of the farms in the area. This movement downhill which some farmers' children make before marriage is a permanent move for many of them, as indicated by the fact that 54 per cent of all married children live at lower altitudes than their parents.

Only one unmarried child was encountered who had left home and moved uphill; but a number of married children had done so, mainly to take up farms. In effect, the uphill movement of the unmarried child was for a similar purpose. He had left home (where he was the eldest son of a large family, with parents who were still young) and had gone to live with his fiancée and her parents on a farm at a higher altitude. He may still have to wait a number of years before his fiancée's parents are willing to retire, but his alignment with them, rather than with his own parents, suggests that he considered there was a better chance of obtaining their farm than that of his father. Three daughters and one son had moved uphill at marriage, but not to farms. They had all moved down in social status by marrying into non-farming families.

[1] This theme is developed further in the next chapter.

OCCUPATIONAL MOBILITY OF FARMERS AND THEIR KIN

Inheritance of occupation

The inheritance of the farming occupation is stronger in this area than is the inheritance of farms. All but one of the single farmers, 81 per cent of the married farmers and 69 per cent of their wives[1] have fathers who are or were farmers.

Not all the farming fathers had been full-time farmers, the proportions of them who had been full-time, dual business or other-work farmers[2] being very similar to those of the current farmers (Table 41).

Table 41: Farming employment categories of farmers
and their farming fathers

Type of farming employment	Farmers %	Farming fathers of the farmers %	Farming fathers of the farmers' wives %
Full-time farming	66	66	61
Dual business	9	10	5
Farming plus other work	25	24	34

This is not due to the current farmers following their fathers' occupation exactly, for 40 per cent of them are in a different farming employment category from their fathers.[3] The similarity between the two generations is the more remarkable when the time span involved is considered. Some of the farming fathers are farming concurrently with their sons and daughters, and the others range from those who have recently retired to those who had ceased farming 30 or more years previously.

Entry to farming from other occupations has been mainly by people from outside the area and unconnected with agriculture. Few sons or daughters of farm *workers* have become farmers, compared with children of people in other employment (Table 42). This

[1] The proportion of farmers and wives with farming fathers differs significantly at the 1 per cent level.

[2] The slightly lower proportion of full-time farmers amongst the farming fathers of wives, and the lower and higher proportions of dual business and other-work farmers respectively, may be due to errors in definition or omissions from the information given. For example, a father described as 'farmer and mason', would have been classified as an other-work farmer unless there was firm evidence to the contrary, but he may have been a self-employed master mason, i.e. a dual business farmer under the definition used in this study.

[3] This comparison is treated in greater detail in Ch. VII.

Table 42: Occupations of fathers who were not farmers

| | Fathers of farmers | | | Fathers of farmers' wives | | |
	Living in area	Living elsewhere	Total	Living in area	Living elsewhere	Total
Farm worker	1	3	4	4	2	6
Other worker	7	18	25	12	23	35
Total	8	21	29	16	25	41

probably arises from the small number of farm workers in the area and surrounding districts who are not actually sons of farmers, rather than from any disadvantage farm workers suffer in comparison with other workers.

It appears that differential movement of land and people is maintaining a balance between the proportion of farmers able to farm full-time, the proportion who operate a dual business, and the proportion who farm and have another job. The land resources are more or less fixed in amount and relatively inflexible in their alternative farming uses; but people move occupationally and spatially and exchange land. A proportion of loosely attached land moves between farms, and farmers move from one farm to another and into and out of other employment, to fit in with their changing family and economic circumstances. In each generation, some holdings too small to maintain a family are farmed full-time by 'incomplete' families. As these families die out, or move away, others take their places, although not necessarily on the same holdings. Some of the holdings vacated by the 'incomplete' families are taken by part-time farmers, and others are amalgamated permanently or temporarily by full-time farmers. The rest are taken by families who become 'incomplete' if they continue for any length of time to farm them as full-time units. Over a period of time, the *number* of farmers in the area may be reduced,[1] as economic circumstances affecting agriculture raise the threshold of farm-size necessary to make a living, whether as a full-time or as a part-time farmer. But the *proportions* of farmers in the different farming employment groupings will probably remain the same.

Work experiences of farmers and wives

Although the majority of farmers are sons of farmers, a high proportion of farmers and their wives have been exposed at some stage in

---

[1] Compared with 1837 the number of farmers in most parishes appears to have been reduced (see Ch. II). Between 1939 and 1955 there was a reduction of 2·5 per cent in the number of holdings in three of the parishes included in the survey (private communication, M. A. Dennis, Agricultural Land Service).

their lives to values, standards of living, and ways of life different from those in their home environment. For example, before marrying, over half of both farmers and farmers' wives were in employment other than farm work at home (Table 43). Much of this em-

Table 43: Occupations of all farmers and farmers' wives
prior to marriage or starting to farm

Farmers	%	Farmers' wives	%
Farm work at home	49	Farm work at home	47
Farm work for others	17	Farm work for others	8
Quarry work	12	Domestic or hotel service	17
Factory work	5	Factory work	17
Transport or goods delivery	5	Shop or office work	5
Rural crafts	3	Teaching or nursing	4
Engineering	2	Other work	2
Other work	7		

ployment was outside agriculture altogether and consisted of domestic service and factory work for the women and quarrying, rural trades, and factory work for the men. A certain proportion of the men, however, were engaged in farm work for other people. Such farm work usually involved 'living in' away from home, as did domestic service. Most other work that was not of a rural nature entailed daily travel to the towns or to another country area, where the quarries and some factories were situated. The farm people employed in these ways were exposed to social experiences and environments which differed considerably from those experienced by the people who never left their parents' farms.

The extent of the intermingling of work experiences amongst married *couples* can be gauged from the fact that the work experiences of both farmer and wife have been confined to farm work at home in

Table 44: Occupations of married couples prior to
marriage or starting to farm

| | Farmers | | | |
Wives:	Farm work at home	Farm work for others	Other work	Total
Farm work at home	41	13	13	67
Farm work for others	6	3	3	12
Other work	21	9	35	65
Total	68	25	51	144

less than a third of the married couples. In a third of the families, either the husband or the wife has been engaged in non-agricultural work, and both spouses have been so engaged in a quarter of the families (Table 44).

Occupations of farmers' children

The greater freedom enjoyed by the farmers' daughters of this generation, compared with their mothers, has increased their occupational mobility. Changes in industrial opportunities for men, however, have not resulted in an increased movement of farmers' sons away from farming.

Prior to marriage, the same proportion of farmers' sons worked in agriculture as farmers themselves had done; but proportionately more daughters took up non-agricultural work prior to marriage, than had farmers' wives. Between the two male generations, the important change has been in the proportions engaging in different kinds of non-agricultural work. Quarrying has decreased considerably as engineering and building have increased and proportionately more sons are engaged in building work than fathers had been engaged in the rural crafts which that work has replaced. Factory work and domestic service, the main non-agricultural sources of employment for women, have not changed in importance between the generations, but proportionately more daughters are engaged in the professions, in shops and in offices. This increase has been at the expense of the number of daughters working on farms and at home (Tables 43 and 45 compared).

Table 45: Occupations of farmers' children, currently or prior to marriage

Sons	%	Daughters	%
Farm work at home	45	Farm work at home	31
Farm work for others	17	Farm work for others	5
Quarry work	5	Domestic or hotel service	16
Factory work	6	Factory work	19
Transport or goods delivery	5	Shop or office	18
Building work	8	Teaching or nursing	3
Engineering	5	Other work	3
Other work	8		

Only half the unmarried daughters are engaged in agriculture, compared with two-thirds of the unmarried sons, but equal proportions of sons-in-law and married sons are farming, or likely to farm,

even though half the married children of each sex are employed outside agriculture (Tables 46 and 47). Those married children who are

Table 46: Occupations of married children of farmers

	Married son	Husband of married daughter	Total
Farm work at home	6	1	7
Farm work for others	2	4	6
Full-time other employment	18	40	58
Farming full-time	6	23	29
Farming plus other employment	3	13	16
Total	35	81	116

Table 47: Occupations of single children of farmers

	Single sons	Single daughters	Total
Farm work at home	44	12	56
Partly at home, partly other work	6	3	9
Farm work for others	17	2	19
Full-time other work	30	19	49
Total	97	36	133

farming are engaged full-time and part-time in the same proportions
as their parents and grandparents, that is, one-third part-time to
two-thirds full-time. This offers further proof of the consistency with
which farmers in the area have adjusted to limited land resources by
working off their farms.

Mobility and single farmers

Single farmers have been the least mobile, both in occupation and
residence. Most of them have inherited small businesses which they
farm full-time. Their lack of mobility, together with their poor
farming and financial status, appears to have restricted their marriage
opportunities. To understand this, we must examine the marriage
trends in the community.

The range of marriage of farmers' daughters is wider than that of
farmers' sons, probably because fewer daughters are employed in

agriculture prior to marriage and more of them work at greater distances from home. Thus, whether they marry a farmer or not, they tend to move to, or with, their husbands, and away from their own homes. Moreover, farmers' daughters tend to marry younger than farmers' sons.[1] Only some of their male peers are in a position to marry at equivalent ages—for instance, those not working at home on the farm; those who elect to leave home and the possible chance of inheriting from parents rather than postpone marriage; and a few sons from the larger farms. Most of the remaining farmers' sons marry eventually when their parents die or retire, or on the death or retirement of parents of similarly placed daughters in 'daughter only' families and in families where a daughter is the child who remains at home.

Some farmers' sons may marry women who come into the area to work, others may be socially mobile by reason of their parents' social status or their own occupations, and thus be able to marry girls from further afield. But even here, although such men may marry girls from other country districts, few of them actually engaged in farm work marry girls from the towns.[2] As one man put it —"The girls from 'Hilltown' think we are 'country gorbies' and we don't go dancing there, but we go amongst our own sort at 'A' and 'B' " (mentioning two villages both within a five-mile radius). Those who marry a girl from another country area[3] thereby deprive someone else in that local area of a bride.

Some farmers' sons are tied to small family holdings by work and filial responsibilities. They are dependent on farming for a living, their knowledge of farming has been acquired at home, or in the immediate neighbourhood, and they have no experience of other work. Consequently their geographical mobility is restricted, and they tend to have a limited number of social contacts. By the time their parents die and they are free to marry, many of their female contemporaries will already be working and residing outside the area, or will have married other farmers' sons not tied to ageing parents and to a limited farming inheritance. Consequently, farmers' sons inheriting small full-time farms are unable to marry at an early age. They are compelled to seek brides younger than themselves, in

[1] The tendency for women to marry younger than men is common throughout our society but the difference in ages of marriage for the two sexes is particularly marked in farming communities; see Rees, *Life in a Welsh Countryside*, Williams, *Gosforth*, Williams, *Ashworthy*, and Arensberg, *The Irish Countryman*.

[2] See Table 36.

[3] Those who did so and remained farming in the survey area are not numerous, for out of 111 farmers who lived in the survey area prior to marriage, only seven have wives who lived in other country areas prior to marriage.

competition with younger men, who have all the advantages of youth, as well as superior social and economic circumstances. It is not surprising, therefore, to find that most of the 16 per cent of farmers who are unmarried, live on small full-time farms and that more than half of them are over 45 years of age.

CHAPTER V

SUCCESSION TO FARMS

THE analysis of mobility developed in the previous chapter will be extended further in this and the two subsequent chapters, by examining the spatial, social and occupational mobility of the various types of farmer in the area, together with the mobility of members of their families.

It was shown in Chapters II and III that the farmers in the area can be broadly classified on the basis of the sizes of their farms, and upon whether or not they, or members of their families, work off their farms. Throughout the next four chapters, references will be made to the farmers classified in this way. The five categories of farmers to be discussed are:

Full-time farmers:

a *Larger-business farmers* who work full-time on their farms, and who have sizes of farm business of 15 cow-equivalents and over.

b *Small-business farmers* who work full-time on their farms, but have sizes of business less than 15 cow-equivalents.

c *Family-earning farmers* who work full-time themselves on their farms but have one or more members of their families working off the farms.

Part-time farmers:

d *Dual-business farmers* who have another business in addition to farming.

e *Other-work farmers* who have full-time occupations off the farms. Most of these farmers have small sizes of farm business.

GENERATIONAL CONTINUITY ON FARMS

In this farming community, there appears to be an implicit scale of values which awards high prestige to size or quality of farm on the one hand and, on the other, to the length of family connection with the area. Furthermore, irrespective of size of farm, full-time farming confers higher prestige than does part-time farming. Accordingly, the extent of a particular family's social prestige is a resultant of a number of factors in combination, that is:

1. Size of farm and its geographical situation.
2. Length of family connection with the area.

3. Family connections with other farmers in the area.
4. Whether the farmer, or another member of his family, works off the farm.

Thus, one farmer at the top of the scale lives in the parish situated at the lowest altitude and operates two farms with a total acreage of over 200 acres. He has a number of brothers and brothers-in-law who have large farms in the district; some of the other 'larger-business' farmers are closely related to him; his family has connections with the area which extend back for more than 300 years, and all his sons and daughters work, or have worked, at home on the farm. At the other extreme is an incomer living on an isolated small farm, at an altitude of 1,600 ft. He is not related to any local inhabitant, nor is his wife. He works full-time off his farm at a factory in the town, and his sons work outside the area at occupations unconnected with farming. He has lived in the area for less than three years and, prior to taking the farm, he lived and worked in a large town over 30 miles away.

The degree of social differentiation recognized varies from one parish to another, in accordance with local conditions. For example, on the fertile land at low altitudes, full-time farmers with large farms, who have all their children living and working at home, are in the highest stratum; and farmers whose children work off the farm (particularly at non-farming occupations) are in the lowest stratum. At higher altitudes, where working off is more frequent, more emphasis is placed upon whether or not people are recent incomers to the area. Because greater changes in population composition have occurred at the higher altitudes, a connection with the area only one generation deep is likely to be accepted there as 'old-established'. On the better farming country, this designation is reserved for those with a longer family connection.

That these distinctions are real ones to the local people is apparent from the conversations of farmers. In response to my comment that all his children went out to work, one small-business farmer on the lower country replied, "Better that than live in poverty", to which his wife added, "Aye, but our children are 'nowt' round here now, millhands they call them." In another discussion with a farmer's wife (again on the lower country) I inadvertently implied that a local cattle dealer with a large farm was her social equal. The farmer's wife, by remarking "Oh, *James* ——", instantly made clear that her acquaintances were not in his class. By contrast, while discussing farming with me, a very respected 'dual-business' farmer from the highest altitude parish remarked that there were not many of the old inhabitants about nowadays. As an example of one of these, he instanced "Joe ——", a single man who farmed full-time, despite the difficulties of the area and the situation of his farm. On further investigation, I found that, although Joe had been reared in the parish, his parents had come there from another county. Furthermore, his father had always gone out to work from his farm, as had Joe himself until his parents died and left him a farm sufficient to support himself and his sister without other work. By virtue of a lifetime spent in the parish, together with his current full-time farming activities, Joe enjoyed a high prestige.

Economic and social pressures both operate to encourage larger-business farmers to remain in the area, and to enlarge their farms, if possible. These pressures also provide incentives for parents to want to pass on such farms to their kin, and for children to be content to stay at home and inherit. This is evident from the greater proportion of larger-business farmers who have family connections with their farm extending to three or more generations. Thirty per cent of them have such connections compared with 14 per cent of the part-time farmers[1] (Table 48).

Table 48: Type of farmer and generational association with farm

Family connection of farmer or his wife with present farm	Larger-business farmers	Small-business farmers and family-earning farmers	Dual-business farmers and other-work farmers	Total
Own generation only	22	31	37	90
Two generations	10	23	14	47
Three or more generations	14	13	8	35
Total	46	67	59	172

Dual businesses do not show a high tendency to persist over the generations. None of the farmers on 'three generational' farms are

[1] There is no difference between the proportions of larger-business, small-business and family-earning farmers currently occupying farms with which they or their wives have no previous family connections. This is partly a function of farm-to-farm movement amongst some of the larger-business farmers and partly due to the tendency for small-business and family-earning farmers to follow parents on their farms, without such family connections persisting into a third generation. This point is discussed in detail later in this chapter, in the section on succession to small full-time farms.

sons of dual-business farmers, and only two grandsons[1] are likely to have a dual-business of the same nature as their grandfathers. These two businesses, cattle dealing and corn selling, are both directly connected with farming, but other types have not survived to the third generation. This is not surprising, since the dual-business farmers have more varied contacts and a wider range of movement. Together with the chances their businesses give them to acquire capital (or to dissipate it, in the case of some cattle dealers), this ensures that sons and daughters will be 'set-up' as full-time farmers, marry into farming families, or move away from farming into other occupations for which they have probably been trained in their father's business. The main feature of the dual businesses is the advantage by which the people who operate them are enabled to rise to farming and/or financial positions better than they could have achieved by following exclusively either their farming or their other trades.

Compared with the other farmers, a greater proportion of other-work farmers are currently occupying farms with which neither they nor their wives have previous family connections. This is largely due to the higher proportion of them whose fathers were not farmers, and who could not therefore have obtained a farm from parents. When farmers with farming fathers are considered alone, no significant difference appears in the proportions of full-time and part-time farmers who have family associations with their farms.

'MARRYING IN'

Although dual businesses and farms where the farmer worked off did not persist for three generations to the same extent as large full-time farms, marrying in ensured that family associations on such farms were often extended into the second generation. Proportionately more part-time than full-time farmers began farming on, or eventually took over, a farm previously occupied by a parent or relative of their wife.

The attractions of 'marrying a farm' are obvious; but, if it is only a small one, those who have another source of employment are more likely to be interested than are those thinking in terms of full-time farming. Such a farm, with a wife accustomed to doing the work on it, fits in very well with full-time employment off the farm by the man, and it provides the first step on the farming ladder for those who otherwise may not obtain an opportunity to farm. If the farm is not

[1] Out of *all* the grandsons (i.e. taking into account the sons of siblings of farmers whose fathers were dual-business farmers).

too big, the wife can cope with the routine daily jobs over and above what the husband may do night and morning. Furthermore, at busy times, such as haymaking, their joint labour is adequate to handle the extra work. Often amongst the part-time farmers who have married in, the parents of the farmer or his wife have also been part-time farmers and their children are continuing a tradition of combining industrial work with farming. Two of the part-time farmers who married daughters of similarly placed farmers are different generations of the same family—son-in-law and father-in-law. Their case-histories illustrate the marriage patterns of this class of farmer, and the different approach they have to farming compared with full-time farmers.

The father-in-law, an eldest son, is not of farming stock but was reared on a farm and worked there for a few years after leaving school. He then went to work in a local factory, and met there the eldest daughter in the large family of a stone mason and part-time farmer. She, too, had worked in farm service for a time but had turned to factory work. They married when both were aged 20 and set up home in a cottage near the factory. They had six children and whilst the children were still under working age, moved to a bigger house—a farmhouse not very far from the farm of the wife's mother. This farmhouse had a considerable area of land attached, but they tenanted the house only and the land was let to another farmer. The disadvantages of this house were its distance from a hard road and its situation in a hollow—which made the journey to work difficult, particularly in snowy weather. Soon after the eldest child was of working age, a brother of the wife moved to another farm, vacating a small farm which was a quarter of a mile nearer a hard road. The family moved up to this and stayed for a few years until the adjacent property, next to the road, became vacant. This property had been tenanted by the wife's family for many years but, after they left it for a property on the main road to the nearest factory, another person had tenanted it for a time. When he vacated it, the present occupiers moved in and started to farm in a small way for the first time; in addition, all members of the family of working age went out to work, most of them in factories. The cycle was repeated in the next generation. At the age of 19, the only surviving daughter married a farm-reared factory worker. They went to live in the large farmhouse at a distance from the road, kept store cattle on the land, and the husband continued to go out to work. Later, the property nearer the road again became vacant. They bought it and moved up there, still keeping a house-cow and store stock. Since this survey was completed, the grandmother in the property on the main road has died.

To date, no further 'general post' has occurred, although the marriage of one of the two unmarried sons of the middle generation could precipitate three more moves, since the families now own all three properties. This son could set up home on the smallholding which is at a little distance from the road, replacing his sister whose family is outgrowing the small house. She could move to the property next to the road, and thus be in a better position when her first-born starts work in three years time. The father, mother and remaining brother could move to the grandmother's farm on the main road. This could be advantageous to the father, who would have easy access to his work for the last 10 years of his working life. It would also solve the problem of who was to look after the mother's un-married brother, left alone after the death of his mother (the grand-mother).

To farmers such as those discussed above, marrying a part-time farmer's daughter does not involve a decline in their social status. Others however, by marrying in, marry down socially. Some sons of full-time farmers are ready for marriage before their parents are ready, or willing, to retire. In such circumstances, some of them marry the daughters of small full-time farmers. They thus exchange the certainty of a share in their parents' inheritance (with a strong possibility of remaining single) for immediate marriage with a small stake in farming, whilst retaining some hope of patrimony at a future date.

Two examples serve to illustrate the circumstances under which such marriages occur. Both concern small-business farmers' daugh-ters who remained at home with ageing mothers after their fathers died. One is an only child of a late marriage; the other is the youngest daughter of a family of four girls. Sons left under such circumstances often remain single, for few women are available who are willing to share a small house and a small income with a mother-in-law who owns the house and controls the means of obtaining the income. But local girls of marriageable age are at a premium in the marriage market, particularly if they are experienced in farm work and likely to inherit a farm. Consequently, these daughters provided marriage partners for two eldest sons, both from 'all-sons' families and both with fathers who continued to farm after the sons had married. The father of one son had a medium-sized farm and, at the time the son married, was unlikely to retire for a number of years. The eldest son, however, was already nearly 30. The youngest son in this family, in his early twenties, worked on the home farm and was still single. Thus he was better placed than the eldest son to take over the family farm eventually, and yet also to marry at a reasonably young age.

The eldest son has changed his status considerably through his marriage. Not only is his wife's farm much smaller than that of his father; but also, in order to adequately support his wife, children and mother-in-law, he had been obliged to take up factory work, whereas prior to marriage he worked solely on his father's farm.

The other example concerns the eldest son of a farmer with two large farms and four other sons, three of them single. The eldest son, and the other married brother, through marriage, are now each established a few miles away from their father's properties, but travel backwards and forwards night and morning to work for their father. The father is reluctant to 'let go the reins' and the two married sons are equally reluctant to sever connections with home, in view of the size of the possible inheritance and the effect on their share of it, if they do not continue to work for their father. Their reluctance to leave home is understandable for they have both married down, socially, and neither of the farms into which they have married is big enough to give them more than a very poor living, compared with even a fifth share of their father's properties.

This eldest son and his wife have very different economic backgrounds. He had been able to afford a car and had moved around the district: "I've been to every one of the 11 villages round here." The wife had been wholly confined to the family farm before marriage, because of the dependence of her invalid father on the resources of herself and her mother to maintain the farm and provide a living for them all: "Many a time I've seen my mother working out beforehand how much the milk cheque would be so she knew what she could afford to spend on 'corn' and groceries." The wife was in her late thirties by the time her parents died and she was free to marry, and

Table 49: Marriage in and social mobility at marriage

Social mobility at marriage	Farmers who took over the farm of wife's parents or relatives	All other married farmers	Total
Married someone of equivalent social status to themselves	16	57	73
Married someone of higher social status	9	18	27
Married someone of lower social status	6	39	45
Total	31	114	145

her husband was about the same age. Both had, in fact, barely escaped celibacy.

These two examples show how some men whose chances of inheriting a farm and marrying at the same time are slight, may achieve marriage and a farm by marrying 'down'. These are exceptions, however, and it is noteworthy that more of the men who married a wife with a farm married 'up' than 'down' (Table 49). Such upward social mobility[1] through marriage was usually unobstructed by the wife's family so long as there were no sons; but these marriages could create considerable family tensions when a father chose to retire in favour of his daughter and her husband, thereby excluding his son or sons.

SUCCESSION TO SMALL FULL-TIME FARMS

The two socio-economic groups with the highest proportion of farmers who followed their own parents or relatives on the farm on which they began[2] are the groups of small-business and family-earning farmers (Table 50). In other words, those who started their farming career on a farm inherited from their own parents or relatives are more likely to be either farmers currently dependent entirely on a small farm business for a livelihood, or farmers whose farm business is inadequate to support a family. It is not surprising, therefore, that

[1] This measure is a comparison of the social status of the parents of each of the two partners at the time of the marriage, based mainly on occupation, but attempting to assess the situation by the standards of the people concerned, rather than by arbitrary 'social class' standards thought up by the investigator. Thus, if a full-time farmer's daughter from a small farm married a part-time farmer's son, the parents both being 'local' and living in one of the high altitude parishes, this would not be considered an upwardly mobile marriage on the part of the man, for going out to work and alternating between full-time farming of small farms and working off is a normal practice in such a parish. If a similar marriage had occurred in one of the lower altitude parishes, however (or even between a daughter from a large farm and a son from a small farm), this would have been considered upward social mobility, since social divisions at these altitudes are more related to farming status.

[2] The discussion of generational continuity in the first section of this chapter was related to the farms *currently occupied* by the farmers, as distinct from those farms on which they may have started to farm. The discussion included those farms where family continuity had been maintained by a man marrying into a farm inherited by a daughter. In this section, we look at the position at the time farmers started to farm on their own account, that is, before movement from farm to farm obscured the original pattern of succession. By confining this analysis to a comparison between those farmers who succeeded their own parents or relatives and those who failed to do so, a strong generational association emerges amongst small-business and family-earning farmers.

the group of small-business farmers includes a high proportion of incomplete or small families, and the family-earning group is composed either of small families with one member (not the farmer) working off the property, or of medium-sized families with more than one member working off.

Table 50: Succession to farm of own parent or relative

	Larger-business farmers	Small-business farmers and family-earning farmers	Dual-business farmers and other-work farmers	Total
Farmer began farming on own account on farm where he started farming and where he succeeded parent or relative at retirement or death	18	37	12	67
No succession as above	28	30	47	105
Total	46	67	59	172

Small full-time farms in this area will not wholly support more than two adults, even at a moderate level of living. Many of the occupants of such farms are either a pair of siblings, a childless couple, a widowed mother and her son, or a single person living alone. These are the only categories of people likely to be able to make a living when left with the burden of a small farm, an inherited tradition of farming, and a knowledge of no other trade. Married men who inherit small farms will be able to live adequately (by the standards of the area) only until such time as they have children; once their family increases, they are forced to go out to work, or to bring up their children in poverty. It is noteworthy that, compared with small-business farmers, a higher proportion of family-earning farmers had worked at occupations other than farm work prior to marriage (Table 51). This occupational mobility appears again later in their life cycle, for a higher proportion of them also changed their occupation during their farming career[1] compared with other full-time farmers (Table 52). Their children too, show a like tendency to work off the farm, thus helping to relieve the financial pressure on the family.

[1] That is, from full-time farmer to part-time farmer and vice-versa.

A striking feature of the inheritance process involving farms of inadequate size is that occupancy tended to be confined to two generations only. After this, the family lost connection with the farm, which then became available for amalgamation, or for occupancy by

Table 51: Full-time farmers' occupations prior to marriage or starting to farm

Occupation prior to marriage or starting to farm	Small-business farmers	Larger-business farmers	Family-earning farmers	Total
Farm at home or for others	33	38	16	87
Other work	8	8	10	26
Total	41	46	26	113

another unfortunate family, for whom the process was repeated. Thus, the family with an only son, who worked at home and did not inherit the farm until his father died, often gave rise to the incomplete family of the next generation—the son remaining single, or marrying

Table 52: Occupation changes since starting to farm

	Small-business and larger-business farmers	Dual-business farmers	Family-earning and other-work farmers	Total
No change	80	6	37	123
Change at some time	7	10	32	49
Total	87	16	69	172

late to someone his own age, or someone much younger. If he married someone his own age there was, in consequence, a reduced chance of producing children. If he married someone much younger than himself, who bore a number of children, these, being obliged to go out to work, were then more likely to leave home, and the family connection with the farm would be broken on the death of the parents. Alternatively, one of the male children might stay at home and be left single with a widowed mother. The various stages and variants of this process can be seen in the case-histories of the farmers in the two groups.

Of the small-business families who started farming on the farm

H

of the farmer's parents or relatives,[1] 11 out of 19 are single farmers living alone, or with a brother or sister, or with aged or widowed parents. Then there is one barren couple; a widower living alone (his children having married and left him) and a couple approaching 70 whose children have left home for urban employment. There are two families with a child living at home who has not yet taken over the farm from his parents. Both families comprise a farmer, his wife, and an only son; and, in both cases, the age-difference between the parents is such that the son is likely to be left to look after his widowed mother, and will eventually remain as a single farmer, unlikely to marry. The three other families are all in the early phase of their family cycle, all have one child only and all are finding it difficult to make a living from a small full-time farm.

The 10 families on family-earning farms and in which the farmers started farming on the farm of parents or relatives, are made up as follows:

1. An unmarried farmer with his married sister and her husband. The brother-in-law works off the farm.
2. A barren couple with the wife's brother. The brother is single and works off the farm.
3. A married couple with an only son working off the farm. The son intends to marry and take a farm elsewhere.
4. Two widows, one with sons working off, and one with a grandson and granddaughter, both nearly 30, working partly on the farm and partly elsewhere.
5. A married couple with one remaining unmarried son (a cripple in his thirties) living at home, but working off.
6. Four families (comprising parents and one child) where the ages of parents and children are such that the children are likely to remain permanently single, after caring for their widowed or aged parents.

Noticeable features common to those 'inheriting families' on small-business and family-earning farms are the marked changes—in attitudes, in material well-being and in mental and physical health—which accompany successive stages in the family life cycle. With the progress of the cycle even the conditions of the farms and the dwellings deteriorate, as confidence yields to doubt and doubt to despair. It was difficult to probe deeply into the intimacies of individual family histories, but a picture of the cycle of changes occurring can be constructed by examining details of families currently at different stages in the process. The following cases illustrate the conditions.

A married couple were in the early stage of the family cycle with

[1] Excluding four who had retired to a small farm from a larger one.

an only daughter who was still at school. The couple had married early but had not taken over the farm until the farmer's father retired several years afterwards. They complained that it had taken them a number of years to 'find their feet': capital was short and building up stock numbers by breeding was a slow process (the inheritance had been split between brothers and at the time of this survey the couple had eight cows). They were cheerful, the farm and house were well cared for and it appeared likely that, if they had no other children and the daughter married 'away', they would not experience difficulties until old age.

Another couple with an only son were on a smaller farm, on poorer land. The farmer complained: "There's enough work to keep me at home but we get nothing for it. Sometimes the milk cheque doesn't pay the corn bills." He expressed doubt about the future of farming 'up here', and thought "the Government ought to do something about it".

A family, in which the husband was considerably older than his wife, had one married daughter living in an urban area, a daughter working off the farm and a son working at home. The farmer had heart trouble, and his wife was of low intelligence. The farm was neglected, all the hens had died, the cows had reacted to the T.B. test and the farmer had only been able to afford to buy six replacements. They were living under very poor conditions and the daughter was the sole source of income, apart from the farm. When she married (a strong possibility since she worked in town and appeared attractive), their living conditions were likely to deteriorate still further. On the death of the father, the son would be left with a poor farm, no money, no other training, and a relatively young mother to look after for many years. It appeared almost certain that, when his mother died, the son would be too old and too poor to marry and perpetuate the poor conditions into another generation.

An only son of a late marriage had recently taken over the farm from his aged parents, thus enabling them to draw the old age pension. All three lived together in reasonable comfort. The son was in his early twenties, and wanted to leave farming. In the son's presence, the father said his advice was to "get out before it is too late". Later, when the son was not there, the father expressed misgivings as to "what we shall do if the lad gets married, as neither the house nor the farm is big enough for two families". The fate of the son was very much bound up with the life-expectation of his mother, who was younger and healthier than his father. Should the son marry and leave farming before either parent died, he would leave them in difficult circumstances. Conversely if he delayed marriage until after their death, a delay of 10 years or more would put him into an age category where the will to change would be diminishing exactly at the time when marriage prospects were becoming even more slender. Whatever he did, either he or his parents would suffer. Looked at impersonally, in terms of farming continuity, the chances were high that the farm would pass out of this particular family in the present, or the following, generation.

One case was of a son in poor health (with heart or respiratory trouble) living with his widowed mother. Although left on a medium-sized farm when the father died, they had to leave it, because the size of the inheritance was inadequate to meet the extra expenses of attestation. The father had risen from small beginnings until he had managed to rent a medium-sized farm, which he bought when the estate was sold. The death of the father was followed by attestation demands which were too much for the son (then in his forties) and the aged mother. As the son put it: "When the mortgage was paid off, there was enough for a deposit on this one"—'this one' being a smallholding on which they kept a couple of cows, two or three young stock, and a few hens. It was hard to see how they lived without work or assistance; the son implied that other people took National Assistance but not them, "although my mother's pension of £2 8s. 0d. helps a bit".

The 'end of the road' for the previous farmer was exemplified in a single farmer living on his own. His father had died in his early fifties, soon after the son had left school. A sister married three or four years later, leaving the son and mother on the farm. The mother died when the son was in his mid-thirties and soon afterwards the married sister left the district. Ten years later the farmer was living in squalor in one room of the farmhouse, surrounded by the debris of meals long past: with a 'parlour' just as the mother had left it, except that it was inches deep in dust. Attestation and the need for building alterations were making demands which he could not meet, as he had no security to offer for a loan. He was managing to live because his farm was big enough to support him at the low level to which he had fallen; but it was difficult to see him managing for the 20 years which separated him from the pension. Men were not the only 'victims' of demographic circumstances, for only daughters or youngest daughters too could be left caring for their aged father if their mother died early. Not as many of them were left on their own, however. To be in her thirties was not the barrier to matrimony for a woman that it often was for a man, particularly if she had inherited a small farm and was accustomed to doing farm work. Even those who were left alone were more resilient than the men, as they were trained for both farm and housework (unlike the men, who may have been good at the one, but were useless at the other). Old age, the rigours of the climate and lack of money caught up with the few single women on small farms too, however, and they were likely to have at least 10 difficult years before the pension brought some relief.

Occasionally, the early death of parents could lead to great distress for unmarried daughters. Once such example concerned a youngest daughter who was in her early 'teens when her mother died. Her other brothers and sisters married at young ages and left her looking after the father, to whom she was devoted. As she put it: "He was mother and father to me, and I could not leave him on his own." The father lived for over 20 years after his wife's death and towards the end of this time the daughter had two illegitimate children by one of the father's friends. Suddenly the father died, leaving the daughter with debts, a heavily mortgaged farm and two young children. Rejected by her relatives and her neighbours because of her 'sin', the woman could not turn to her lover who had his own farm, wife and family. At the time of the survey she did not know how she was going to live after the farm had been sold to pay the debts incurred by having to 'go attested'. In this case, demographic circumstances combined with Government policy had released a farm for amalgamation, or perhaps for part-time working, but the cost was being paid in terms of human misery.

CHAPTER VI

MOBILITY IN RELATION TO LAND
AND LOCALITY

AMALGAMATION OF LAND

THE misfortunes of some members of the farming community provide others with opportunities for land amalgamation.

Relatively few farmers have given up land to other farmers from their current holdings. Those who have relinquished land tend to be small-business farmers, with an incomplete family structure. Seven of the nine small-business families who have given up some land to neighbours are incomplete families. Other sources of land for amalgamation are farms vacated by farmers who retire or retreat to small holdings. But this movement is not very great in the area. Consequently the bulk of land for amalgamation becomes available on the death or retirement of its former occupiers, of whom many are the incomplete families of the previous generation.

The propensity and ability to amalgamate land is strongly associated with the socio-economic status of the farmers. Thus the dual-business farmers have been most active, the larger-business farmers fairly active, and the small-business farmers least active (Table 53).

Table 53: Amalgamation of land and type of farmer

	Small-business farmers	Family-earning farmers other-work farmers	Larger business farmers	Dual-business farmers	Total
Amalgamated land	8	19	24	13	64
Not amalgamated	33	50	22	3	108
Total	41	69	46	16	172

It would appear, then, that amalgamation of land is being carried out by those farmers best able to make a success of it, that is, those who have been well trained in farming, who have a reasonable amount of capital for their business, and who have adequate resources to enable them to utilize their increased land area.

The outstanding position of the dual-business farmers suggests that their combination of farming with a service to farmers places them in an advantageous position for acquiring land. They travel about the area a good deal in the course of their second business activities and thus are likely to hear of land becoming available before other interested parties. Their businesses give them a chance to build up capital from non-farm sources, and in some cases they have settled with a creditor by taking over some of his land and/or stock. Two cases will serve to illustrate the process by which amalgamation occurs.

An eldest son of a farming family, who was working away from home, married in his early twenties, whilst his brothers and sisters still lived at home with his widowed mother. He took a village smallholding of a few acres which had frequently changed hands in the past, kept a couple of cows on it, and continued to go out to work. Some years later he exchanged properties with a farmer on a small farm, who wanted to retire and whose children did not work on the farm. Later, an adjacent property (rather larger, but not big enough to support a family) became vacant on the death of its occupier. This man had no children following him on the farm and his widow could not run it herself. This property was incorporated with the other holding. At some stage the farmer started to deal in cattle, increasing his size of business and, presumably, strengthening his capital position. Still later, the land of another small farm became vacant, and this also was incorporated. Eventually therefore, over a period of 20 years, three small farms, each incapable of adequately supporting a family, were combined together into one compact holding providing a reasonable living, and employment, for a farmer and his family. It should be noted that this 'natural' process of amalgamation fitted in with the stages in the family developmental cycle of the amalgamator, and with those of the people from whom he obtained land. Furthermore, the availability of the smallholding in the village was an important factor in the initiation of the whole process.

The son of a part-time farmer was drafted on war work away from his home area. Whilst away, he learnt the building trade, which came naturally to many of the part-time farmers in the area who were only one generation removed from the masons of the past and may well have worked with stone in local quarries. On returning home, he married a farmer's daughter. They set up house in a cottage attached to her father's smallholding, and the men went out to work. On the death of the wife's mother, the father gave up farming and went to live with relatives. The son-in-law rented the land and started up in business as a building contractor. Two or three years later a piece of land about a mile away became available and this also was rented. This land was owned by the single daughter of the previous occupier and she continued to live in the house. Later still, a relative of the farmer's wife retired, and his land (which adjoined the original holding) was rented. Finally, another small accommodation field was rented. This belonged to a bigger farmer, but was at a distance from his property. In all, 50 acres of land were acquired over a period of 10 years. The farm is still not big enough to support a family without the other business, which is the dominant business of the two. Nevertheless, land which had previously been in parcels too small for effective use by its previous occupiers is being utilized for the partial support of one family. Probably a third of it will be lost again on the deaths of the owners; but, by that time, the farmer's children will be working and the family's need for land will have diminished.

MOVEMENT OF PEOPLE AND LAND
TO MEET FAMILY NEEDS

The needs of a farming family vary with different stages in the family developmental cycle and with the number of persons in the household. The adequacy with which a particular farm meets the needs of a family living on it varies with changes in economic conditions affecting agriculture. To meet increased family needs, or to meet constant needs when farm income is reduced, a family farmer has several courses of action open to him.

He may attempt to increase the production from his current farm.
He may attempt to acquire more land.
He may try to move to a larger farm.
He may either go out to work himself or allow some of his family to do so.
He may leave farming for other employment.
He may take no positive action and consequently have to accept a reduced standard of living.

In a marginal farming area, such as the one under consideration here, it is often difficult to increase production from a fixed area of land, because of limitations of fixed resources (for example cow 'standings' and acreage available for hay) or because of a shortage of investment and working capital. Evidence presented in Chapter II suggests that the small-business farmers, whose need to increase their farming intensity is the greatest, are operating their farms at the lowest level of intensity. If this had been the situation in the past, some farmers were likely to have attempted other means of adjustment, and some would have been forced to adopt other means, or live in poverty.

It has been shown in the previous section that dual-business and larger-business farmers have been most active in amalgamation. To some extent, this states the obvious, in that those farmers originally on small farms who acquired enough land to raise them out of the 'small-farm' category, will inevitably be classified currently as having medium or large-sized farms. The effectiveness of amalgamation in changing the socio-economic status of farmers can be seen, however, by comparing the size groupings of farms before and after amalgamation (Table 54). This comparison indicates that larger-business

Table 54: Farm size changes consequent upon amalgamation

Farm size before and after amalgamation		Small-business, larger-business and dual-	Family-earning and other-	
Before	After	business farmers	work farmers	Total
Small to	small	14	12	26
Small to	medium or large	9	4	13
Medium to	medium	4	3	7
Medium to	large	9	0	9
Large to	large	7	0	7
Total		43	19	62*

* Excludes two farms where more land was given up than was amalgamated.

farmers have been able to achieve large-farm status by means of amalgamation, but 'small-business' farmers have not been as successful in changing their farming status. Amalgamation has been even less effective in changing the farming status of other-work and family-earning farmers.

In contrast to the above, very few farmers who started farming on medium to large farms have moved to bigger ones, for the majority of those moving to better themselves (85 per cent) started out on small farms. Of these, 63 per cent have changed their farming status from the small-farm grouping to the medium or large grouping as a result of one or two changes of farm during their careers (Table 55). The farmers who have been least successful in moving out of the 'small-farm' category are the current other-work and family-earning farmers. For those people who started on small farms, moving to another farm has been a more effective way of increasing their farm land resources than has amalgamating land, judging by the numbers who have changed from small to medium or large farms by the two methods (compare Tables 54 and 55).

Table 55: Farm size changes consequent upon movement
from smaller to larger farms

Size group of farm		Small-business larger-business and dual-business farmers	Family-earning farmers	Other-work farmers	Total
Original	Current				
Small to	small	3	4	5	12
Small to	medium or large	14	5	2	21
Medium or to large	Medium or large	4	1	1	6
Total		21	10	8	39*

* Only includes those farmers who had moved to their current farm to better themselves.

It would appear that, in this area, about half the farmers starting on small full-time and small dual-business farms, and about two-thirds of all farmers starting on small farms, could not expect to progress beyond a small farm during their career, whether they moved to another farm or amalgamated land into their original holding.[1] It is not surprising, therefore, that 19 per cent of all farming families (comprising mainly those on small, full-time farms) are living in poor circumstances, or that so many of the families on small farms have the farmer, or some other family member, working off the farm.

Working off the farm by the farmer, or his family, will be considered in detail in the next chapter, when occupational mobility within and between generations is discussed. One point should be

[1] This statement assumes that the numbers of farmers in these categories were the same in the past as they are in the present. It also assumes that movements of farmers into the area for larger farms are balanced by movements out of the area of farmers from small farms going to larger ones elsewhere. Twenty-three full-time and dual business farmers in the sample had progressed from small to medium or large farms by farm-to-farm movement or by amalgamation. Currently, the sample contains 49 small full-time and dual-business farms. Similarly, 21 farmers starting on small farms had progressed to a larger farm by farm movement and 13 had progressed by amalgamation and there are 104 small farms in the sample.

noted here, however. Compared with full-time or dual-business farmers, other-work and family-earning farmers have not been as successful in progressing from small to medium or large farms whether by farm movement or by amalgamation. Case-study material suggests that some of these families may have adopted the alternative of working off after unsuccessfully attempting to obtain an adequate income from farming consequent upon moving to another farm or amalgamating land. Others had accepted at the outset that work off the property would be necessary. Consequently, if these farmers moved to another farm, or added some land to their original farm, they were not under the same compulsive need to move out of the small farm category as were farmers who were unwilling either to work off their farm themselves or to allow members of their family to do so.

It is much easier to adjust income to family needs, if going out to work by the farmer or his family, or having another business, is accepted as normal and as an alternative to acquiring more land or moving to a larger farm. A farmer is likely to run into difficulty, however, if he and his wife start out on a full-time farm large enough to provide for the needs of a married couple and two children, but they then proceed to have a large family, or the wife develops 'extravagant' tastes,[1] or the husband starts to drink heavily (three circumstances which may well be interrelated). Their difficulties will be particularly acute if the farmer does not supplement his farm income by other work. There may be a number of reasons why such a farmer does not go out to work. He may be too idle to seek or retain other work or he may have a disability which prevents him from working off the farm. He may not have experience of any occupation other than farm work or he may fear the disapproval of his relatives and friends if he takes other employment and runs his farm on a part-time basis. There are practical difficulties, too, in the part-time operation of a dairy farm when the farmer's wife has a number of young children. With the man away all day, the wife is responsible for much of the routine work about the farm. This may prove too much for her if she is bearing one child, nursing another and trying to control the rest. How many of these people had to leave farming cannot be ascertained from a study of mobility which from practical necessity is based on the people who remain in an area. That these

---

[1] These need be no more than the standards to which she had become accustomed before marriage, or which she sees being adopted around her by her neighbours who have money coming in from work off the farm. Such standards may be 'extravagant', however, relative to the earning capacity of the farm she is living on.

circumstances occur is evident from the case histories of six families still living on the survey farms, and from the remarks made by the (successful) occupiers of holdings previously held by such people:

> "It was all beer and whisky with him and he drank himself out of the door."
> "Our ways were not good enough for his wife, and he could not carry on at her level."
> "They had 'fairish' of kids, she wouldn't help and he went banked."[1]

Some trends are suggested by the distribution of the lengths of occupation of present occupiers, by details of the types of people who had remained for long periods on small full-time farms, and by the meagre information which was obtained about what happened to previous occupiers.[2]

In common with other-work farmers, a high proportion of small-business farmers have occupied their farms for 10 years or less, and a lower for 11–20 years, compared with other farmers. Of the 23 small-business farmers who have been on their farms for 10 years or less, eight are married couples in the early stage of their family developmental cycle, 11 are single farmers, and there are three other incomplete families and one semi-retired couple who have unmarried daughters living at home.

On the eight small-business farms occupied for 11–20 years there are two families living under poor conditions, and who have children at home, three single farmers, one widower living alone, one barren couple and one retired couple. The 10 families who have been on their full-time small farms over 20 years, consist of five in the middle stage of the family developmental cycle and three in the late stage, one barren couple and one single farmer living alone.

Superficially, the above would appear to suggest that quite a few families have managed to survive on full-time small farms. Further examination of the past circumstances of the married farmers on small farms which they have occupied for over 20 years shows, however, that six of them have children who worked off the farm in the past. The two exceptions are families of mother, father and only son. Even the barren couple claimed that they were not there of their own free

---

[1] i.e. they had a lot of children, and he became bankrupt.

[2] The failure to obtain more information about the economic and family circumstances of previous occupiers is a weakness of the study. If a reliable method of obtaining accurate information on this could be devised it would be valuable. Because present occupiers may be relatives of past occupiers who had to leave, and in some instances may have been instrumental in getting them out, a much more subtle technique would be needed than the obvious one of asking the present occupier or neighbours—a method fraught with difficulties, as I quickly discovered.

will. The husband explained forcibly: "My father made me promise when he was on his death-bed that I'd come back to the farm, and I did. There is nothing I can do about it now—who would employ me at nearly sixty? But as soon as I'm 65 I'll be out, maister, as fast as I can."

This analysis suggests that few married couples with families managed to survive on small farms throughout the family developmental cycle, without some member going out to work. It also indicates that few single farmers stayed long on one farm. Some may have married, although it is possible to visualize only two doing so out of the 11 single farmers on farms occupied for 10 years or less. Some may have gone out to work or have come to some arrangement to live with a relative—there were five of these on small farms in the survey—but some must have left. Some clues about what happened to these can be obtained from remarks made about them by other farmers. Thus one farmer, in commenting on a former neighbour, said: "Oh, he's a road sweeper now in Hilltown. He couldn't carry on after his mother died, it was only her pension that kept them going."

People certainly left farms for other employment but there is no definite trend linked to size of farm, although amongst previous occupiers of farms at the higher altitudes (where the farms were poorer) a much higher proportion had short lengths of occupation and had left for other work than amongst previous occupiers of farms at the lower altitudes. Many of the present occupiers of the holdings at high altitudes are 'incomers' and work off their farms but, without obtaining much more information about them, we do not know how many of the previous occupiers had been of this type, and how many had been full-time farmers with small resources relative to family size.

With the exception of the family-earning farmers, there is a definite consistency in the proportions of farmers in all the socio-economic

Table 56: Type of farmer and length of occupancy of farm

Length of occupancy by present occupier	Small-business farmer	Larger-business farmer	Family-earning farmer	Dual-business farmer	Other work farmer	Total
10 years and under	23	20	6	5	26	80
11–20 years	8	16	9	7	8	48
Over 20 years	10	10	11	4	9	44
Total	41	46	26	16	43	172

groupings who have occupied their current holdings for over 20 years. Twenty to 25 per cent of them have been on their holdings this length of time, compared with 42 per cent of the family-earning farmers (Table 56). Many of the family-earning farmers worked off their farms in their younger days, before their children were of working age. Now they work at home, and some of their children work off the property. Such farm families have thus supplemented farming with other earnings for a considerable time. This may be having an effect on the proportion of them remaining on their farms for over 20 years.[1]

Another factor influencing periods of occupation of holdings is that of succession to parents or relatives. Previous occupiers who were relatives of current occupiers had longer lengths of occupation than had non-relatives (Table 57).[2] This suggests that there are two groups

Table 57: Length of occupancy by previous occupier
and generational link with farms

| | Generations farm has been in same family | | | |
	Present generation only %	Two generations %	Three generations %	Total %
10 years and under	45	11	9	28
11–20 years	22	32	11	22
Over 20 years	33	57	80	50

[1] Most of the farm families in this category are in the middle phase of the family developmental cycle, and none is in the early phase. By contrast, about a third of all married farmers are in the early phase, and therefore not likely to have been on their farms over 20 years. This characteristic of 'family-earning' farmers may be having an effect on the relative proportions.

[2] Table 57 shows that 80 per cent of the farms with which the current farmer has family associations extending to his grandparental generation and beyond (i.e. a three-generational association) had previous occupiers (i.e. the parents or relatives of the current farmer) who were on the farms for over 20 years. This proportion is significantly greater than that of 50 per cent for the previous occupiers (again the parents or relatives of the current farmer) on farms with which the current farmer has family associations extending to his parents' generation, but not beyond (i.e. a two-generational association).

Most parents or relatives of current farmers occupying the three-generational farms were likely to have started their farming careers on those farms at the death or retirement of *their* parents or relatives (i.e. the grandparents, grand-uncles, etc., of the current farmer). Consequently they would have spent the whole of their farming careers on those farms. Some parents or relatives of current farmers on two-generational farms, however, could have come to those farms

of farms—those which 'turn over' at a relatively slow rate and pass from one relative to another; and those which 'turn over' at a faster rate and pass between non-relatives.

Those current farmers occupying their first farm are much more likely to be related to the previous occupier of their farm than are those farmers who are currently occupying their second or third farm (Table 58). These mobile farmers are more likely to have followed

Table 58: Whether farmer has had more than one farm
and generational link with present farm

No. of farms worked by farmer	Generations farm has been in family			
	Present generation only	Two generations	Three generations	Total
Present farm only	53	37	30	120
One or more other farms	37	10	5	52
Total	90	47	35	172

Table 59: Number of farms worked by present occupier
and reason for previous occupier leaving

	Present occupier has worked	
	present farm only %	one or more other farms %
Previous occupier:		
Went to another farm	23	38
Retired	35	21
Died	29	17
Left farming for other occupation, had to leave, etc.	13	24

previous occupiers who themselves had moved away, either in search of another farm, or to take up other employment outside farming altogether (Table 59). In other words, mobile farmers tend to follow each other on the same holdings, and they remain on their farms for shorter periods than other farmers.

A survey of current farmers cannot provide adequate information

part-way through their careers, or even towards the end of them. This difference in the mobility of parents or relatives would account for the lower proportion of them who had occupied current two-generational farms for over 20 years.

on the degree of turnover of farms in the past. Nevertheless, the existence of the relationship outlined above is substantiated by independent research carried out in three of the survey parishes, and in three nearby parishes.[1] The six parishes contained 252 farms. Sixty per cent of these (151) had one or more change of occupier over the period 1939–55. These 151 farms had 199 changes in occupants. Eight farms (having three or more changes) accounted for 26 changes, another 30 farms (having two changes) accounted for 60, and 113 farms had one change. In other words, 25 per cent of the farms which had changes of occupier accounted for 43 per cent of all changes in the period.

One important reason given for leaving these farms during the period was 'management and financial difficulties'. More tenants than owner-occupiers left because of management and financial difficulties; but the figures do not help us to determine whether this was due to tenants getting into difficulties more frequently, or to owner-occupiers being less able to cut their losses and leave. Tenants also left more frequently to go to other farms than did owner-occupiers who tended to stay on their farms until death or retirement (Table 60A).

When we compare the reasons for leaving farms given in Dennis's study with those in my study, we find that 'death or retirement' accounted for approximately the same proportion of the reasons in both. A lower proportion of previous occupiers had left because of management difficulties, or to seek other work, in my study than in Dennis's study and in mine more had left to take up other farms (compare Tables 59 and 60A). Some of this difference may be due to the greater difficulty farmers experienced in moving from farm to farm during wartime; and some of it may be due to the compulsory powers of dispossession and direction of labour which were exercised during the war. The relative proportions may also have been influenced by the 38 moves in Dennis's study for which no reasons were given.

This other study further confirms the impression of mobile farmers following mobile farmers. 'One-change' farms had a high proportion of previous occupiers who died or retired and 'multiple-change' farms had a high proportion of farmers who changed farms or left for other reasons.

In Table 60B owner-occupiers and tenants are classified according

---

[1] M. A. Dennis, of the Agricultural Land Service, provided the information on this piece of research, and I calculated from this the various proportions mentioned. The information covers all farms in the six parishes, and was obtained from various official sources and not by direct enquiry from farmers in the area.

Table 60: Reasons for occupiers leaving farms* in six
parishes in and adjacent to survey area, 1939–55

A

Reason for leaving	All farmers	All owner-occupiers	All tenants	All leaving one-change farms†	All leaving multiple-change farms‡
Death or retirement	89	32	57	68	21
Move to other farm	29	5	24	12	17
Management or financial difficulties	26	3	23	13	13
Sale of farm at profit	4	4	0	0	4
Other reasons (mainly return to town or to be near other work)	13	7	6	3	10
Total	161	51	110	96	65

* For all moves for which information was available comprising 161 out of 199 moves.
† Farms with only one change of occupier in the period.
‡ Farms with more than one change of occupier in the period.

B

	Owner-occupiers leaving one-change farms %	Tenants leaving one-change farms %	Tenants leaving multiple-change farms %	Owner-occupiers leaving multiple-change farms %	Total %
Death or retirement	84	64	35	26	55
Move to other farm	9	14	33	11	18
Management or financial difficulties	3	19	24	11	16
Sale of farm at profit	0	0	0	21	3
Other reasons	3	3	9	32	8

to whether they had left 'one-change' farms or 'multiple-change' farms, and the groups arranged in descending order of the importance of death and retirement as a reason for leaving. The group of owner-occupiers leaving 'one-change' farms had been the least mobile group, tenants leaving 'multiple-change' farms had left more frequently than the others to go to other farms, whilst owner-occupiers leaving 'multiple-change' farms had left most frequently for reasons not directly connected with farming.

In 1951, a large-scale changeover from tenancy to owner-occupation occurred in three parishes included in both studies. This change did not occur in the other three parishes included in Dennis's analysis. For this reason, the differences between owner-occupiers and tenants demonstrated above are likely to have been applicable generally to my survey area up until 1951, but may not have been applicable necessarily after that time when the proportion of tenants changed from two-thirds to one-third.

Previous analysis has shown that most of the farmers in the survey area who moved from one farm to another in order to better themselves, had been tenants prior to 1951. This agrees with the proportions shown in Table 60B, and suggests that the changeover to owner-occupation may well restrict in the future the mobility of farmers wanting to improve their situation by a move to a better farm. Many of them will not only have to find a suitable farm available to which they can move, but will also have to find a purchaser for the one they want to vacate. Furthermore, they will need extra capital for the larger farm. This is likely to increase still further the element of chance involved when people attempt to move from farm to farm to fit in with changing family or economic circumstances.

MOVEMENT OF PEOPLE INTO THE AREA

Over two or three generations, replacement of local families who have 'died out' or moved away has resulted in a higher proportion of unrelated people living at the higher altitudes than at the lower ones, and consequently occupying the part-time farms as compared with the full-time ones. Nineteen per cent of all farmers came into the area from either urban locations or from other country areas. It has been noted earlier (Ch. III, page 61) that 19 per cent of all the farms sampled were operated by 'problem' families living under poor conditions, and in demographic and economic circumstances which were likely to result in the farm passing out of the family. If in the short run the number of farms in the area did not change and there was no surplus of farmers' sons wanting to farm, the farms which become vacant when problem families moved out or died out would provide a source of farms for incomers. This could be either a direct source or an indirect one, which created the opportunity for a farm-to-farm movement of existing farmers and thus caused vacancies for incomers to enter farms of various types and sizes. The concordance of the proportions of incomers and of problem families supports the replacement calculations presented at the end of Chapter VIII.

Two-thirds of the incomers had taken up farms at the higher altitudes, and rather half of them work off their farms. A higher proportion of them have been on their farms for shorter periods compared with the locals and there is a tendency for incomers to follow 'short-length' previous occupiers.

On the poorest farms, incomers have definitely followed one another and sometimes in rapid succession. For example, one farm in a remote situation had five occupiers in 10 years. Although the turnover of incomers is greater, some obviously stay, otherwise there would not be a quarter of them who have been occupying their current farms for over 20 years.[1] The example has already been quoted, on page 40, of someone who was actually an incomer 30 years previously, being regarded as an 'old inhabitant'.

Analysis of the full list of farmer's names from which the survey farms were drawn shows that for the parish at the highest altitude (mainly above 1,300 feet), 65 per cent of the names occur once and 35 per cent occur twice. For a parish lying mainly between 1,000 and 1,100 feet 43 per cent of the names occur once and 57 per cent twice or more. Of these, one name occurs seven times, three names five times, one name three times and seven names twice. One smaller parish at an altitude of 900 to 1,000 feet (which has mainly full-time farmers on farms of medium to large size) has a seventh of its farmers with the same name.

In these circumstances it is not surprising that the farmers at the lowest altitudes tend to dismiss all those at the higher ones as 'strangers, townies, layabouts and factory hands', whilst the latter, in their turn, consider the farmers 'down there' to be 'an inbred lot, you don't know who's related to whom, and none of them have been further than——(the local village)'. Of course, in reality, the position is not like this at all. At all altitudes there are good farmers and poor ones, inbred families and 'outcrossed' ones, full-time and part-time farmers. In the determination of attitudes, however, the dominant trend is taken as applying to all.

It is true that most of the incomers at altitudes of below 1,100 feet are from country areas, and consequently are more likely to be

[1] Note that this is the same proportion as that for all farmers, see Table 56.

accepted by the locals. On the other hand, those from country areas are equally likely to have gone to the higher altitudes as to the lower ones in search of a farm, and they are as likely to work off the farm themselves or to have some family member work off as they are to farm full-time. Most of those from country areas who are farming full-time are on medium to large farms, and a rather higher proportion of all incomers compared with locals have previously had another smaller farm and have moved into the area to obtain a larger farm. Unless they had relatives in the area, however, the full-time farmers who came in were likely to have obtained only those farms which had not been taken up by a local because of poor access or a bad reputation (wet, or subject to deficiency diseases for example).

A greater movement from one part of the area to another and in from neighbouring parishes is indicated when we define mobility in terms of distance from birthplace rather than by area of origin. With this measure, least mobility is shown by the small-business farmers (Table 61).

Table 61: Type of farmer and distance living from birthplace

Distance of present abode from birthplace	Small-business farmers	Other-work farmers	All other farmers	Total
2½ miles and under	31	15	53	99
2¾–5 miles	6	12	13	31
Over 5 miles	4	16	22	42
Total	41	43	88	172

The general tendency to move uphill relative to the location of parents has been discussed in Chapter IV. The other-work farmers are the only ones to show greater uphill mobility. This is to be expected, in view of the proportion of incomers in this group, of whom three-quarters lived at lower altitudes prior to moving into the area.

In the general tendency to divide people into 'us' and 'them', or 'townies' and 'country folk', the interchange of experience between town and country which has occurred, is often forgotten. Some countryborn men worked in an urban area, and then returned to the country, whilst many of the wives had worked in urban areas prior to marriage and a number had lived there. Considering husbands and wives together,[1] one or both partners have lived in an urban area prior

[1] Only four of the single farmers have lived outside the area, and only one of these four has lived in a town.

to marriage in a quarter of all the married pairs. A relatively high proportion of dual-business families have either the husband or wife who has lived in an urban area prior to marriage (Table 62). This is

Table 62: Type of farmer and where husband or wife lived before marriage

Where husband or wife lived before marriage	Married other-work farmers	Married farmers with a dual-business	All other married farmers	Total
Urban area	16	6	14	36
Country area	23	9	76	108
Total	39	15	90	144

despite the fact that all of the 'dual-business' husbands are sons of local farmers.

The presence in the area of 25 per cent of families who have one or other person accustomed to urban living is likely to have an influence on the 75 per cent with a rural background, for consumption in some things can be even more conspicuous in the country than in the towns. In an area not served by electricity, a farmer who possesses an electric generator can literally be seen for miles around. When a major topic of family conversation is what the neighbours are doing, or going to do, any changes in standards of living or ways of life are quickly noted, even if to outward appearances they are apparently deprecated and ignored.

CHAPTER VII

OCCUPATIONAL MOBILITY

ALTHOUGH more than 80 per cent of the farmers in this area are sons of farmers, this broad continuity in occupation conceals a great deal of social and occupational mobility. Not all farmers' sons remain in the industry, and those who take up farming do not necessarily follow exactly their fathers' type of employment. In certain circumstances one farmer in his lifetime may progress up the 'farming ladder' from part-time farming at a high altitude to full-time farming on a large farm in the valley. Such a movement within one lifetime is uncommon; but a family may progress in this way over the generations. Conversely, well-to-do farmers may move down the 'farming ladder' through accident, or ineptitude; or sons may prove unable to maintain the same standards as their fathers. This kind of family progress, whether up or down, may be associated with particular marriages; a son from a small farm may be fortunate enough to 'marry into' a family of higher farming status, or a son from a large farm may marry down socially and thereby find himself compelled to farm under much poorer circumstances than his father. Moreover, the picture of the social and occupational mobility occurring amongst farmers is complicated by recruitment into local farms of persons from outside the industry—a recruitment which is more frequent at the lowest farming level (namely part-time farming) than at any other.[1]

The process of mobility is continuous and a cross-sectional study —such as this—in fact comprises a number of persons at varying stages in the process. Some are unlikely to change their present farming employment or to move to another farm, for reasons of age, incapacity or lack of capital; others will move either up or down the farming and social scale in the future. The 'farming ladder' in this area does not consist of a simple series of steps from small to large farms, but is a complicated interaction between size of farm, opportunity and capacity for other employment, size of family, prospect of inheritance, and chance demographic and economic factors. Inevitably, therefore, the picture of mobility presented in this chapter is complicated.

---

[1] Part-time farming does not confer a high prestige upon the person practising it, but it frequently gives him a higher income than that of many full-time farmers, see Ch. II, Table 8.

A number of features can be distinguished. These are:

1. The operation of the 'farming ladder', within and between generations.
2. The recruitment into farming from outside the industry.
3. The occupational mobility of farmers before and after they start to farm on their own account.
4. The social and occupational mobility of farmers' wives.

THE OPERATION OF THE 'FARMING LADDER' WITHIN AND BETWEEN GENERATIONS

The proportion of part-time to full-time farmers in this generation is approximately the same as that in their fathers' generation, two-thirds full-time to one-third part-time. This does not mean, however, that current farmers in each socio-economic group have followed exactly their fathers' type of employment. Continuity of occupation between father and son (in the sense that a current farmer is follow-ing exactly the type of farming employment of his father) varies considerably from one socio-economic group to another. Thus, there are 113 full-time farmers in the sample, and 74 of these (65 per cent) are the sons of full-time farmers. On the other hand, there are 59 part-time farmers, but only 20 of these (34 per cent) are the sons of part-time farmers. In other words, continuity of occupation is much more marked amongst the full-time farmers; and part-time farming is clearly the avenue through which outsiders enter the industry (Table 63). This continuity of occupation between the generations of full-time farmers is apparent whatever category of full-time farmer we consider, whether they are larger-business farmers, small-business

Table 63: Type of farmer and occupation of father

| | *Father's occupation* | | | | | |
Farmer's type of farming	*Full-time farming*	*Dual-business farming*	*Farming plus work off*	*Farm work*	*Other work*	*Total*
Full-time farmer	74	8	20	3	8	113
Dual-business farmer	8	3	5	0	0	16
Other-work farmer	13	3	9	1	17	43
Total	95	14	34	4	25	172

farmers or family-earning farmers. There is no significant difference between the proportions of current farmers in each of these categories who had fathers who were full-time farmers.

Part of this continuity of occupation amongst full-time farmers comes from a direct passing on of full-time farms from father to son. It was shown in Chapter V that full-time farmers are more likely than part-time farmers to have previous family associations with their farms. This relationship is also apparent when we examine together the inheritance of occupation and the inheritance of farms. Of the 74 full-time farmers who are sons of full-time farmers, 42 (57 per cent) started to farm on their own account on a farm previously operated by their parents or relatives. By contrast, out of the 20 part-time farmers who have remained in their father's type of employment, only five (25 per cent) started their farming career on a family farm. Thus, inheritance of property and farming upbringing, combine to retain many sons of full-time farmers in full-time farms. Whether or not they remain at the same economic level as their fathers depends upon factors such as their working histories prior to achieving independence from home, the marriages they contract, and chance economic or demographic circumstances. These other factors are also operative in determining the movements of those full-time farmers' sons who pass down the 'farming ladder' into part-time farming and of those sons of part-time farmers who move upwards into full-time farming.

The 'farming ladder' is usually visualized as a process whereby—within his own lifetime—a farm worker, or a person in an occupation other than farming, can work his way up from being a hired worker, through successive sizes of farm until he achieves independence and property on a reasonably sized farm. It is apparent from the foregoing discussion, and from Table 63, that such a ladder is not characteristic of this area. Indeed, it is doubtful whether this notion of mobility within the farming industry has any basis in reality anywhere.[1] In this area, a few farmers were able to start as part-time farmers and work their way up to full-time farming in a lifetime; but most men who started at the bottom remained there, or progressed only a step or two upwards. A real move from the bottom to the top usually took two or more generations. And, parallel to this upward movement through the generations, was another movement from the top to the bottom. Some of the sons of full-time farmers have moved into dual-business or other-work farms and some of the grandsons have moved out of farming altogether.

This up and down movement can be illustrated from the experi-

[1] See Ashby and Davies, 'The agricultural ladder and the age of farmers', *Welsh Journ. of Agric.*, Vol. 6, 1930, pp. 5–19.

ences of the current farmers. If we consider only those farmers whose fathers had themselves farmed, it appears that the number and proportion of part-time farmers' sons who have moved up the 'farming ladder' into full-time farming is more or less balanced[1] by those sons of full-time farmers who have moved down into part-time farming. It might be thought that the latter are farmers' sons, who for various reasons have not followed their fathers, but are using part-time farming as a stepping stone back to full-time farming. This supposition does not apply to the eight who are dual-business farmers, who appear to have developed their non-farming occupation as a means whereby to increase the size of their businesses in relation to family needs, and to the availability of family labour and farming resources. For example, three of them have taken up agricultural contracting, a business arising out of their farming operations and utilizing farm equipment and family labour which was likely otherwise to be under-employed. Another three are dealing in cattle, a useful and profitable complementary business to their dairy farming, whilst one of the remaining two has a building business and the other a public house. None of these farmers appear likely to give up their profitable other business for the rather doubtful advantage of becoming a full-time farmer.

Only four of the thirteen other-work farmers who are sons of full-time farmers have obvious intentions of trying to achieve a full-time farm in the future, and even these have no certainty of achieving it. All are unlikely to succeed to their parents' farms, for other brothers are already there. Also, they or their wives own their present farms; in consequence, a move to another farm (with a chance of achieving the goal of full-time farming) depends on their being able to sell the one they are at present occupying. One of them has already experienced difficulty in this respect. He rented a farm large enough to provide a living for his family without work off, but had to relinquish the tenancy after a year, because he could not dispose of the small farm he owns.

Some of the others may at some stage have had ideas of becoming full-time farmers, but currently none of them appear likely to do so. Considering the circumstances of both their families of origin and families of procreation, it is doubtful, in any case, whether they would benefit financially by becoming full-time farmers. Some have married wives with urban backgrounds, others either come from large families, or have themselves large families, and the whole impression gained from their case histories is that they have accepted work off

[1] Relatively, and absolutely, rather more have moved up than down; but the difference is not statistically significant at the 5 per cent level.

the farm as an obvious way to make a living in their present circumstances. One of them, who has a family of ten and whose father went bankrupt, said: "They say up here that the first thing you have got to learn is how to live. . . . You cannot farm here in the way you can down-country: and there are plenty of farmers not earning a labourer's wage. . . . There is one thing that most people are interested in having nowadays, and you don't get far without it—money. . . . I couldn't have reared a large family without another job." This statement sums up the dilemma faced by many farmers in the area. Full-time farming confers high social prestige, but often those who strive to achieve, or to maintain, this status are financially worse off than their neighbours who go out to work. Furthermore, by placing a high evaluation on their full-time farming status and connections, they encourage their children to remain in full-time farming, despite its obvious financial disadvantages for all except the limited number of larger-business farmers. Those children who have been brought up to consider other-work as being on a par with farming, are quite likely to leave the industry, but, in socially ambitious families who have achieved the goal of full-time farming, sons, at least, identify themselves much more closely with farming than with other occupations.

The case history of one part-time farmer, whose farm has been in the family for three generations, illustrates the slowness of the progression from part-time to full-time farming status through the generations and also shows the complex nature of the forces which determine the occupational mobility of different members of a family.

The present farmer's grandfather was a mason with a small farm. He had four sons, and, when his family was young, moved to the holding on which his grandson was living at the time of the survey. This was a larger farm, but still not big enough to support a family without other work, and, until his death, the grandfather continued to farm and work off. His sons all worked off the farm, three at quarrying and one in farm service. The last married a 'small-business' farmer's daughter (also in farm service), rented a small holding, and went to work in the quarries. In the depression, he moved to a larger rented holding, but still cycled 10 miles a day to and from the quarries for £2 a week. He also sold eggs in the local market to buy the week's meat for his wife and six children. Soon after his elder children started to work, his father died, and he took over the tenancy of his father's farm. The acquisition of this additional land enabled him to become a full-time farmer, employing each of his children in turn before they married. Eventually, he bought both holdings together with part of another one.

Two of his three daughters married part-time farmers, and one married out of farming. Two sons married local girls and the youngest son remained at home working on the farm. One married son helped his father and occupied his grandfather's house. The other lived in a cottage and worked off the farm. After the accidental death of one married son, the father 'set up' the other on the grand-father's former holding. This son's wife had always done farm work at home, and she ran the holding while he went out to work.

It was likely that the youngest son would marry in his early thirties, after the death or retirement of his parents, and thus become a full-time farmer from the start of his married career, the culmina-tion of a process extending over three generations.

RECRUITMENT TO FARMING FROM OUTSIDE THE INDUSTRY

The bottom rung of the 'farming ladder' in this area is the part-time farm situated at a high altitude. Persons who wish to become farmers can most easily enter the industry at this level, for such farms can be obtained, and worked, with the minimum of capital. Accordingly, we find that of the 43 other-work farmers, almost half (18) are ex-ternal recruits. In contrast, only eight out of 113 full-time farmers are external recruits who actually started their farming careers as full-time farmers (although three others have managed to progress to full-time farming status from an original entry as part-time farmers). Two of the eight who started as full-time farmers have also progressed from small to larger farms. In other words, only a small proportion of external recruits to farming in this area had either the capital, the initiative, or the connections, to help them climb the 'farming ladder'. The importance to an external recruit of a wife who is experienced in the needs and duties of a farm is exemplified by the fact that, although only one of these recruits to full-time farming 'married into' a farm, five others have wives who are farmers' daughters.

Of the 18 recruits who came into part-time farming, only four intend to try and achieve full-time status. Even for this ambitious group, success is by no means certain, for two of them have already attempted to be full-time farmers but have been forced to abandon the attempt and go out to work in order to maintain a growing family. For most of the remaining 14, part-time farming is an end in itself, and is not considered as a first step on the road to full-time farming. Half these recruits to part-time farming married farmers' daughters, but proportionately more of them than the recruits to full-time farming 'married into' small part-time farms (5 out of 18).

The analysis indicates that there are three categories of recruits to part-time farming, viz., those who see part-time farming as the first rung of the 'farming ladder'; those who are content to remain as part-time farmers; and those who either have no alternatives, or who are using a farm as a temporary refuge.

A few of this last category are transients attracted by the cheap housing and the remoteness of some of the isolated farms situated at high altitudes. These transients tended to be men who were either 'between wives' or between jobs, and they frequently gave a 'bad name' to their area of residence which was out of all proportion to their numbers. In the sample there are only three such farmers,[1] yet their brushes with 'authority', and with their neighbours, have been such that they will be remembered long after they have returned to the towns. The notoriety of such transients has helped to perpetuate a myth amongst the more prosperous full-time farmers that part-time farmers on the highest altitude farms are feckless and morally irresponsible. Nevertheless, some members of these families have managed on occasions to settle into farming when a son has become interested in farm work, or a daughter has married a local farmer. But, in general, they were transients; as one old-established farmer put it: "A good gust of wind, or the first fall of snow, sends them back to where they came from." However, at any one time, there are always some of these people present in the area and often enough they follow each other on the same farms. Less often, they take over from a local who has died or moved away, obtaining the farm largely because it was offered at a price or rent considered exorbitant by the local people. The rapidity of the movements of transients into and out of farms, and the gossip their activities attract, tends to create the impression that they are more numerous than they actually are.

OCCUPATIONAL MOBILITY OF FARMERS BEFORE AND AFTER STARTING TO FARM

Many sons of farmers engage in farm work before they achieve independence from home by marriage or by starting to farm on their

---

[1] This suggests that there are probably half a dozen of them, or less than 2 per cent on farms in the whole area, the sample being a 50 per cent random sample of people living at farm addresses. There may be more living in remote cottages not scheduled as agricultural. Their numbers cannot be large, however, as there are few habitable properties outside the villages which are without land, and any with five acres or more would have been included in the population from which the sample was drawn.

own account. Some work at home, but only the largest farms can provide opportunities for two or more sons to work at home simultaneously. Consequently, some sons of full-time farmers will work on the farms of other farmers, preferably for relatives. Some sons of part-time farmers may work at home, but most of them either work on other farms or in other occupations.

The type of work engaged in prior to achieving independence from home has an effect on the subsequent career of farmers, irrespective of their family backgrounds. There is, of course, a strong connection between the family background of current farmers and their working history. For instance, a greater proportion of those whose fathers were full-time farmers had worked on the home farm than had those whose fathers were part-time farmers (Table 64). Nevertheless, despite this

Table 64: Occupation prior to marriage or starting to farm of farmers with farming fathers, and occupation of father

| Farmer's occupation prior to marriage or starting to farm | Father's farming occupation | | | Total |
	Full-time farming	Dual-business farming	Farming plus work off	
Farm work at home	70	5	8	83
Farm work for others	11	3	8	22
Other work	14	6	18	38
Total	95	14	34	143

association, there are exceptions. No less than a quarter of those whose fathers were full-time farmers had worked off their home farms (either at farming or other work) and, conversely, a quarter of those whose fathers were part-time farmers had worked full-time on their fathers' farms.[1]

For this sample of farmers the highest proportion who worked off their parents' farms prior to achieving independent status is found among the dual-business and other-work farmers and the lowest among the larger-business farmers; small-business or family-

[1] Information on the working histories of brothers of current farmers was not obtained in sufficient detail to enable a satisfactory analysis of their work histories to be made. Consequently, it is not known what proportion of *all* sons of the parental generation had worked at home, at farm work or at other work. This information was obtained, however, for all sons of current farmers and is presented in the next chapter.

earning farmers falling between these extremes (Table 65).[1] Hence, it appears that work histories had a greater effect on the mode of farming employment of current full-time farmers than had inheritance for a significantly higher proportion of the small-business and family-earning farmers inherited their farms from parents than did larger-business farmers.

Table 65: Type of farmer and previous occupation, for farmers with farming fathers

Farmer's occupation prior to marriage or starting to farm	Larger-business farmers	Small-business and family-earning farmers	Dual-business and other-work farmers	Total
Farm work at home	30	38	15	83
Other work off the home farm	9	25	26	60
Total	39	63	41	143

Unfortunately, it was impracticable to obtain on a systematic basis the size of parents' farms, but such evidence as is available, particularly from the occupations of current farmers' sons, indicates that sons from larger farms were those most likely to work at home. Some of the sons from these larger farms who did not inherit the family farm were 'set up' on farms of their own by their parents, who helped either to buy a farm outright or to stock a rented one. Whether or not this farm was of equivalent standing to that of their parents depended on a number of factors—for example, the availability of farms in the area at the time, and the amount of capital that parents could spare. The careers of brothers of current larger-business farmers suggest that those who did not work on the home farm, or in other farm work, tended to find employment further afield before they married, and that they also tended to settle at a distance from home. Certainly those sons from larger farms who were either unable to farm or else did not choose to do so, could find little alternative work locally which would have been acceptable socially to their parents, relatives or friends. As a result, a non-farming brother from such families was more likely to become an auctioneer or a retail trader in a nearby market town than a farm worker on the family doorstep.

[1] Farmers whose fathers were not farmers could not have worked on their fathers' farm, and therefore are excluded from this analysis.

The occupational adjustments farmers made during the course of their farming careers, to meet changes in family economic circumstances, appear to be related to what their own home and work environment had been before starting to farm. Thus, few of those who had worked at home prior to farming on their own account had changed their occupation since starting to farm compared with those who had worked away from home (Table 66). Although some of

Table 66: Previous occupation and occupation changes whilst farming

Farmer's occupation prior to marriage or starting to farm	Whether occupation changed since starting to farm		Total
	Yes	No	
Farm work at home	13	70	83
Other work (farming parents)	23	37	60
Other work (non-farming parents)	13	16	29
Total	49	123	172

those who had only worked at home had inherited or acquired farms of sufficient size to make it unnecessary for either themselves, or their children, to go out to work at any stage in their family developmental cycle, not all are in this fortunate position. There are 33 farmers, with a small-business per family member, who had only worked at home prior to starting to farm on their own account. Only half of these have the farmer, or some family member, working off the farm to supplement the family income. In comparison, there are 48 farmers with a small-business per family member who had worked off their fathers' farm before starting to farm. In 40 of these cases the farmer or some other family member works off the property. For such farmers, considerations of social prestige are not important in determining whether or not the farmer or other members of his family work off the farm. For the others with only farming backgrounds, however, their social standing and farming reputation in the community is tied up with the maintenance of a full-time farming status. To go out to work, keep two or three cows, and let your land revert to rough pasture, is one thing, if you live at an altitude of 1,500 feet surrounded by many neighbours who are doing the same. It is quite another thing to do so if you live at 900 feet, surrounded by full-time farming neighbours, and it is considered *déclassé* for even your daughters to go out to work, let alone you or your sons.

It is significant that, of the 13 farmers who had worked at home and then changed their occupation after they had started to farm on their own account, six had developed dual businesses. Five of these are all closely connected with the farmers' normal farming operations and the requirements of their neighbours, for instance, cattle dealing, corn selling and agricultural contracting; another is a building contracting business, again providing a service to neighbours. All the other seven farmers who went out to work after starting to farm are, or have been, farming at the higher altitudes. One of them had been faced with the dilemma of how to reconcile high family needs with a small farm in a full-time farming area where kin and neighbours did not go out to work. He had solved his problem by moving from a property in the area where he had been born and brought up to the area he is currently farming in. There his social antecedents were unknown, and farming and working off the farm was the accepted norm. He and his family have not, however, forgotten his origin, as is evident from the work histories and marriages of his children. All his daughters are married to farmers and his sons are either working at home, working on farms elsewhere, or farming on their own account.

SOCIAL AND OCCUPATIONAL MOBILITY OF FARMERS' WIVES

The occupational skills of farmers are associated with a particular locality and often with a specific farm. Their farming knowledge is limited, to a large extent, by the boundaries of their local area, and most of their contacts with other farmers occur within these boundaries. In addition, they are often dependent on patrimony for a farm, which may be directly inherited from parents or acquired for them by parents. Consequently, a farmer can most easily acquire high social prestige by obtaining a farm and developing his farming skills within the area of his upbringing and at the particular level of farming where his training was acquired and his farming contacts are most numerous. Farm women, on the other hand, are not as restricted as men in their choice of occupation prior to marriage, and the skills which they contribute to a family farm are more transportable, for the acquisition of such skills does not depend on an intimate knowledge of a particular farm or locality. Furthermore, farming areas usually have a net shortage of young women, because more women migrate to urban areas than men. Hence the women who remain in farming have a wider choice of marriage partners than have men; and thus women have greater opportunities for upward social mobility.

Half the farmers in this area married 'within their class'; but, of those who married across class or status lines, 62 per cent of the wives married 'up' compared with 38 per cent of the husbands.[1] There are equal proportions of farmers in all the current socio-economic groupings who married 'within their class' but different proportions of them have been socially mobile 'up' or 'down'. Amongst the larger-business, dual-business and other-work farmers, approximately the same numbers have been mobile upwards as downwards, but amongst small-business and family-earning farmers most of those who have been socially mobile married down (Table 67).

Table 67: Type of farmer and social mobility at marriage

Social mobility	Small-business and family-earning farmers	Larger-business, dual-business and other-work farmers	Total
Upward	4	23	27
Downward	21	24	45
Total	25	47	72

This is not to say that those who 'married down' are necessarily worse off economically than their peers who married within their class or upwards. In many instances, a son who 'married down' married a woman who had work experience outside farming. Such a woman may have worked at domestic service in a nearby town, or in the house of a well-to-do country resident, or she may have lived at home but travelled each day to work in shop, office or factory in the town. The experience she gained is likely to affect her family's future, for such a wife has a wider view of occupational opportunity than a wife whose whole previous work experience has been confined to the boundaries of her parents' farm. Hence, the wife's non-farm experience often appears to have been the deciding factor in determining the occupational choice of the children. That is to say, in such families the parents encourage the children to go out to work, rather than to stay at home and continue to farm and live at the low standard typical of families on those small farms where neither parent has any work experience apart from that on their parents' farms.

Certainly there are a few examples where the evidence indicates that a cross-class marriage adversely affected a farmer's prospects.

---

[1] This measure was a comparison between the social position of parents at the time of marriage of the farmer and his wife—see Ch. V, page 94.

K

For example, one farmer's son lost his father's farm through 'marrying down' against the wishes of his parents, and another who 'married up' had not thereby obtained his wife's parents' farm.

Some people were at a disadvantage in the 'marriage market' compared with their peers, owing either to the general social and economic circumstances of their families, or to the effects of birth order, age of parents, or other demographic factors. Where those people came from the socially superior categories, 'marrying down' could be the only alternative to remaining single. For instance, three brothers and a sister, all over the age of 30, between them ran a large farm for their aged father. One of the brothers married a servant girl from a neighbouring farm and thereby incurred the strong disapproval of his father and his siblings. The couple left the district to take up farm work 'down country'. Ten years later they returned in a position to buy a farm of their own. They had children to succeed them and had an independent farming status. But the three remaining siblings still lived on the family farm, were still unmarried, and continued to squabble over the inheritance.

A comparison of the farmers on the basis of the occupation of

Table 68: Type of farmer and occupation of fathers of
farmer and wife

Occupations of fathers of farmer and wife	Larger-business farmers	Small-business and family-earning farmers	Dual-business and other-work farmers	Total
		A		
Both farming full-time	22	12	9	43
Both farming part-time	4	7	3	14
Both not farming	4	2	8	14
Other combinations of occupations	12	28	33	73
Total	42	49	53	144
		B		
Both farming full-time	22	12	9	43
Both farming, but one or both part-time	8	23	15	46
One or both not farming	12	14	29	55
Total	42	49	53	144

their parents and their wives' parents indicated that assortative mating[1] occurred in about a half of all the marriages (Table 68A). This is in agreement with the figure quoted earlier for social mobility at marriage. Such an agreement is not surprising, in view of the close relationship between occupation and social prestige in this particular society. The current larger-business farmers show the highest degree of assortative mating (71 per cent), and the current dual-business and other-work farmers the lowest (38 per cent). This difference is largely due to the high proportion of the larger-business farming couples who followed their parents' occupation compared with the part-time farmers (52 per cent compared with 6 per cent).

Movement up the 'farming ladder' between generations is clearly indicated. Dual-business and other work farmers had the highest proportion of non-farming parents (whether their own or their wives') while small-business and family-earning farmers had the highest proportion of part-time farming parents of one spouse or the other (Table 68B). A downward movement is indicated by the greater number of parents on both sides farming full-time than farming part-time, amongst the dual-business and other-work farming couples (Table 68A).

Although fewer wives than husbands had fathers who were farming full-time, approximately the same number of farmers and wives had fathers with dual-businesses, or who worked off their farms. The greater number of wives with non-farming parents, however, had married in at all levels. The same proportion of them had married full-time farmers' sons as had married part-time farmers' sons, a result of the upward and downward mobility occurring amongst the full and part-time farmers' sons and daughters (see Table 69, 'All farmers').

As was to be expected, in view of the greater number of wives with parents who were not farmers, fewer wives than their husbands had been engaged in farm work before marriage, whether at home or for other people. The only farmers with a significantly lower proportion of wives who had not engaged in farm work are the larger-business and dual-business farmers. As far as the married farmers themselves are concerned, a lower proportion of those who farm full-time (of whatever socio-economic category), than those who farm part-time, have had other work experience before marriage. Considering separately those wives with farming parents, the proportion who had

---

[1] Assortative mating is the marriage of people with similar social origins and upbringing. For the purpose of this analysis, I have assumed that assortative mating occurred if the farmer and his wife had fathers who were both full-time farmers, both part-time farmers, or both non-farmers.

Table 69: Type of farmer and occupation of fathers of
farmer and wife

Type of farmer and father's occupation	*Occupation of wife's father*			
	Full-time farming	*Dual-business or farming plus working off*	*Not farming*	*Total*
Small-business and family-earning farmers Father:				
Full-time farming	12	11	9	32
Dual-business or farming plus working off	5	7	2	14
Not farming	0	1	2	3
Total	17	19	13	49
Larger-business farmers Father:				
Full-time farming	22	2	3	27
Dual-business or farming plus working off	2	4	2	8
Not farming	3	0	4	7
Total	27	6	9	42
Dual-business and other-work farmers Father:				
Full-time farming	9	5	7	21
Dual-business or farming plus working off	7	3	5	15
Not farming	2	7	8	17
Total	18	15	20	53
All farmers Father:				
Full-time farming	43	18	19	80
Dual-business or farming plus working off	14	14	9	37
Not farming	5	8	14	27
Total	62	40	42	144

farm work experience is highest for those married to larger-business and dual-business farmers, and lowest for those married to small-business and family-earning farmers. A relatively high proportion also of such wives of other-work farmers have worked on farms in the past.

Most of the wives on the larger farms had parents who were themselves full-time farmers. It is scarcely surprising, therefore, that a high proportion of these wives had worked on farms before marriage, for such women were the ones most likely to be married by farmers' sons from reasonably sized farms, in that they were experienced in farm work and lived in proximity. In the same way, it is understandable that many dual-business and other-work farmers sought wives with farming experience. Some of these men, with experience of other work, married into a small part-time farm where the daughter was accustomed to farm work. Others married daughters from small farms who had experience of farm work, and then set up as part-time farmers. These arrangements were useful to both parties. The wife could maintain her interest in farming and her connections with her kinsfolk in the area, while the husband could work full-time off the farm. By such a division of labour between farm and other work, the couple were usually able to earn a better living than by the only alternatives open to them. These were either to work a small farm full-time, or to give up farming altogether and seek employment outside the industry. The first alternative condemned them to a low income; the second usually meant leaving the area, for there were few houses available locally and job opportunities were scarce for people who could not bring specialized skills to the labour market. With such economic considerations acting as a spur to marriage, farmers' daughters from small farms had no greater difficulty in finding husbands than had daughters from the larger farms. In other words, farmers' daughters (from whatever size of farm) were at a premium in the local 'marriage market'. Farmers' sons from small farms, however, had the opposite experience for, without a suitable farm, or alternatively, an acquired skill whereby to earn money outside farming, they were not in an advantageous position to offer marriage and set up a home and family.

The evidence presented in this section suggests that there are two opposing forces acting upon farmers and their wives. Through assortative mating there is a tendency to perpetuate the existing social and economic strata in the farming community. But occupational mobility works against this stabilizing influence. Some farmers and wives move up and down the 'farming ladder' in relation to the farming status of their parents; work experiences other than farming modify their attitudes to farming and to other industrial opportunities and affect both the advice they give to their children and the home environment which the children experience. Interchange at marriage of work experience and different family backgrounds is not evenly distributed throughout all strata of the farming society, however, but tends to be concentrated more amongst part-time than full-time farmers. Thus, migration of farmers' children to other occupations is more likely to occur from that sector of the industry which contains the newest entrants than it is from the old-established farming families.

CHAPTER VIII

MOBILITY OF FARMERS' CHILDREN

IN the previous chapter, the emphasis was placed on the working history of present farmers and their wives, and on the occupations of their parents. In other words, the present situation of farmers was related to their family and work environment in the past. Sufficient systematic data are not available to extend the analysis so that the working histories and farming status achieved by current farmers can be related to the precise farming status of their parents. Such an analysis can be made, however, for the future generation of farmers, namely, the children of current farmers. This is the object of this chapter, in which the figures in the tables refer to the number of sons and daughters and not to the number of farmers.[1]

The children of the survey farmers are of all ages. They range from those who have only recently been born to those who are married and have a home and family of their own. Very few in the last group, however, have passed out of the phase of expansion in their family developmental cycle. Consequently, the population of farmers' children available for this analysis has by no means completed its spatial, occupational and social mobility. Therefore we do not know what will be its ultimate mobility pattern. Inevitably, we cannot make the same types of comparison as were made between the current farmers and their parents; but we are able to make comparisons between the *precise* farming status of parents, and the working history and mobility—to date—of *all* their children who are at work. This avoids two of the weaknesses in the comparisons made between present farmers and their parents, viz., that the precise farming status of parents was not known, and the analysis related only to a selected sample of their children (namely the ones who happened to be farming in this particular area at the time of the survey).

For comparative purposes, the farmers' children of working age

---

[1] Because of the relatively small number of married sons and single daughters further classification by the farming employment of parents resulted in rather small numbers in some sub-groupings. Consequently, although trends were sometimes detected which were supported by case history information (or by supplementary information obtained about conditions in the area generally), these could not always be substantiated by a statistical test at the 5 per cent level of significance. Where the supporting evidence was strong, a 10 per cent level of significance was accepted as evidence of a trend and in some instances case material only was used to suggest a possible trend.

can be grouped according to sex, marital status and present occupation. In addition, for those who are married, details are available of their working histories prior to marriage. From the available data we can look at the relationships between the present farming status of farmers and *a.* the occupations before marriage of all their children of working age; and *b.* the present occupations of their married children. We can also look at *c.* the 'farming ladder' and mobility of children, and *d.* the replacement of the parental generation of farmers by the filial generation.

OCCUPATIONS OF CHILDREN PRIOR TO MARRIAGE

The farmers in this area are dependent almost entirely on their own families for labour to operate their farms. Only full-time farms require extra labour over and above that of the farmer and his wife, and sons are more often employed on farm work at home than are daughters. In addition, sons on full-time farms are likely to stay and work at home, in the hope that this will further their chances of inheriting the farm from their parents, or of being set up on independent farms of their own. Such sons are more limited in the occupational and spatial range within which they seek a wife than are sons from part-time farms, or daughters from most farms. Consequently, we would expect to find a lower proportion of married sons than married daughters from full-time farms, and a higher proportion of married sons amongst the sons of other-work farmers than amongst those from farms where the business size is such that it requires additional labour to that provided by the farmer and his wife.

Of the 21 single[1] sons of the other-work farmers, only three work on their parents' farm. The father of one of these also works full-time on the farm, but the mother works off. The other two, both about 30, have one or other parent with a farming tradition extending back for a number of generations. By contrast, 35 out of 49 single sons of larger-business and dual-business farmers work at home, and even on the smaller full-time farms, 12 out of 27 single sons are working at home.

There are 38 full-time and dual-business farmers with medium to large farms, who have sons and daughters of working age,[2] married

---

[1] The term 'single' (as used throughout this chapter) means 'unmarried'. When referring to a son from a family in which there are daughters but only one son, the term 'only son' is used, and similarly for daughters. When referring to a son or daughter who is the only child in the family, the term 'only child' is used.

[2] There are 121 of these children; but at the time of the survey three of them were unfit for work.

and single. The majority of these farmers (30) have one or more children working at home on the farm. Six of the eight exceptions[1] illustrate the circumstances under which children do not stay and work at home, even when their parents are operating farms of a size capable of employing more than one person. One of the six farmers was over 30 when he married a girl of 18; they have a large family. The other five all married young; one owns only a part-share in his farm, two were relatively young when their sons were ready to marry, and two have daughters but no sons.

The farmer with a large family has 10 children. His farm is of medium size, but not adequate to provide for a household of 12. Consequently, as each child has reached working age, he or she has left home—the boys to work and 'live in' on farms at lower altitudes, and the girls to work in the town. The children of school age have helped their parents to run the farm. By these means, the farmer has avoided the payment of Unemployment and National Insurance on family workers, and the burden of a large family has been reduced slightly each time a child of working age has left home.

The farmer with only a part-share in his farm is in partnership with his wife's brother, who is single and works full-time on the farm. His mother-in-law also lives in the household. The farmer and his wife have only one child (a son), who worked at home for a number of years after leaving school. This son left home in his early twenties, preferring a career in the armed services to farming, in which "he could see no future for himself".

The two farmers who were relatively young when their sons were to marry are both 'self-made men'.[2] Their sons worked at home but, like their fathers before them, left at an early age to marry and start a farming career independently of home.

Another self-made man, whose children are all daughters, is not a native of the district. He moved to his present isolated farm after selling a small farm situated in a much better farming area. His daughters were courting at the time of the move and did not stay long helping on the new farm, but proceeded to marry sons of farmers from their area of origin.

The other farmer with a family of daughters is tenant of quite a

[1] One of the remaining two exceptions is a farmer with a daughter working off, and a son not yet of working age. The other has none of his own children of working age, but has two stepsons at work. Neither of these sons lives or works at home.

[2] 'Self-made men' are those farmers who started out in a very small way and, by their own efforts, progressed from smaller to larger farms, supplementing their income, where necessary, by going out to work, but finishing up as full-time farmers when their children had reached working age.

large holding, but his three daughters have all married and left home. In the past, there would have been an inducement for one daughter to remain working at home on such a farm, for, by doing this, she would have been likely to attract a husband willing to work for her father until such time as he could take over the tenancy. This was likely because, until recently, the main concern of landlords in the area was to acquire a tenant who would pay his rent regularly, who would not poach game and who would be content with the minimum of repairs and maintenance to houses and buildings. The son of a satisfactory tenant, or the son-in-law where there was no son, could often obtain the tenancy, if he were careful to impress upon the agent that he had the same deference towards the landlord's policy as had his father or father-in-law. But, in recent years, rent restrictions have been relaxed and the principal landlord is no longer resident in the district. Under these changed circumstances, the dominant characteristic looked for in a tenant now is a willingness to pay a much higher rent, plus interest on any capital spent on improvements. Such tenants are more likely to be found if the field of selection is widened, rather than if it is restricted to the sons and sons-in-law of conservative existing tenants, who have been accustomed to paying low rents. Consequently, sons have no certainty of obtaining their fathers' farms and daughters have little inducement to stay at home in the hope of attracting a husband.

Single daughters are less firmly held to farms by occupational ties than single sons. Even on the larger farms, fewer of them work at home compared with sons.[1] Except for one daughter who is an only child, no other single daughter works at home on such farms, without a brother also doing so. This suggests that, for daughters, status considerations are also important in determining whether or not they stay at home. This is supported by the fact that most of the married daughters who worked at home prior to marriage, and all the 12 single daughters currently working at home, have fathers who are farming full-time (on farms of all sizes) or are 'dual-business' farmers. The daughters of this class of farmer who go out to work show a greater tendency to take up high prestige jobs in offices or in professions, than do the daughters of other farmers. It is noteworthy that the daughters of full-time and 'dual-business' farmers who take

[1] The comparison was made between all sons and daughters on these farms, based on their occupation at the time of the survey (for those who were single) and prior to marriage (for those who were married). Comparisons between single sons and single daughters, or married sons and married daughters, are difficult to interpret, because of the differences in numbers of sons and daughters in the various age groups.

up domestic work or factory work come from the smallest farms, or
have fathers who are self-made men. Those from the smallest farms
have to take whatever work is available, and the self-made men have
not been averse themselves to doing any sort of work on their way
up (Table 70).

Table 70: Occupation of married daughters prior to
marriage and father's type of farm

Occupation of married daughters prior to marriage	Small-business, larger-business and dual-business farmers	Family-earning farmers	Other-work farmers	Total
Working at home	23	1	1	25
Professional	2	2	0	4
Office	6	1	2	9
Shop or service industries	0	4	0	4
Farm service	1	1	2	4
Domestic service	2	10	5	17
Factory work	5	7	5	17
Total	39	26	15	80

Only one of the married daughters of 'family-earning' farmers had
worked at home prior to marriage, and only one single daughter of
these farmers works at home (and she merely part-time). Almost half
the single sons of these farmers work at home, however, despite the
general tendency for the farm resources per family member to be
low. That working at home on small farms may be an impediment
to marriage for the sons who do so is suggested by the fact that none
of the married sons of these farmers had worked at home prior to
marriage.

If we consider all small full-time farms, we find that the proportions of married sons who had engaged in non-agricultural work
before marriage is higher than the proportion of single sons currently
employed on non-agricultural work. This suggests that those sons who
are engaged in farm work find it rather harder to marry than do those
sons employed in occupations not connected with farming. A farmer's
son whose work experiences are confined to farming is not able to
marry and to start farming on his own account whenever he wishes.

He is dependent either on the retirement of his father, or on the retirement of his prospective wife's father; or he has to try and find a suitable non-family farm within his means. All these alternatives involve an element of uncertainty, which may mean that he has to wait some time until the appropriate opportunity occurs. These considerations do not apply to the same extent when a son with another trade at his fingers wishes to marry. Wherever he lives in the rural area, it is likely that he will have to travel some distance to work. Some parishes will be more convenient for work than others, but his choice of where to live should not be as limited as the choice of a son who has to find both a place to live and a place to farm. Moreover, his 'marriage isolate'[1] will tend to be wider in geographical area, in terms of occupation, and in range of favourable demographic circumstances, than that of a farm-based son wishing to marry and find a suitable farm at the same time. The chances are, therefore, that a farmer's son employed in non-agricultural work will marry sooner than a son wishing to farm who is either employed at home or engaged in farm work elsewhere.

The lowest proportion of single sons engaged in farm work, either at home or elsewhere, is found amongst the sons of other-work farmers; the highest proportion is amongst sons of dual-business farmers and full-time farmers on the larger-business farms.[2] Sons of full-time farmers on small-business farms[3] fall between these two extremes. That these employment patterns have an effect on marriage opportunities is suggested by the rather smaller proportion of married sons of dual-business farmers and full-time farmers on larger-business farms, compared with the proportion of married sons of other-work farmers.[4] By contrast, no difference is apparent in the proportions of married daughters to single daughters according to the farming employment of their parents.

OCCUPATIONS OF MARRIED CHILDREN

The types of farm employment of married sons and sons-in-law follow the same patterns as for single sons—except that 'farming on their own account' takes the place of 'working at home'. Thus, the highest

---

[1] A 'marriage isolate' is a defined range of contact within which people meet and marry. It can be expressed in terms of time, space, occupation, social distance, or any other plane upon which social contacts occur between people.

[2] These include the larger-business farmers and those family-earning farmers who have a size of farm business of over 15 cow-equivalents.

[3] These include the small-business farmers and those family-earning farmers who have a size of farm business of under 15 cow-equivalents.

Thirteen out of 62, compared with nine out of 30.

proportion of married children who are farming are children of dual-business, larger-business and small-business farmers, and the lowest are children of other-work and family-earning farmers (Tables 71 and 72).[1] Furthermore, a higher proportion of married children

Table 71: Occupation of married sons and father's type of farm

Occupation of married sons	Small-business, larger-business and dual-business farmers	Family-earning farmers	Other-work farmers	Total
Farming on own account or on father's farm	12	0	3	15
Other work	5	9	6	20
Total	17	9	9	35

Table 72: Occupation of husbands of married daughters and father-in-law's type of farm

Occupation of husbands of married daughters	Small-business, larger-business and dual-business farmers	Family earning farmers	Other-work farmers	Total
Farming on own account or on father's farm	23	7	2	32
Other work	16	13	9	38
Total	39	20	11	70*

* See footnote [1] on this page.

with parents on the larger farms are farming than those with parents on the smaller farms (Tables 73 and 74). This is to be expected, for the parents of the children from the larger farms (or the parents of their spouses) would be in a better financial position to set them up on a farm.

[1] These figures for married daughters exclude five daughters of one part-time farmer, all of whom married farmers (this was the farmer, cited in Ch. VII, who had moved to the area from a full-time farming district) and six of one widow on a medium-sized farm, all of whom went out to work, and none of whom married farmers.

Opportunities to marry and to farm are about equal for sons and daughters from the larger farms; but, on family-earning farms, daughters have been more successful in obtaining a farmer for a husband than have sons in achieving independent farming status and marriage at the same time. A third of the daughters have husbands who are farming (or likely to take over their parents' farm), but none of the married sons are either farming on their own account or

Table 73: Occupation of married sons and size of parents' farm

Occupation of married sons	Size of farm occupied or retired from by parents		Total
	15 C.E. and over	Under 15 C.E.	
Farming on own account or on father's farm	10	5	15
Other work	4	16	20
Total	14	21	35

Table 74: Occupation of husbands of married daughters and size of farm of parents-in-law

Occupation of husbands of married daughters	Size of farm occupied or retired from by parents		Total
	15 C.E. and over	Under 15 C.E.	
Farming on own account or on father's farm	24	8	32
Other work	14	24	38
Total	38	32	70*

* See footnote [1] on page 141.

working on their parents' farm (compare Tables 71 and 72). Some of these daughters have probably been socially mobile upwards, like their mothers before them (Table 67, Chapter VII), but the sons probably had to choose between marriage and remaining in agriculture. Few of these daughters from family-earning farms had worked at home before marriage, and their experiences reflect the general tendency—namely, that proportionately more daughters than sons who 'worked off' before marriage are farming on their own account (even though in total, for both sons and daughters, a higher proportion of those who had worked at home achieved independent farming status—Tables 75 and 76). It was shown in Chapter IV that

Table 75: Occupation of married sons before and after marriage

| Occupation of married sons | Occupation before marriage | | Total |
	Farm work at home	Other work	
Farming on own account or on father's farm	13	2	15
Other work	1	19	20
Total	14	21	35

Table 76: Occupation of married daughters before marriage and their husbands' current occupation

| Husbands of married daughters | Occupation of married daughters before marriage | | Total |
	Farm work at home	Other work	
Farming on own account or on father's farm	20	17	37
Other work	4	39	43
Total	24	56	80*

* One married daughter was an invalid prior to marriage.

very few farmers born and brought up in the country had sought a wife in the towns, since few of them had wives who were born or brought up in towns or who had gone to live in the towns from the country. Similarly, for the married sons of the farmers, most of those who intended to farm were likely to have chosen a wife from amongst the ranks of women brought up on farms. But (as will be shown later), there were fewer farmers' daughters than farmers' sons who had only worked at home. Consequently, some sons would marry farmers' daughters who lived at home but worked away from it.

MOBILITY OF CHILDREN AND THE 'FARMING LADDER'

The differential movement into and out of farming by children of the various types of farmer is relevant to the 'farming ladder' discussed in Chapter VII. It indicates two main trends. First, that those families which have entered farming most recently, generationally speaking,[1] are the ones from which the 'wastage' of children out of farming is the highest. Second, that those farming families whose family size and family resources are not well equated are losing children from farming at a greater rate than those which have a better balance between their farm resources and their family size. This second loss should help to increase the efficiency of farming and improve living conditions for future generations of farmers. By pressure of circumstances, single children are working off those farms where limitations of capital, shortage of land or lack of ability keep farming productivity low. The effect of working off is to increase greatly the chances that such children will not farm when they marry. Although the demand by children for available farms is relieved in this way, there is still a big problem created by those children, predominantly male, who remain working at home on farms where resources are low. These are likely to become problem farmers of the following generation.

The majority of the present unmarried farmers have followed their parents' occupation of farming and are operating small farms with limited capital resources, as are the couples who married late in life and whose sons are thus likely to become the unmarried farmers of the next generation. Twenty of the present unmarried farmers followed their parents on the same farm; of these, 13 took over small farms, six took over medium-sized farms, and one took over a large farm. A prediction was made of the possible number of unmarried farmers likely to arise from the families included in this sample of farmers. This prediction indicates that there may also be 20 unmarried farmers who succeed current farmers. Of these, 14 are likely to follow their parents on small-business farms and six on farms of medium size.[2]

[1] That is, the other-work farming families.

[2] A prediction of this nature, involving families at all stages of life, is a hazardous one; but I consider it worthwhile in view of the strong economic and demographic relationships in the past histories of current farmers. The prediction was made on the basis of an overall assessment of the circumstances of each family at the time of the survey, but could not take account of future non-predictable occurrences, such as the early death of one parent. Any statements as to future movements were taken into account, however. For example, in one case, from the age difference between parents and the age of the son, it appeared that the son would be left unmarried on the farm. The parents stated, however, that the son did not want to farm and that they were going to retire to a cottage, in order to give him a chance of obtaining another job without having the farm to worry about. There seemed a reasonable chance that they would be in a position to do this, and consequently the case was not counted as likely to lead to an unmarried farmer.

Because of the conservative nature of the estimates, the position can be regarded as the minimum one.

The family-earning farmers have the highest average number of children per completed family (Table 77). Consequently, although proportionately more children are leaving farming from this group than from other full-time farms, the group is producing relatively

Table 77: Type of farmer and size of family
(for complete families)

	Number of children	Number of families	Average family size
Small-business, larger-business and dual-business farmers	113	43	2·63
Family-earning farmers	80	21	3·81
Other-work farmers	57	18	3·17
Total	250	82	3·05

more children and thus maintaining a residue of sons working at home.

Superficially, the relatively greater loss to farming of children from amongst the newest entrants might be considered unfortunate, on the theory that it is a loss of 'new blood' to the industry. This view does not stand up to detailed examination. The influence of the family and work environment on children's attitude to farming is more likely to be of importance than is any addition of new genetic material or any dilution of 'rural values' with 'urban ideas' brought in by newcomers to the area.

The marriage mobility of farm people indicated in Chapter IV does not suggest close inbreeding. Except for a few families with a morbid recessive,[1] no other recessives were encountered which were apparently genetically linked. And the 'urban values' are there already, as is inevitable in a society exposed to radio, T.V., the cinema, and so on, and which has many members with work experiences not confined to farming. The closed rural society may exist somewhere, but certainly not in the area studied here.[2]

The importance of the new blood from outside the industry is that

[1] Muscular dystrophy occurred in some families when two particular family lines intermarried.

[2] A statement made by one farmer illustrates the degree to which people in this rural area are exposed to so-called 'urban influences'. He said that one particular parish was a very good place to farm in because: ". . . there are four first division football clubs within a 30-mile radius, and you are half-way between Scarborough and Blackpool."

L

those incomers who have survived a lifetime in farming have progressed through hard work and frugal living to the status of a full-time farmer[1] or are in a position to give one or more of their children a chance to start up as one. Such children are only one generation removed from a reference group which is likely to be geographically and occupationally wider than that of the old-fashioned farming families. But they have been brought up on a farm in the area and consequently are likely both to be aware of the difficulties of farming there, and to have the local contacts and acceptance as a local so necessary in a farming community where physical and economic conditions are relatively unfavourable.

It is fair to say that the high wastage of new entrants to farming at the lowest level—part-time farming—has resulted in a survival of the fittest. Fittest, because they have learnt the difficulties of the area from personal experience on their parents' farm, and probably on other farms too, for these are the people who at some stage in their parents' family developmental cycle would go out for a time to work on other farms. Fittest, too, because the habits of hard work, frugal living and saving, which their parents practised (virtually the only way of amassing capital from small beginnings in this area), would have been instilled in them from an early age.

Of course there is a high wastage, because many are unwilling to accept the hardships involved in making a success of farming from small beginnings. For every self-made man there will be more than one who finds it easier, and more profitable, to go out to work and farm part-time, or who gives up the attempt and returns to town. Also, not all the children of self-made men are themselves willing to make the sacrifices, or put up with the drudgery they have witnessed, and no doubt shared, at home.

It is a reflection on the different impact farming under difficulties has on men and women, that 17 out of 22 of the sons of the self-made men in the sample are farming or likely to farm, compared with only 9 out of 19 of the daughters. One daughter has parents who have not experienced as difficult a time as have some of the other 'progressives', and whose current farming and living conditions are very good. She summed up the views of those daughters who quit farming in the words: "Me farm! No fear! I've seen my father work—work with nothing for it: no holidays, no rest, no nothing; and my mother slaving away. You'll not get *me* doing that."

It was shown in Chapters IV and VII, that many of the married

---

[1] Obviously, any children of these would come under the group 'full-time farmer' for analysis purposes, since this group contains the self-made men who have successfully climbed the farming ladder in their own lifetime.

farming couples have either origins, or work experiences, on the part of one or other of the spouses, which are different from the types of farming employment currently practised by the farmers. The occupational and marriage mobility of children of farmers provides a possible explanation of this.

It was shown in Table 75 that a close relationship exists between the possibility of married sons farming and their working at home before marriage. There are 64 sons who have worked at home but only 37 daughters have done so. If we consider this sample of farmers' children as a 'marriage isolate', and assume that, ideally, those sons who are going to farm would, for social and farming reasons, prefer a wife who had also worked at home, under the current demographic conditions there are insufficient potential wives of this nature. Obviously, therefore, even if some of the potential farmers remain single, a proportion of others will have to marry wives who have not worked at home.

If we assume that the discrepancy in the numbers of male and female children of working age is a temporary phenomenon,[1] and consider the situation on a proportionate basis, we find that 48 per cent of the sons have worked at home compared with 32 per cent of the daughters. Consequently, even if the total numbers of sons and daughters had been the same, some sons would still have to marry daughters who had not worked at home.[2]

In reality, the situation is even more complicated because the 'marriage isolate' of the daughters is geographically wider, judging by where married daughters are currently living compared with married sons, and where single daughters are living and working compared with single sons.[3] This further reduces the available females of the desired background, for the wider work dispersion of single and married daughters occurs irrespective of the farming employment of their fathers. For example, married daughters of larger-business farmers have (proportionately) fewer local spouses than have married sons; and more of them worked in urban areas prior to marriage (Tables 78 and 79).

Although a greater *number* of daughters left the area at marriage,

[1] It was indicated in Ch. III and App. 4 that the discrepancy is probably related, either to a chance sampling fluctuation, or to the incompleted nature of some of the families in which there are children above and below working age. That this phenomenon is probably only a temporary one is suggested by the numbers of boys and girls under 15 years of age, 77 and 75 respectively.

[2] Assuming that the greater resultant number of daughters would have been employed at home in the same proportions as the actual number of daughters have been employed.

[3] See Ch. IV, Table 40.

and married non-local spouses,[1] the sons who married had not ranged further afield in search of wives, either geographically or occupationally. This suggests that, at some stage, all the available

Table 78: Location of work before marriage of sons and daughters of full-time farmers on larger farms (15 C.E. and over)

	Sons	Daughters	Total
Country area	8	17	25
Urban area	1	21	22

Table 79: Origin of spouse of sons and daughters of full-time farmers on larger farms (15 C.E. and over)

	Sons' wives	Daughters' husbands	Total
Local	8	19	27
Non-local	1	19	20

daughters for any particular age cohort of sons will be married, some locally and some out of the area, before all the sons are married, thus creating conditions whereby some of the sons will remain single.

REPLACEMENT OF THE PARENTAL GENERATION OF FARMERS BY THE FILIAL GENERATION

Some measure of the degree of internal replacement can be obtained from a comparison of the number of children of working age likely to go farming with the type and number of farmers likely to die, retire or otherwise vacate farms. There are 66 farmers with children all of working age.[2] Of these, 50 have some children still living at home, 35 of them have one child or more working at home and 15 have children living at home but not working there. The remaining 16 farmers of the 66 have no children working or living at home. There are seven childless couples with the wife past the age of child-bearing (over 45),[3] and 16 unmarried farmers over the age of 45 and there-

[1] Due to the much greater number of married daughters than married sons.

[2] This category was taken in order to consider only the farmers at roughly the same 'replacement stage' in their family developmental cycle, and also because the numbers of male and female children in it are approximately equal.

[3] These seven childless couples, together with the 16 farmers with no children remaining at home, constitute those 23 farmers who were classified in Ch. III as being in the late stage of their family developmental cycle.

fore unlikely to marry and have children. In all, 89 farmers over the age of 45 can be considered.

The 66 farmers with all children of working age have 100 sons and 103 daughters. Of these, 49 sons and 53 daughters are not likely to farm, compared with 51 sons and 50 daughters who are already farming or likely to farm.[1] Nine of the married sons who are farming do not farm with their parents, and (because they have another brother working at home) a further nine of the single and married sons will probably be compelled to farm elsewhere, a total of 18 farmers' sons likely to farm away from home. Seven of the daughters living at home are likely to take over from their parents. In all then, for the 89 farms considered, 40 (45 per cent)[2] are likely to be taken over by sons or daughters living at home,[3] compared with 43 (48 per cent) of the current farmers who took over from parents or relatives of the husband or wife. Of the seven farmers' daughters who are likely to take over from parents, two may marry farmers' sons who have worked at home,[4] but who will probably farm away from home. There are 18 of these non-inheriting farmers' sons, and of them, another four are likely to farm away from the area.[5] This leaves 12

[1] These estimates were made on the assumption that sons and daughters who are single are likely to go farming in the same proportions as those who are married have gone farming relative to their occupations prior to marriage. Thus there are 15 married sons farming and 20 not farming; 36 single sons work at home and 29 do not. Thirteen out of 14 of all married sons who worked at home prior to marriage, and two out of 21 of those who did not, have gone farming. Applying these proportions to the single sons in these categories for the group considered here, 35 out of the 36 who are working at home are predicted as likely to farm, and three out of the 29 who are not working at home, making 36 predicted as likely to farm. Together with the 15 married sons, this gives 51 sons likely to farm. Similarly, for daughters, $\frac{20}{24}$ of the single daughters working at home and $\frac{17}{56}$ of those not working at home gives 15 singles likely to farm, and 11 likely not to farm. Added to the married daughters, this gives 50 daughters likely to farm and 53 likely not to do so.

[2] Thirty-three by sons and seven by daughters.

[3] There is no way of estimating how many sons and daughters not currently living on parents' farms will eventually return and farm there. We know, however, that, for all the farmers, the numbers who started to farm on their parents' farm are approximately the same as the numbers currently occupying a parents' farm, those moving away from such farms being approximately balanced by those moving to them (see Ch. IV).

[4] Of the 31 current farmers who took over farms from their wives' parents or relatives, nine had worked on their own parents' farm before marriage. Applying this proportion ($\frac{9}{31}$) to the seven daughters likely to inherit farms from parents gives approximately two who may marry farmers' sons currently working at home.

[5] Of the 13 married sons who worked at home before starting to farm on their own account, one farms outside the area. Applying this proportion to the 33 single sons working off their fathers' farms gives three, (to the nearest whole

sons[1] available for 49 farms, a discrepancy of 37 (or 42 per cent of the 89 farms). This is a measure of the farms likely to be available for those farmers' sons in the area who start their married life in an occupation other than farming, but who may wish to farm on their own account at a later date; for incomers from outside, with or without farming background; or for amalgamation by existing farmers in the area who wish to expand their size of business. Most of the farms available for these people will be those currently occupied by single farmers, barren and deserted couples, and farmers whose children, although still at home, do not intend to follow their parents. As shown in earlier chapters, these farms are mainly the smaller poorer ones, where it is difficult for a family to make a living by farming full-time.

Despite the reduction in family size which has occurred between the families of origin and the families of procreation,[2] the predicted future position is not appreciably different from the current position where 36 (40 per cent) of the 89 farmers are local farmers' sons who worked at home before starting to farm. This compares with a predicted figure of 42 (47 per cent) of the sons who worked at home and who are farming or likely to farm locally.[3]

It appears that the pattern of replacement of farmers by the rising generation is being determined by a combination of demographic and

---

number), who may farm outside the area. Together with the one son already married and farming outside the area, this makes a total of four who are likely to farm outside the area.

[1] Eight of these are already married and farming in the area, but it is considered a fair assumption that another eight similar to them will be available from amongst other farmers' sons in the area who are at the appropriate demographic stage.

[2] The average number of children is 4·88 in the families of origin and 3·35 in the families of procreation which have been fertile and are completed (i.e. in which the wife is over the age of 45).

[3] Statistically, these proportions are not significantly different. Even if the 7 per cent difference had been significant, it would probably be reduced somewhat by virtue of the movement of some of the 'predicted' farmers out of farming, or out of the district, for the comparison is between current farmers at the latter end of their farming careers, and 'predicted' farmers at the commencement or in the early stages of theirs.

Throughout the analysis presented in this section no account has been taken of farms becoming available due to the movement of farmers from one farm to another. There is no need to allow for this, as usually such movement merely involves a re-shuffling of the farming population. One farmer may die or retire, and another move into his farm. This may create a whole chain reaction of moves, but there will still have been only one absolute vacancy, and the movement will stop when someone who has not previously farmed elsewhere in the area takes up the farm at the end of the chain of movement.

environmental influences. A quarter of the families are not producing any children,[1] and, whilst three-quarters are producing more than enough to replace themselves and the other quarter, only half these children are likely to commence their adult careers as farmers. Because of the movement of children out of farming,[2] and because of the incidence of celibacy and childlessness, over half the farms are not likely to remain in the same family from one generation to the next.

The individual influences on farmers and their children, and the complex interactions between influences which result in particular types of mobility form the subject of the next two chapters.

[1] Of the 89 farmers, 18 per cent are unmarried and 8 per cent are childless.

[2] Of the 66 farmers with children, 16 have no child remaining at home and another 10 have no child likely to take over from them. These 26 amount to 29 per cent of the 89 farms.

CHAPTER IX

DEMOGRAPHIC FACTORS INFLUENCING MOBILITY

IT has been shown in previous chapters that the mobility patterns of the farm people, occupationally, spatially, and socially, are complex and interrelated. The mobility of people at one point in time is likely to influence their own mobility in the future and also that of other people. Discussion of the various kinds of mobility has indicated the multiplicity of influences and the 'feed-back' effects of one type of mobility on another. In such circumstances it would be unrealistic, and misleading, to attempt to establish in quantitative terms the relative effects of each influence on each mobility. The small size of the sample makes it impossible to 'hold everything else constant', and it is doubtful whether this technique would have given very meaningful results, even if the sample had been very much larger. Such an apparently 'scientific' approach neglects the realities of the situation, which suggest that particular mobilities are determined by a constellation of influences acting over time.

Short of a highly complex mathematical treatment, involving a large number of variables and attributes (a procedure beyond either my capabilities or the suitability of the material), it has not been considered possible to measure the degree of relationship involved between 'influences' and 'mobilities'. Consequently, the influences on the different types of mobility are discussed in general terms, and significant simple relationships established. In addition, the combined effects of various influences are indicated in the narrative, and illustrated by reference to case material.

Some of the influences to be considered are specific to particular types of people (for example an only child), whilst others (such as the nature of the farming process) have more general application. To avoid repetition, and also to bring out the particularity of some influences and the universality of others, the discussion will be centred on the influences themselves and their relation to the different socio-economic and mobility groupings of farmers. Wherever necessary, however, the reverse procedure will be adopted of considering the total influences acting upon people in a particular grouping.

The influences to be considered can be broadly classified as demographic factors, the home and family, and the world outside the home. Demographic factors are those which place an individual into a particular relationship with other individuals, by processes or events, some of which he cannot control and some of which (although he can exercise a certain control over whether they occur or not) he cannot alter once they have occurred. Within the home and the family (and, in family farming, this includes the farm work environment which is inseparably associated with the home), individuals endowed with a particular demographic background come under the influences of other family members and of the home environment—itself a result of the interaction of the family members and the home and farm circumstances. These particular individuals react to, and upon, the others and the environment. Demographic factors, the home and family influences thus separate people into different 'mobility potential' categories. Social, economic and fortuitous circumstances in the world outside the home then provide opportunities for mobility or immobility, according to the particular situations of people with differing potentialities for mobility.

In this chapter demographic influences will be considered; and in the next chapter environmental effects on mobility and their interaction with the demographic influences will be discussed.

No individual determines his own birth. Nor can he determine at what point he is born into a family, how many siblings he will have, or which amongst them will be male and which female. The ages of his parents and siblings in relation to his own are independent facts which he is powerless to alter. Although he may precipitate his own death, that of others of his kin is more likely to occur despite, rather than because of, his own actions.[1] Some, or all, of these demographic occurrences or attributes may, however, have profound effects on an individual's career. This is particularly so in farming in which the occupation, and frequently the farm, the livestock and the equipment necessary to pursue the occupation, are passed on from one generation to the next.

---

[1] That occasionally this may not be so is suggested by the grim jocular references to 'soaping the stair', which were heard on a number of occasions when people in the area were discussing children waiting to inherit a farm from parents. A similar reference is contained in the autobiography of Dominic Behan, *Teems of Times and Happy Returns*, London, 1961, p. 123. Mrs. Behan, from Dublin, and Mrs. Kelly, from the country, are talking by the bedside of an old woman. Mrs. Kelly says: "If y'e'd only take that pillow from under her head, she'd be gone soon enough. In the country M'am, we'd have none of this unnatural nonsense (i.e. waiting for a person to die). . . . Do what I say an' whip the pillow from under her head!"

BIRTH ORDER AND SUCCESSION

Where the inheritance is small, usually only one child will take over from the parents. Which child this will be is considerably influenced by demographic circumstances. Let us consider the hypothetical case where a farmer has married at 24 and had a number of children within the first 15 years of married life. If the eldest child is a boy born within a year of marriage, he will be 25 when his father is 50. Unless the father is willing to retire early, or the son is willing to stay at home single until he is over 40, the eldest son's chances of taking over will be small. On the other hand, a youngest child born, say, when the father was 40, will be 25 when his father is 65 and consequently in a better position than the eldest son to marry and still to succeed his father.

When applied to the farmers surveyed, this theoretical expectation is confirmed, for relatively more farmers who are the youngest or intermediate sons have taken over from parents who had married young,[1] than have those who are eldest or only sons (Table 80).

Table 80: Sibling position and age of father at birth of first child
(for those who took over farm from parents only)

| Age of father at birth of first child | Sibling position of farmer | | Total |
	Eldest or only son	Youngest or intermediate son	
Under 25	3	11	14
Over 25	25	17	42
Total	28	28	56

Even the three eldest sons who took over from parents who were still relatively young only managed to do so by presenting them with a *fait accompli*. Two sons married girls who conceived children prenuptially, and the other married against the wishes of his parents. One father moved to a larger farm thus allowing his son to marry and take over the smaller one; but this was done only after the birth of an illegitimate child. Another father split his holding in two, the son taking one part and the father retaining the other. In the third case,

---

[1] Exact data could not be obtained on the age at marriage of parents of farmers. Ages of farmers' siblings were known, however, together with the age of parents currently, or at death. From these, the age of parents at the birth of their first child was calculated. This measure was taken as an approximate indication of the relative ages at which parents married. It will be in error where the parents had not had a child until a number of years after marriage.

the two families attempted to live together and farm jointly but abandoned this after a short while. In the words of the father: "More than one woman in the same kitchen doesn't work."

Although demographic circumstances were against them taking over from *parents* at an early age, some eldest or elder sons were able to take over from *grandparents* under certain circumstances. At the present time, there are only two cases where the children of farmers are living with their maternal grandparents, but there are a number of instances where this had occurred amongst the farmers, their wives and siblings in the past. Usually, but not always, it was the eldest child of an eldest child who was 'granny-reared'. As one second child in a family described it: "When I was six months old, my aunt Annie, who was only about 12, came to help my mother, and she fetched me back to my granny's, and there I stayed." The aunt Annie was the youngest in the grandmother's family and, by the time she had married and left home, the child of the eldest child was of an age to help the grandparents. Where both parents and grandparents had married young, this arrangement relieved the young mother of the burden of one child, whilst the grandmother was still young enough and at a state in her own family developmental cycle to care for, and appreciate, a young child. Later, the grandchild helped with the work when all the grandparents' children had left home. He or she, therefore, stood a much better chance of inheriting a farm from the grandparents, than directly from the parents. Whilst convenient for the two families concerned, the possibility of the inheritance skipping a generation was not always viewed favourably by the uncles or aunts who, unlike the grandchild, did not consider that the help given to the grandparents by the child merited the right of inheritance to the property.

The greater possibility of youngest sons taking over from parents is not confined to those whose parents married young. Irrespective of the age at which parents married, more youngest sons have taken over from parents than have farmers who occupied other sibling positions in their family of origin (Table 81). This needs further explanation, for there is a wide variation in the ages of marriage, retirement and death of parents; in the spacing of children; and in the ages at which children have succeeded parents. If the relative ages of parents and children were the only major factors concerned, some of the variation between ages which occurs would be more favourable towards succession of children who were not the youngest in the family. For example, if a farmer married late (say at 35) had a number of children over a period of 10 years, and then died at 60; an eldest son aged 25 would be more likely to take over from his father than a youngest son aged 15. This assumes that the eldest son had remained at home working for his father. But it has been shown that many of the farms are not large enough to employ all members of the family on them and that, once a child worked away from home, his chances of taking over from parents were much lower than if he had remained at home. Both these factors favour youngest and only

Table 81: Sibling position and succession to parents

Whether farmer took over from own parents	Sibling position in own sex in family of origin*				
	Only one	Youngest	Eldest	Inter- mediate	Total
Yes	14	19	17	9	59
No	14	14	29	25	82
Total	28	33	46	34	141

* Includes woman farmers.

sons taking over from parents rather than eldest or intermediate sons.

In families with a number of children, the first child to reach working age, whether a boy or a girl, would tend to be employed at home, but would often be replaced later by a younger child. Sometimes, the availability of another child to work at home enabled the elder child to marry, or to take up work off the farm. Sometimes, an elder child working at home would marry and leave, thus creating a labour gap which would be filled, either by the next child to reach working age, or occasionally by a child who was working off the farm returning to work at home. There was an economic pressure encouraging elder children in the family to work off the farm in order to help family finances: they had an incentive to leave home if they wanted to marry at a reasonable age; and they were subject to a replacement pressure as the younger children came of working age. The youngest children, on the other hand, were not under the same economic pressure to leave home, because their elder siblings were already contributing to family finances, or had left home and thus reduced the family requirements. In addition, the necessity for the youngest children to work at home increased as their parents became older and were more in need of help on the farm.

The replacement of elder children by young is clearly shown by the employment pattern for single sons of the farmers surveyed.[1] Although, over a period, probably as many eldest or intermediate sons worked at home as did youngest and only sons, at any one point in time we find fewer of them working at home simply because eldest and intermediate sons have had a longer working life available in which to marry and/or move away from home into other employment (Table 82a). The position is even more marked when only those

Table 82: Sibling position and occupation

Sibling position in own sex	Working at home	Other work not on home farm	Total
(a) Single sons of farmers			
Youngest or only one	29	19	48
Eldest or intermediate	15	34	49
Total	44	53	97
(b) Married daughters before marriage			
Eldest	11	13	24
Youngest or only one	11	22	33
Intermediate	2	21	23
Total	24	56	80

farmers with children all of working age are considered.[2] Amongst the 14 families who have more than one son and who have at least one son working at home, there are eight families with only the youngest son at home, one with the two youngest sons at home, two with all boys at home, and three with an eldest or intermediate son at home.

Two other subsidiary factors contributed towards keeping a relatively higher proportion of farmers who were youngest sons living and working at home, and thus in a position to take over from their

---

[1] Information about the siblings of farmers was not obtained in the same detail as for the farmers themselves. Consequently, in the analysis presented in this chapter, evidence is sometimes used from the past history of the farmers themselves, and sometimes from the history and current situation of their children. Although there is some evidence to suggest that the trends in one generation are similar to those in the other, evidence presented for one generation should not be taken as proof that precisely the same pattern occurred for the other generation.

[2] A situation whereby replacement of elder or intermediate sons by youngest sons could have taken place.

parents. These were the fertility gap which occurred in some families, and the effect of a father marrying twice and having children by each marriage.

The larger average family size in the families of origin of farmers, compared with that in their families of procreation, suggests that contraception was either not as widely practised by the parents as by the present generation, or that it was not as reliable. Under such circumstances, families often consisted of a run of children spaced at intervals of two years or less, then a period when no children were born for a number of years, followed by a final run of one or two children.[1] This accentuated the difference in age between the first and last-born children, and so reinforced the tendency for younger children to remain at home.

When a parent married for a second time, the youngest son of the second marriage usually obtained the farm.[2] Here again the effect of the second marriage was to increase the possibility that older children would move away from home, and that the youngest child would remain at home to work for, and to support, both his parents in their old age, and (later) probably remain to care for his widowed mother. Also, where there was property of any substance to inherit, it was likely that the second wife would favour her own child or would bring pressure to bear upon her husband to provide for him, rather than for the step-children of the first marriage.

Table 81 shows that half the farmers who were only sons had not commenced farming by taking over from their parents, whereas we might have expected that these farmers would have taken over from parents in higher proportions than other farmers, because they had

[1] Some indication of the prevalence of this was obtained by taking all those families of origin with uneven numbers of children and, for those where the ages of all the farmers' sibs were known, ascertaining the difference between the ages of the first child and the middle child, and between the middle child and the last child. Out of 42 families, there were 28 with a greater age difference between the last and the middle child than between the first and the middle child; eight where the reverse applied; and six where the first and last children were the same number of years older and younger, respectively, than the middle child. In 13 out of the 28 families, there was a difference of four or more years between the differences in age of youngest and middle, and middle and eldest children. Out of the eight families where the reverse applied, only one had a difference figure of more than three years—and this was a family of three children, where there was a 12-year gap between the eldest child and the middle one, and a two-year gap between the middle and the youngest.

[2] There were five families of origin of farmers in which the father had been married twice, and which had more than one son in the family. In four of these, the youngest son (who was by the second marriage) had taken over from parents. In the other family, the fourth son of the combined family (who was eldest of the second marriage) had taken over.

no brothers to compete with them. The explanation is partly economic, and partly demographic. Some of them had parents who had small farms only or who had gone bankrupt. Consequently, the sons were more likely to improve their situation by starting up on their own account away from home, or by 'marrying a farm'. Others had chosen to marry and leave home, rather than wait until their parents retired and, by waiting, run the risk of remaining single.[1] The rest had not taken over from parents because they were illegitimate children, or because one or other of their parents had died young and the surviving parent had left the farm.

The lowest proportion of farmers taking over from their parents were those whose sibling position was other than only, youngest, or eldest. These intermediate sons (like eldest sons) were more likely to work off their home farm than were youngest and only sons. Also, as they were closer in age to the eldest sons, vacancies on the home farm were not as likely to arise for them as for younger children, by reason of an eldest son marrying and leaving home. Consequently, some of them were never employed at home (except on the largest farms, which could provide employment for all members of the family). Others were employed at home for a time, but later were displaced as younger family members reached working age and started their working career on the home farm. These intermediate sons could claim neither the privileges of an eldest son nor the indulgences accorded to the youngest. They were thus less likely to stay at home and inherit the farm.

Birth order in the family also affected the careers of farmers' daughters. It influenced what work they did before marriage, and so (indirectly) influenced their choice of marriage partner and their connections with farming after marriage.[2]

A higher proportion of 'eldest' than 'other' daughters had worked at home before marriage (Table 82b). The main factor responsible for this appears to have been the requirements of the farm, rather than the requirements of the home. Of the 11 eldest married daughters who had worked at home before marriage, 10 were also the eldest child in the family. Nine of them lived on large farms where their labour was required for farm work before brothers had left

---

[1] It is of significance that, of the 14 farmers who were only children and who took over from parents, six were unmarried and seven had married late and succeeded late to their parents' farm. The only son to succeed and marry at an early age, had taken over from his widowed mother, who had lost her husband soon after the son was born.

[2] Those married daughters who had worked off the farm before marriage are more likely to have husbands who are not farmers, than are those who worked at home (see Ch. VIII, Table 76).

school, or because they had no brothers. One was from a large family, where she helped in the home and on the farm, and the one who was not eldest in the family was from a large farm where all the children had worked at home before marriage. By contrast, of the 13 eldest married daughters who had worked away from home, six were not the eldest in their families and five were from small farms where the labour requirements were not such as to make it necessary for a daughter to stay at home.

Like intermediate sons, intermediate daughters were the ones least likely to work at home before marriage. This can be explained by an argument similar to that used above for sons, with an added effect due to the greater likelihood of eldest daughters, rather than others, working at home. In families where the eldest daughter worked at home, she would tend to be more tied to home by filial duties and responsibilities, than would an intermediate daughter. Consequently, when the intermediate daughter came of working age, her elder sister would probably still be unmarried and living at home and the intermediate daughter would be free to take up employment off the farm. This would tend to increase the geographical area and broaden the occupational range within which she could meet a potential husband. By travelling to work at a distance from home, and probably by working in a town, her chances of meeting men of her own age would be greater than those of her elder sister working at home, whose social contacts were confined to farmers' sons and men in rural employment. Consequently, she may well marry before her elder sister and thus never have to take up duties on the home farm. Rather more youngest daughters, however, would still be single and thus in a position to take over home duties when an eldest sister married. This helps to explain their position in the analysis between eldest daughters at one extreme, and intermediate daughters at the other (Table 82b).

Birth order is a stronger determinant of whether children work off the farm or not than is the size of the family. It has been indicated in previous chapters that there is a tendency for household size and farm resources to be equated, and for sons to work at home, irrespective of farm size. Daughters are much more likely to work off than sons, and a higher proportion of them work off from the largest families than from the others; but there is no similar relationship between family size and sons working off (Table 83). Even for daughters, the relationship is not a simple one, for a higher proportion of them work off from the smallest-sized families, than from the intermediate-sized ones. This is probably associated with a tendency for the intermediate-sized families to be on the intermediate-sized farms

Table 83: Size of family and working off

	Work currently or prior to marriage	Size of family of procreation			Total
		One or two	Three or four	Five or more	
a.	Farmers' sons				
	At home	17	19	22	58
	Working off	18	22	34	74
	Total	35	41	56	132
b.	Farmers' daughters				
	At home	7	17	12	36
	Working off	16	17	47	80
	Total	23	34	59	116

which are the ones dependent on family labour and which would therefore be likely to employ daughters on farm work when sons were not available.

AGE AT MARRIAGE AND AGE AT SUCCESSION

The combination of demographic circumstances which resulted in a particular child succeeding his parents on a farm could have effects beyond the filial generation, for the age at which such a son succeeded largely determined his opportunities for marriage. Succession at a young age enabled him to marry, have a family and, in turn, hand over the farm to a son young enough to repeat the process. But the longer a son had to remain unmarried and waiting for a farm, the greater would be his chances of not marrying at all, and therefore of not producing a legitimate heir. Furthermore, if an inheriting son did marry at a late age, he tended to marry someone much younger than himself, and thereby created conditions which could lead to *his* son remaining unmarried on the farm after the death of both parents. These conditions could arise because of the age-difference between husband and wife, combined with the longer expectation of life amongst women. Thus, if the father died before the mother, she would then require support in her old age. An unmarried son would be available to give this support. Such a son, if he worked full-time on the farm, would be likely to remain single until his mother's death, for most of the small family farms in the area were inadequate to provide a three-generation household with either housing or a living. By the time his mother died, the son would be at an age when

M

it would be difficult to find a bride. It seems rather more than co-incidental that four of the present farmers who had been placed in a situation like this had all married late, immediately before or immediately after the death of their mother, and all of their wives had conceived children before marriage.

Particulars for the farmers surveyed illustrate the effects discussed above. A higher proportion of those farmers who succeeded parents started to farm at the age of 35 or over than did other farmers. This occurred irrespective of birth order in the family, for there is no significant difference in the proportion of farmers succeeding to parents at 35 or over according to their birth order in the family. Compared with other farmers, a higher proportion of those farmers who inherited at a late age are single and, of those who are married, proportionately more have wives considerably younger than themselves (Table 84). Of the 29 farmers referred to in Table 84, six had

Table 84: Marital status of farmer and late age of succession

	Single	Married with wife 9 years or more younger	Married with wife other age	Total
Farmers who succeeded to parents' farm over the age of 34	12	8	9	29
All other farmers	15	17	111	143
Total	27	25	120	172

married under the age of 35 before succeeding to the farm. Of these, three had fathers with farms of over 30 cow equivalents and lived in separate accommodation on or adjacent to the farm; two had fathers with small farms and had brought a wife to the farm on the early death of one of the parents; and one had married and moved away from home, returning only after the death of both his parents. Eleven of the others had married after the age of 35, immediately before or after succeeding their parents. Ten of these have wives seven or more years younger than themselves[1] and only one married a woman of his own age.

---

[1] In the original classification punched onto Hollerith cards, the extreme limit of age-difference between husband and wife was fixed as 'husbands nine years or more older than wives'. In Table 84, eight farmers are shown under this classification heading. But two of the other farmers who inherited at a late age have wives younger than themselves by seven and eight years respectively. These

The association between late age of succession, taking over from parents or relatives, and remaining single emerges clearly for farmers in the survey (Tables 85 and 86). All the demographic circumstances

Table 85: Marital status and age of succession of farmers who succeeded their own parents or relatives

Age of succession	Single farmers	Married farmers	Total
Under 35	8	30	38
35 and over	12	17	29
Total	20	47	67

Table 86: Marital status and succession of farmers with fathers who were farmers

	Single farmers	Married farmers	Total
Took over from own parents or relatives	20	47	67
Did not take over from own parents or relatives	6	70	76
Total	26	117	143

associated with this cannot be presented in simple 2 × 2 tables, for a number of different combinations of circumstances lead to the same result. These are presented in full in Table 87 for 19 single farmers who directly succeeded their parents, for two others who effectively succeeded them, and for a brother-and-sister pair, where the brother succeeded the parents, and the sister succeeded the brother. As suggested at the beginning of this section, a wide gap between the ages of parents tended to be associated with single farmers, but other circumstances are important, too. The early death of a father is likely to leave either an eldest or an only son with his mother; youngest children stay on with ageing parents; and brother-and-sister combinations occur where the mother had died young.

It is not suggested that demographic circumstances were solely

---

two farmers also did not marry until over the age of 35. The effects on the succession of their children are likely to be the same as for children of the other eight. Consequently, they are considered with the other eight in the above discussion.

Table 87: Demographic circumstances of 23 single farmers

Code number of single farmer, and whether parents alive or dead	Current household composition	Birth order in own sex	Size of family of origin	Ages of parents at birth of first child		Age difference between parents (years)	Which parent died first	Age at death of first parent to die	No. of years between deaths of parents	Age of succession of child
				Father	Mother					
Both parents dead										
149	Self and housekeeper	Eldest of two boys	2	26	28	−2	Father	39	37	50
121	Self and single sister	Only boy	3	32	33	−1	Mother	37	33	36
119	Self and single sister	Third of four boys	5	20	33	−13	Mother	64	32	37
168	Self, single brother and single sister	Eldest of three boys	4	35	29	6	Mother	40	28	36
105	Alone	Only girl	1	NA	NA	NA	Adoptive father	73	20	43
091	Self with children	Youngest of two girls	4	25	26	−1	Mother	45	20	35
071	Alone	Youngest of three boys	6	27	19	8	Father	71	17	39
013	Alone	Only boy	2	29	23	6	Father	56	16	33
042	Self with married sister and family	Second of five boys	10	22	19	3	Mother	56	14	29
002	Self with single sisters and widowed brother	Youngest of three boys	5	35	26	9	Father	80	13	40
085	Alone	Seventh of eight girls	12	27	22	5	Mother	65	13	40
087	Alone	Second of four boys	12	27	22	5	Mother	65	13	40
164	Self and invalid sister	Youngest of three boys	7	39	29	10	Father	70	11	26
109	Self and single sister	Youngest of two boys	4	26	31	−5	Father	70	1	33
062	Self and single sister	Eldest of two girls	2	37	35	2	Father	80	1	44

									Years parent been dead	
125	Self, mother, married sister and family	Youngest of two boys	3	31	23	8	Father	67	20	49
049	Alone (mother with married sister)	Eldest of two boys	3	35	29	6	Father	79	10	34
012	Self and mother	Only boy	1	27	32	−5	Father	74	3	44
154	Self and mother	Eldest of two boys	2	26	24	2	Father	71	2	45
056	Self, father, brother and sister	Eldest of three boys	4	32	26	6	Mother	55	1	27
Both parents alive									Present age of farmer	
134	Self, mother and father, brothers and sisters	Third of five boys	8	28	29	−1	—	—	35	34
073	Self, mother and father	Only boy	2	43	41	2	—	—	35	25
031	Self, mother and father	Only boy	1	46	43	3	—	—	24	22

Notes:
NA: not available.
A minus sign in the column 'Age difference between parents' indicates mother older than father.

responsible for the existence of single farmers; sometimes the size of the property likely to be inherited had effects too. For example, farmer 154 stood to inherit a large farm by remaining single at home with his parents, his younger brother having married and left the family home, whilst the brother-sister partnerships of 134 and 168 are on medium or large-sized farms. Nevertheless, it is pertinent to the argument that only four of the 22 single farmers who inherited from parents have farms of over 15 cow equivalents in size, and some of them are living in very poor circumstances, not likely to encourage anyone to stay at home for reasons of economic gain. Low intelligence or the illness of one or more siblings, combined with poverty, is holding some unmarried siblings together, as for instance 164 and 002, but it is still those whose demographic position fits in best with the circumstances who remain at home.

Initially, some sons who remained unmarried and lived at home with their parents may have chosen deliberately to do so, either from a sense of filial duty or with an eye to the main chance. But with each year that passed their opportunities for alternative action diminished. Their parents grew older and more dependent upon them, their female peers married or moved away from the immediate neighbourhood, and their own horizons narrowed. In time, the interaction of demographic circumstances and environment transformed what may have been a relatively free-choice situation into one confined within ever-narrowing limits. Thus, a decision to remain with parents in order to inherit their farm often resulted in celibacy. Conversely, a decision to marry young often resulted in a son not inheriting from parents, for, once such a decision had been taken, it was affected similarly by a series of probabilities which limited the number of alternative outcomes likely to result. The relevant factor was the willingness of the father either to retire at an early age or to

Table 88: Succession to parents and age of father when present farmer married (for those with fathers who were farmers)

| | Age of father when present farmer married | | |
	Under 55	55 and over or dead	Total
Farmers who took over from parents	4	36	40
Farmers who did not take over from parents	26	50	76
Total	30	86	116

move elsewhere in favour of his son. A few fathers were in a position to divide their farms or move to another; but the majority were not able or willing to do this if their sons married when they (the farmers) were still relatively young. Consequently, few sons who married when their fathers were under the age of 55 succeeded to their parents' farms (Table 88). Looked at in terms of the farmers' ages at marriage, a lower proportion of those who had married under 30 as against those who had married over that age had succeeded to the farm of a parent or relative (Table 89).

Table 89: Succession to parents or relatives and age at marriage (for those with fathers who were farmers)

| | Age at marriage | | |
	Under 30	30 and over	Total
Started to farm:			
at death or retirement of parents or relatives	24	23	47
other than at death or retirement of parents or relatives	53	17	70
Total	77	40	117

PRE-NUPTIAL CONCEPTION, MARRIAGE AND SUCCESSION

The foregoing has been presented as though a son had a free choice between early marriage, with a risk of losing his parents' farm, and late marriage (or no marriage at all) with a chance of inheriting the farm. In some cases the choice was open; but, in many others, the son, his future wife, and both their parents, were all placed in a forced-choice situation due to a pre-nuptial conception, which in fact occurred in 40 per cent of all marriages. Consequently, irrespective of whether there was a farm available for them at the time, over a third of the farmers who were sons of farmers had little choice but to get married.[1] Having to get married reduced their chances of obtaining a farm at the time of marriage, as appears from the num-

---

[1] Usually the parents of a girl who became pregnant could be fairly certain who was responsible and could bring pressure on the man to marry. In one case, however, two youths had been courting the same girl and there was uncertainty as to who was responsible. One of the youths was likely to inherit a reasonable farm from his parents if he married at the right time and into an acceptable social class. By agreement between all parties concerned, this youth acknowledged paternity but refused to marry, although he agreed to pay an allowance for the child. The other youth who had no patrimony to lose then married the girl.

bers of them who did not start to farm until after marriage, compared with those who did not have pre-nuptially conceived children (Table 90).[1] This is not difficult to understand for to begin farming required

Table 90: Pre-nuptial conception, marriage and commencement of farming (for farmers with farming fathers and where birth status of first child known)

Started to farm	First child pre-nuptially conceived or illegitimate	First child conceived in wedlock or no children	Total
At marriage	15	40	55
Before marriage	4	11	15
After marriage	24	12	36
Total	43	63	106

a farm, and farms were not easily obtainable at short notice. Many of the pre-nuptial conceptions occurred when the man or woman (or both) were under the age of 21 (Table 91). It was unlikely that

Table 91: Age at marriage of husband or wife and pre-nuptial conception (for all farmers where birth status of first child known)

Age at marriage	First child pre-nuptially conceived or illegitimate	First child conceived in wedlock or no children	Total
One or both under 21	22	13	35
Both over 21	29	66	95
Total	51	79	130

such minors would have parents on either side who were in a position to retire in their favour or willing to do so in the circumstances. Moreover, the likelihood of obtaining a non-family farm was much greater when a potential farmer could spend a year or more looking for one, than where he had to try and find one in a hurry. Consequently, those who delayed marriage until they obtained a farm could marry and start to farm at the same time; but those who were

[1] 'Commenced farming after marriage' refers to starting a farm on his own account at least one year after marriage. In many cases, it was considerably longer than a year before such farmers managed to obtain a farm of their own.

forced to get married often had to wait until some time after marriage before they could start to farm on their own account.

The evidence of this study does not support the explanation sometimes advanced to account for the higher proportion of pre-nuptial conceptions recorded in country areas compared with urban areas. This explanation holds that where inheritance was important, a proof of fertility was required before marriage would be undertaken.[1] If 'fertility testing' had been common in this area before children inherited from parents, we could expect to find a higher incidence of pre-nuptial conception amongst those taking over from parents or relatives, than amongst others. There is no such relationship (Table 92). The farmers with the lowest ages at marriage have

Table 92: Succession to parents or relatives and pre-nuptial conception (for farmers with farming fathers and where birth status of first child is known)

Took over from parents or relatives	First child pre-nuptially conceived or illegitimate	First child conceived in wedlock or no children	Total
Yes	22	38	60
No	20	26	46
Total	42	64	106

the lowest proportion taking over from parents or relatives and the highest incidence of pre-nuptial conception (Tables 93 and 94). This

Table 93: Succession to parents or relatives and age at marriage (for farmers where birth status of first child is known)

Took over from parents or relatives	Age of farmer at marriage			Total
	Under 26	26–30	Over 30	
Yes	18	19	23	60
No	20	13	13	46
Total	38	32	36	106

fits more closely with an explanation linking high rates of pre-nuptial conception with the younger ages of marriage where potential fertility is higher.[2]

[1] See, for example, Rees, *Life in a Welsh Countryside*, p. 89.
[2] Data from the Family Census of 1946 indicates that a high prenuptial

Table 94: Age of farmer at marriage and incidence of pre-nuptial conception (for farmers with farming fathers and where birth status of first child known).

| | Age of farmer at marriage | | | |
	Under 26	26–30	Over 30	Total
First child pre-nuptially conceived or illegitimate	21	5	16	42
First child conceived in wedlock or no children	17	27	20	64
Total	38	32	36	106

It is possible that, amongst farming people, a 'normal' rate of pre-nuptial conception (associated with young ages of marriage and high total fertility) may be increased by two other causes. Firstly, as a result of the late ages of succession to farms, some of the men either remain single permanently, or do not marry until they are in their mid-thirties, or over. These single males tend to be restricted in their social contacts to the immediate area of their upbringing. Furthermore, rural women marry at earlier ages than rural men and marry over a wider spatial and occupational range. Consequently, there is an absolute shortage of unmarried women to the unmarried men of equivalent age. These discrepancies in the number of unmarried men and women may lead to sexual experiences of a periodic and unplanned nature amongst some of the unmarried males. This may result in the late marriage of some apparently confirmed bachelors to women much younger than themselves after such women have become pregnant.[1] This tendency is illustrated by

conception rate is associated with a high total fertility; and that, within social status categories, there is a close association between early marriage and a high frequency of pre-nuptial conception.

D. V. Glass and E. Grebenik: *The Trend and Pattern of Fertility in Great Britain*. Papers of the Royal Commission on Population, Vol. VI, Part I: Report, p. 143, and Table 8, p. 145.

[1] Rees, op. cit. dismisses this possibility by referring to the low illegitimacy rate in Ireland, despite the high numbers of unmarried males. Apart from the need to make a judgment on the basis of prenuptial conception rates as well as illegitimacy rates, the case of emigration from Ireland should not be discounted. Babies born to unmarried Irish mothers in the homes and hospitals of London, Liverpool and Manchester may well have been conceived in the bogs of County Mayo, and could be one compelling reason for the higher rate of emigration of Irish country girls compared with boys. Support for this contention is provided by statistics on the origins of unmarried mothers who had babies in London hospitals in 1961. Many of these mothers came from Ireland. Annual Report of the Medical Officer of Health, London County Council, 1961.

figures for this sample of farmers. Amongst the 15 farmers who married after they were 30 and whose wives had conceived before marriage, 11 were seven or more years' older than their wives.

Secondly, pre-nuptial conception may, in some cases, be planned in advance, as a means of forcing the hands of otherwise reluctant parents, who must then provide a home (and maybe a farm) for a son or a son-in-law. Certainly (as has been indicated already), some parents, when presented with a *fait accompli*, responded by either splitting up their farm, by moving to another farm in favour of a son or son-in-law, or by setting up the pair on a farm of their own. In addition, there were cases where a couple had an illegitimate child and did not marry until years later on the death of one or other of the parents, at which time they took over the parents' farm. Circumstantial evidence suggests that in these cases there had been parental opposition on one side to the marriage. During the course of research, a number of remarks were overheard and gossip was encountered, concerning planned pre-nuptial conception. One farmer who failed in his attempt to obtain a farm by these means and, as a consequence, was still on a small full-time farm, remarked, in effect: "You may copulate yourself into a farm, but you don't procreate yourself out of one." A remark is also pertinent which was overheard at a dance where a number of farmers' sons from surrounding areas had congregated. One young farmer was asked the question "hast gotten thyself a farm yet?" One of his friends answered for him by saying, "No, but he's — (copulating) hard enough."

Some families were very 'touchy' when discussing sons or sons-in-law who had been set up on farms at an early age. Frequently the sons or daughters in question had married down the social scale. Such indirect evidence, and the gossip, suggests that people in the area recognized (not necessarily with approval) that planned pre-nuptial conception was one way of obtaining a farm.

It should not be thought that the male was the only one who stood to gain from any planned pre-nuptial conception. The daughter of young parents in reasonable financial circumstances could obtain the man of her choice at an earlier date than otherwise and she would stand a fair chance of still sharing in the family inheritance. The daughter of poor parents would either raise her social status, or, if she stood to inherit a small property, would have security and a husband to work for her whilst still of marriageable age, rather than run the risk of being left a spinster on an inadequate holding, after the death of her parents.

For those who did not take over from parents, marriage (whether occasioned by pre-nuptial conception or not) meant that they had a number of alternatives. They could live with one or other of the parents and the husband could work on the farm, or go out to do other work; they could start up farming wherever they could find a farm and—depending on its size—the husband could work at home, or find work off the farm; or they could find a house somewhere, and the husband go out to work. Which alternative was available to them, or chosen by them, was affected by a number of factors. These were the size of business of their respective parents, whether other children were already working at home, what accommodation was available either at their homes or elsewhere, the training the husband had received for work off the farm, and what his attitude was to such work. Few of the farms in the area have accommodation on them for more than one family, and fewer still are large enough adequately to support two families, particularly when other children also work at home. What work a person had done prior to marriage influenced what he was prepared to do, or capable of doing, after marriage. Where the couple could obtain accommodation, or a farm, determined the availability of work for the husband; and the size of the farm obtained determined whether work off the farm was required, or not. All these environmental factors interacted with the demographic circumstances affecting individuals, and resulted in particular patterns of mobility. Before studying these interactions further, it is necessary to look much closer at the influences of environment on farm-reared people.

CHAPTER X

THE EFFECT OF ENVIRONMENT
ON MOBILITY

DEMOGRAPHIC circumstances place certain limitations upon
some members of a family and give certain advantages to others.
The circumstances of their home and work environment during
childhood, youth and adulthood, together with influences from the
world outside, provide a framework within which the different
family members make decisions in response to their social and
economic needs.

THE FARM ENVIRONMENT

In industrial communities a boy grows up in a home environment
which is physically separated from his father's work environment,
and frequently there is little direct contact between home and work.
In farming communities, on the other hand, the home environment
and the work environment are inseparable. A boy's home is also his
father's workplace, and even the homes of other relatives are likely
to be farms, if the boy's parents have been reared on farms in the
same area. All this ensures that a farm boy absorbs from an early
age an outlook which is largely restricted to farming, and to the
particular farms amongst which he grows up. His father's work is not
something mysterious carried on away from home but is a familiar
part of the boy's everyday life. He can smell the cows, hear the tractor
and lie in the grass. He helps with the milking, stays at home from
school at haymaking and other busy seasons, and generally acquires
by precept and practice a detailed and intimate knowledge of the
farming in his immediate neighbourhood, and particularly that of
his home farm. In most aspects of his life he is involved in the adult
world. At meal-times the topic of conversation is likely to be farming; at play he is surrounded by the environment in which farm work
operates; and at school his peers have similar backgrounds and
interests. The longer his family connections have been with an area,
or a particular farm, the more intensely he is likely to be exposed to
farming. If his family's past and his own present are dominated by
farming it is not surprising that he sees his future in the same
terms.

At the same time as the boy is identifying himself with the world

173

of farming, his father is likely to be furthering his son's involvement. A full-time farmer has a pride, interest and tradition in the work he does and these he wants to encourage in his son. If he is an owner-occupier he has property and a skill to hand on to the next generation. If he is a tenant-farmer, he will not have land to hand on, but he will have an equity in his farm, in the form of livestock and equipment, which a child may inherit. In the past it was also quite common for children to inherit the tenancy. His encouragement of his son may not be without a certain amount of self-interest, in that a family farmer can ill afford to pay for labour, so that any work done by the children relieves the father of some of the burden, without representing money going off the property. Also, if the father married at about 30, he will be around 45 when the son leaves school. After 15 years or so of hard work for his own father, and another 15 for himself, he will be likely to welcome the opportunity to 'ease up' which should be possible if his son takes up farming and starts to work at home.

A farmer's son thus looks forward to the day when he will be his own master, engaged in an occupation for which he has been conditioned by his experiences in childhood and youth. A farm-reared girl, however, usually reacts differently to the farm environment, and often has aspirations for a life unconnected with farming. If she has no brothers, or is the eldest in the family, she may become involved in the tasks and atmosphere associated with farm work, and as a result have the same interest in farming as a boy. But, more frequently, she will help her mother in the house, and share her work and worries (which are of considerable magnitude, particularly when the family is a large one). Babies, meals at all hours, washing up, dirty clothes and muddy boots; all have to be dealt with and often the facilities are inadequate. Her participation in adult life also starts from an early age but the satisfactions for her are not as tangible as for the son. The mown crop of hay can be seen in the barn, and the full bucket of milk brings a cheque at the end of the month. But housework is continuous and unpaid. To a farmer's daughter, school and the world outside farming often represent an escape from the drudgery of home.

This division of interests and attitudes between boys and girls does not arise only on full-time farms. Many of the people on part-time farms have full-time farming parents on one side of the family or the other. If on the husband's side, he is likely to project his own thwarted farming ambitions on to his son, hoping to regain through him the farming and social status which he has lost by going out to work. When the wife has married down socially, she too will be anxious for her son to regain the status she lost at marriage.[1] Particularly in these latter circumstances, the son may be exposed to as intense a farming environment as on full-time farms, for—with the father away for up to 12 hours a day—the son comes under his mother's farming influence and from an early age will be her main support in carrying out the farming tasks.

A daughter of a part-time or 'small-business' farmer, on the other hand, will be more likely to grow away from farming. When the mother is not of full-time farming stock, or is not a farmer's daughter at all, her urban experiences will not be lost on the daughter, nor will her struggle to obtain some of the material goods to which she has been accustomed, or which she feels entitled to enjoy. Constantly the farm and the home compete for scarce resources. Second-hand car or second-hand tractor, 'bottle gas' cooker or milking machine, cosmetics or udder salve—all involve conflicts which are so often resolved in favour of the farm. Where the mother rather than the father is interested in the farm, she will give priority to farm duties and probably spend more of her time outside on the farm than in the house. In such circumstances, the household chores will fall to the daughter. At busy times outside, she will be expected not only to cope with the indoor duties but also to give a hand in the hayfield or milking shed. School, the pictures, shopping in town and, latterly, television[2] fortify her day-dreams of a working and married life free from the demands, restrictions and deprivations of family farming.

SCHOOL VERSUS FARM

Until a few years ago, school children beyond the primary school stage had been taken from the area into the nearby towns, most of them to secondary modern schools, with a very few going to grammar schools. This involved them in journeys by bus in all weathers and, because of this dependence on transport, there was a tendency within the school for such children to become a group apart. All their school activities had to be geared to the prompt departure of the

---

[1] Allison Davis states: 'Many parents who push children towards social mobility are members of mixed-class marriages . . . a lower-middle-class woman who married a man from the upper part of the working class usually begins to try and recoup her original class status, either by reforming and elevating her husband's behaviour to meet lower-middle-class standards or by seeking to train and propel her children toward the status she once had', in 'Personality and social mobility', *The School Review*, Vol. 65, 1957, p. 137.

[2] Many of the farms have no mains electricity but those with their own generating set produce at least enough power for the milking machine, electric light and a television set.

buses in good weather and their possible late arrival in bad. In addition, country children were very much in the minority within the town schools. Despite the partial segregation of country children from town children in the schools, farmers considered that their sons and daughters were being made into 'townies' and they agitated for the establishment of new secondary modern schools in country districts. The county education authority was sympathetic towards these views and adopted a policy which resulted in a number of schools being built in rural areas, exclusively for the use of country children. Now their children are installed in these schools, mothers can no longer complain that their daughters deliberately miss the bus at night in order to look at the shops, or go to the pictures with their girl friends in the town. Fathers can no longer complain that their sons are likely to leave the farms because of the counter attractions of the town. This latter claim is a doubtful one, in view of the very great influence of the farm environment on the son, as previously shown. Presumably when the children were attending school in the town, it was as easy for them to miss the bus to school on those days when the farm needed extra labour, as it is now when they are attending school in the country. Certainly, comparisons of the present occupations of those farmers' sons who were educated in the towns, and those who were educated in the country, do not support the contention made by farmers that education in the town encouraged their sons away from farming. There is no significant difference between the proportion of farmers' sons working on farms, or at other occupations, between the age cohorts 15 to 16, 17 to 20, and 21 to 25.[1]

The steady loss of hired farm workers to other occupations provides a more likely explanation of the agitation for schools to be sited in rural areas. Farmers' sons on the full-time farms are held to farming by upbringing, filial duty, and the possibilities of either inheriting a farm from parents or of acquiring one with their help. Sons of part-time farmers and of other rural workers are not tied so closely to the industry; but, in the absence of alternative employment, they often become farm workers on the larger farms. Some of the farmers with these farms hire labour throughout all the phases of their family developmental cycle; others require the services of hired youths until their own sons are old enough to help on their farms. These larger-business farmers fear that education in the towns

[1] All those in the age group of 15-16 had attended secondary modern school in a country area. Some of those in the 17-20 range had attended secondary modern school in a country area, and the others in an urban area. All those in the range 21-25 had attended secondary modern school in an urban area.

might deprive them of their labour-force by suggesting other employment opportunities to the sons of part-time farmers and other rural workers. Should this occur, it would throw the labour burden of operating their farms still further upon either their own shoulders or those of members of their families. Hence, the 'larger-business' farmers who occupy positions of power in the rural districts and county councils are under pressure from their relatives and neighbours to further an educational policy which will retain rural youth for farm work. From the point of view of the larger-business farmers this makes sense, but it also helps to perpetuate the small-farm problem, for such a policy ensures that there will always be a plentiful supply of young men with farm training and with aspirations to farm on their own account. These men usually will not have access to the capital sums necessary to purchase a farm of reasonable size or even stock and equip it. Consequently, they will compete for the small full-time farms. In the long run, this may even be to the detriment of the larger-business farmers, because small farms will not readily become available for amalgamation if there is always a demand for them by people wanting to farm them as units and therefore willing to pay more for them (in rent or purchase price) than larger-business farmers may consider worthwhile. The farms which do become available for amalgamation are likely to be the poorer ones situated in remote parts of the countryside, which become vacant on the death, retirement or bankruptcy of single farmers, barren couples and couples with occupational experiences other than farming, whose children have left home for employment outside the industry. Such farms are unlikely to be adjacent to the larger-business farms on the better land, and therefore will not be very suitable for incorporating in the farm business, except perhaps as areas of rough grazing for use by 'dry' stock.

Information about the boys and girls attending the country secondary modern school serving the research area and other surrounding parishes, confirms the impression gained on the farms: that boys are less interested in scholastic achievement than girls. Boys do less well at school work and are much poorer attenders than girls, apart from those farmers' daughters who have no brothers. In fact, 63 per cent of the boys are in B classes against 37 per cent of the girls. Children from the village primary schools were allocated to A and B streams in the secondary school on the basis of their ratings in the 11-plus examination and/or 'Cotswold' tests. Thereafter, they moved into A or B classes according to their progress in secondary school work. The distribution of boys and girls in these classes of the secondary school is indicated in Table 95.

N

The lower standards achieved by boys is well seen in the special class for backward children. In 1960 this class comprised 10 boys and two girls. While both girls had very low Intelligence Quotients, this did not apply to all of the boys. For instance, one of the boys had been recommended by his primary school as a potential A stream pupil but his work was so poor that he never achieved this

Table 95: Boys and girls in A and B classes at local secondary modern school

	Class 1	Class 1/2	Class 2	Class 3	Class 4	Total
Boys						
A stream	10	0	13	11	9	43
B stream	13	10	18	19	14	74
Total	23	10	31	30	23	117
Girls						
A stream	19	0	21	19	10	69
B stream	7	2	12	12	8	41
Total	26	2	33	31	18	110

potential, mainly because of his exceedingly poor attendance record. He was the third son of a farmer with a large family, who farmed a number of holdings under difficult conditions. The father had expanded his land-holding systematically as his sons grew older, his last acquisition had taken place in the year before the boy in question left the primary school. It was the boy's absorption in the work of the farm which distracted him from school work and lay behind his poor attendance. Other boys in this class had equally poor records of attendance.[1]

The children at the secondary modern school can be divided into three categories on the basis of their home addresses: those obviously from farms, those not from farms, and an intermediate group who might be either. Excluding this last (which was a small minority), we find that 69 per cent of the boys and 37 per cent of the girls from farm addresses are in B classes. From the non-farm addresses 58 per

[1] Evidence from the 1947 Scottish Mental Survey indicates that the poorest attenders at school were the children from rural groups, and that a broad correspondence existed between Intelligence Quotient test scores and the incidence of satisfactory school attendance. *Social Implications of the 1947 Scottish Mental Survey*, London, 1953, p. 186.

cent of the boys and 37 per cent of the girls are in B classes.[1] There
is no reason to suppose that any *great* difference exists in inherent
ability between boys and girls of equivalent ages.[2] Consequently, the
gross difference indicated above may be due to differences in attitudes, application and attendance between the boys and girls in
this rural area.

It is unlikely that sons would either regularly stay away from
school or show little interest in school work, unless their parents too
were indifferent to the benefits of education. Even the progressive
farmers in the area appear to value the labour of their sons more
highly than their educational achievements, for many of them keep
their sons at home to help them when labour demands on the farm
are high. As a result, the sons of 'progressives' are as likely to be in
B classes as are the sons of incompetent farmers. Indeed, one of the
leaders of the farming community in the area stated: "Education
beyond 15 hinders a boy from becoming interested in farming at an
age when he is most impressionable, and it can lead him away from
farming, even if he has every opportunity[3] to start up on his own
account."

The divergence in interests and aspirations between boys and
girls in the area is evident from their replies to a questionnaire on
what work they would like to do, what work they expected they
would do, where they would like to live and why.[4]

---

[1] The difference in the proportion of boys from farm and non-farm addresses
in the B classes was not statistically significant at the 5 per cent level.

[2] *Social Implications*, Table 1, p. 6. There was a higher average test-score for
the Intelligence Quotients of girls compared with boys but the difference in
average scores between the two sexes was not statistically significant. In *The
Trend of Scottish Intelligence*, London, 1949, Table X, p. 85, the mean scores for
girls were higher than for boys, but this was stated to be due to the range of
scores being narrower for girls than for boys. Later, on p. 91, the author stated:
'There are, in fact, somewhat more very bright boys than very bright girls, but
considerably more dull boys than dull girls'.

[3] By 'opportunity' he meant availability of land and capital from family
sources.

[4] Six questions were put to the children in their final two years at school. These
were:
What work would you like to do when you leave school?
Why would you like to do this?
What work do you think you *will* do when you leave school?
Why do you think you will do this work?
If you were able to chose, where would you like to live within 10 miles of here?
Why would you like to live there?
The children filled in the answers to these questions on a questionnaire form which
had no indication of its origin, and they did it during the course of an ordinary
lesson on general topics taken by the headmaster. The number of children

Two-thirds of the boys either wish or expect to work on farms and eventually to farm on their own account, compared with one-ninth of the girls (Table 96). Most of the wishes and expectations of the

Table 96: Occupational wishes and expectations of children in their final two years at school

	Would like and expect to do farm work	Would like other work, expect farm work	Would like and expect to do other work	Would like farm work, expect other work	Total
Boys	24	3	12	1	40
Girls	1	3	32	0	36

boys coincide, particularly in relation to farming, but exceptions are revealing: "The work I would like to do is to drive long-distance lorries. . . . The work I think I shall do is farming. . . . I shall do this because it is the work that I have been brought up to do." Another boy who wanted to drive a corn lorry ('corn' is the local term for animal feeding stuffs) wrote: "because you would go to different places, and when you had to fetch the corn you would see the docks where the corn is unloaded". Again, this boy thought he would do farming "because it is the only work available, and office work is too far away". A third boy wanted to go into the police force—"because I like helping other people"—but thought he would actually work at dairy farming, "because there is no other work round here". These three exceptions to the general run of boys who want to farm are all in A classes and all come from the better farming part of the area where full-time farming predominates, but which is not as well served by direct links with the towns. Although not making agriculture their first choice of occupation, they have taken a realistic view of their future opportunities.

Those boys who neither want nor expect to work on farms usually live either in a village, close to a bus route, or near a main road. Popular jobs with them are lorry driver or mechanic.

There is a greater discrepancy between 'wished' and 'expected' jobs amongst the girls, although very few of them wish or expect to work in the country, or to be connected with farming. The effects of limitations of transport are again evident. "I would like to be a

---

concerned is less than that shown for classes 3 and 4 in Table 95, because the questionnaire was answered in the third term when some of the children had already left, whilst others were absent at the time.

dressmaker making dresses and baby clothes. . . . I will work in 'Hilltown' in Woolworths . . . because there is no transport from my village early enough to get into the large towns." (Hilltown has few industries but it is accessible from the area, whereas other towns are not.) Those settling for 'millwork' do so because of the availability of transport and lack of other opportunities—"Because there is no other job near enough to work at . . ." "Because the bus and the taxis come round to pick you up." One girl who wanted to become a children's nurse had resigned herself to the mill "because the bus picks you up". Although a few girls expressed a desire for prestige or fantasy jobs, such as hairdresser or air hostess, many girls want domestic rather than industrial jobs. Thus, peak aspirations are for domestic science teaching and needlework teaching, subjects for which the school has excellent facilities. It also has good teaching facilities for art, pottery and woodwork, but the boys show no desire to become furniture makers, potters or commercial artists.

The wishes and expectations of the majority of the boys do not appear to be dictated by any realization of a lack of opportunities locally, but arise rather from a close identification of themselves with the countryside and farming. Thus—"I would like to be a dairy farmer . . . because I shall be able to do this work . . . because I like it." "I would like to farm because I am interested in farming and like working in the open . . . because I live on a farm, and will in time carry it on from my father." Occasionally—"because I have lived on a farm all my life and my dad says I shall work on the farm", but even this was prefaced by "because I like farming".

Boys with non-farming parents but who live in full-time farming areas are equally certain of what they want to do: "I would like to be a farm worker on a big farm . . . because I like animals and driving tractors and you also get a lot of fresh air . . . because all our family has been one (i.e. a farm worker) and I want to farm." "I should like to go dairy farming . . . because I work on a farm in my spare time and I like it."

Table 97: Occupational and residential wishes of children in their final two years at school

| | Would like to live in town | | Would like to live in country | | |
	Would like farm work	Would like other work	Would like farm work	Would like other work	Total
Boys	4	4	21	11	40
Girls	0	23	1	9	33

In view of the differences in occupational choice between the two sexes, it is not surprising that two-thirds of the girls want to live in the towns as against only one-sixth of the boys (Table 97). This is not only associated with the difficulty girls have in obtaining jobs locally or of transport to those of their choice, but appears to stem from differences in interests and values between the boys and the girls. A measure of these differences can be gauged from some of the reasons given by boys for wishing to live in the country and by girls for preferring the towns:

BOYS

"I would like to live in the open not in the town or village... because I have lived there all my life."

"I don't want to live anywhere else but —— because I like the country-side."

"I like living in the countryside and would not go to live in a town . . . because you see a lot of life and nature, birds are always singing and there is plenty of fresh air."

(A boy who wanted to live away from his own area) "because the ground is dry and I could keep a lot of sheep".

(A farmer's youngest son who was going to farm but expressed a wish to live in a town) "because there are plenty of girls there".

GIRLS

"When you live in the country you have not got much transport to go shopping unless you have a motor or van of your own, but in —— you can just cross the road and you are at a shop. Also you haven't as much walking to do as in the country." (This girl lived 1½ miles from the nearest bus route.)

"I would like to live in —— because it is a nice clean place, there are lots of buses to different places and you can get about." (A farmer's daughter who wanted to be a hairdresser, but was going to work at home.)

"I would like to live there because of the shops, you can go out at night when you go home to look round the shops and on a Saturday to look round the market stalls. Also the pictures, but you can't do that in the country."

(A girl who wanted to live in London) "because there are plenty of good jobs and you can get a better one there than here".

(A girl who was going to work in the mill) "I would not have to pay any bus fare if I lived in the town".

The proportion of boys at the secondary modern school who expect to work on farms corresponds very closely to the proportion of sons of farmers who actually work on farms after leaving school. The proportion of daughters actually working on farms, however, is greater than the proportion of girls who express a desire to engage in farm work after they leave school.[1] Some bias may have entered into the figures for work expectations for girls, because not all the children at school are from farms. All those girls at the school who expect to work on farms are farmers' daughters; so that the number of daughters of non-farmers may be weighting the work expectations towards other work. Nevertheless, the proportion of girls with farming expectations is so low compared with the actual position for farmers' daughters who are at work, that it confirms the impressions obtained from case histories. These suggest that some farmers' daughters, although wishing to work off the farm, have difficulty in obtaining work acceptable to themselves or their parents. Such girls either work at home (even though their labour is not really required) or take casual work for a day or two per week, wherever they can find it in the district, working at home for the rest of the time. Thus, one farmer's daughter works part-time in a shop in the village, and part-time at home; another does domestic work at a nearby farm for two or three days each week; and a third has a part-time postal round. When interviewed, all of them mentioned the unavailability of local jobs and the lack of transport to a centre of employment other than 'the bus to the mill'. This alternative is considered the last resort by parents who themselves have been brought up in a farming tradition. In addition, some daughters from families which lack a son of working age would like to have other jobs but are obliged to stay at home, either to work in the house, or on the farm itself.

In Ch. IV, it was shown that in rather more than half the married pairs, either the husband or the wife had 'other-work' experiences apart from farm work at home or for others. This experience is likely to influence what their children do, either directly because of the experience of, and attitude towards, other work by parents, or indirectly through contacts with grandparents and other maternal and paternal kin, whose experiences, environment and values have not been confined to farming or the immediate neighbourhood. This is reflected in the work histories of single and married daughters. A greater proportion of those daughters, both of whose parents had work experiences before marriage which were limited to farming, are themselves working on farms (or have married men who are doing

[1] 68 per cent of the boys at the school expect to do farm work, as against 69 per cent of the single sons of farmers who are so engaged. Only 11 per cent of the girls at school expect to do farm work, as against 47 per cent of the single daughters of farmers who work on farms and 35 per cent of married daughters who worked on farms before marriage.

so) than daughters of whom one parent, or both, had work experiences *not* confined to agriculture (Table 98). The same trend is evident for married sons, but with a greater tendency towards

Table 98: Employment of parents before marriage and employment of daughters or their husbands (for farmers with all children of working age)

	Employment of daughter's father and mother before marriage			
	Both farm work	One farm work, one other work	Both other work	Total
a. Current employment of single daughters				
Farm work at home or elsewhere	8	3	0	11
Other work	5	5	5	15
Total	13	8	5	26
b. Current employment of husbands of married daughters				
Farming on own account or farm work	29	7	3	39
Other work	13	10	15	38
Total	42	17	18	77

farming (Table 99b). For single sons, however, only those, both of whose parents had other work experiences, show a reduction in the proportion working on farms; and, even amongst these, the proportion farming is one half (Table 99a).

Strong outside influences are necessary to break the link forged for boys by a childhood steeped in the activities and sensory perceptions associated with farming. That some of them may change their views when faced with the responsibilities of marriage is evident from the higher proportion of married sons engaged in other work. One eldest son, who was in his twenties, with a father in his forties, confessed: "If I'd known what I know now, I'd have gone on at school. I could have done so, but I messed about too much, and didn't want anything but to be finished and get back to the farm."

He is one of the few sons to have had higher secondary school education,[1] probably under the influence of an aspirant mother. She was the eldest daughter of a large family in which: "We'd no option but to leave at 14. My youngest sister was the only one to win a scholarship and go to grammar school." The father was an eldest son of a large family. He had married young, left home to take a small farm, and later moved to his present farm, bought for him by

Table 99: Employment of parents before marriage and employment of sons (for farmers with all children of working age)

	Employment of father and mother before marriage			
	Both farm work	One farm work, one other work	Both other work	Total
a. Current employment of single sons				
Farm work at home or elsewhere	22	11	9	42
Other work	9	5	9	23
Total	31	16	18	65
b. Current employment of married sons				
Farming on own account or farm work	12	2	3	17
Other work	3	6	9	18
Total	15	8	12	35

his father. He has a number of brothers, some unmarried, and some in the early phase of married life. Consequently, the chances are very slender of this farmer's eldest son obtaining one of the family farms whilst still of marriageable age. Furthermore, most of the farms in the immediate vicinity are 'tightly held', which reduces the son's prospect of ever farming near home.

Contrary to the fears expressed by farmers, and to the 'selectivity theory' linking rural migration and education, there is no significant relationship (for either sons or daughters) between higher secondary

[1] That is, who have been to grammar schools, technical schools, or colleges of further education.

school education and leaving the occupation of farming. Admittedly, the numbers involved are small. There are only 11 sons and 16 daughters with higher education, and these 27 came from 18 families. Particularly amongst the sons, the influence of the home environment appears stronger than that of school, as witness the example just quoted.

For sons, there is no relationship between possession of higher education and moving away from home; but proportionately more of the better educated daughters, than those with less education, were living at greater distances from home. This suggests that the effect of higher education is to widen the job selectivity area and range for girls, with the possibility of subsequent employment and/ or marriage away from their home district. All three single daughters with higher education who are living away from home are over 20 miles away and one of them teaches abroad.

There is evidence that the educational attainment of parents or of close relatives, together with birth order in the family and the requirements of the farm for labour, are factors influencing the achievement of higher education by children. Thus, of the parents with higher education themselves (having children of working age), all except one have one or more of those children with higher education.[1] Of the other families who have children with higher education, two have close relatives on one side or the other with higher education, five have either 'aspirant' wives, or wives who were in professional or semi-professional employment before marriage, and four have the only, or the youngest, child with higher education, but have no evidence of higher education in the families of husband or wife. Amongst the sons there are no intermediate children with higher education, and amongst the daughters only one eldest child has higher education.[2]

OCCUPATIONAL MOBILITY AND FARMING ACHIEVEMENT

Whether children achieve higher education or not, there is evidence that their occupation prior to marriage is an important influence in determining where they subsequently settle. Very few sons or daughters who had worked in a country area before they married are living in an urban area now. Fewer sons than daughters had worked in

---

[1] There are eight married pairs with all children of working age in which the husband or wife, or both, have received higher education.

[2] It was stated earlier that intermediate sons are those most likely to have to go to work off the farms, and eldest daughters are most likely to be required to stay at home to help on the farm or in the house.

urban areas prior to marriage, but relatively more of the sons who had done so are living there than are daughters, many of whom married into their home area where most of them were living when single (Table 100). On the other hand, of sons and daughters who

Table 100: Working location of farmers' sons and daughters prior to marriage and current living location

Worked prior to marriage	Now living in Country area	Urban area	Total
a. Married sons			
In country area	24	2	26
In urban area	3	6	9
b. Married daughters			
In country area	34	6	40
In urban area	25	16	41

had worked close to home prior to marriage, more daughters than sons are now living farther away from home (Table 101).

Table 101: Distance from parents' home at which married sons and daughters are living, who worked within 2½ miles of home prior to marriage

	Now living 2½ miles or less from parents' home	Now living over 2½ miles from parents' home	Total
Married daughters	18	14	32
Married sons	18	2	20

The greater mobility of daughters than sons appears to be related in part to their being much less tied by marriage to the farms and farming practices of their home area. A farm-reared daughter should have no difficulty in adapting herself to farm life outside her immediate area of upbringing. Her farming contribution to a marriage would be that of her knowledge of, and skill at, the *tasks* of farming and her understanding of the way of life, rather than any detailed knowledge of the *techniques* of handling land, stock and people in a particular area, such as a farming husband requires. Equally, a daughter trained in housekeeping on a farm should have no difficulty in adapting herself to urban housekeeping. The situation is different for the farm-reared man who intends to remain in the farming industry. His training is largely informal, and usually acquired at home.[1] Consequently, his knowledge of farming tends to be confined

[1] This applies to farming in general and not only to the area in question. See D. Sheppard: *A Survey Among Grassland Farmers*, 1960. In a random sample of

to that practised in his home area. This means that a move away from his area of upbringing may well appear to be a step into the unknown. In addition, he is likely to lose the support and help of his parents and relatives if he moves to another district which is too far away for daily contact. Sons are therefore reluctant to go elsewhere for a farm, so long as there is some chance of inheriting, buying or renting a local farm.

The reluctance of farmers' sons to look outside their home area when seeking a farm helps to explain why farmers' daughters who stand to inherit a farm of whatever size have no difficulty in obtaining husbands. Among those 21 married couples where the farmer had 'married in' and he and his wife had taken over the farm when the wife's parents had died or retired, nine of the wives were either only children, or had sisters but no brothers (Table 102). Twenty of the

Table 102: Marrying in and sex composition of
wife's family of origin

Sex composition of wife's family of origin	Took over farm at death or retirement of wife's parents	Others	Total
Only child or all daughters	9	26	35
Other	12	97	109
Total	21	123	144

wives had stayed at home with parents after their brothers or sisters had left home, and 14 of these had, in fact, stayed on with one parent after the death of the other. In these 14 families, a son-in-law was welcomed as a support to both mother and daughter where the mother was the survivor. Where the father was the survivor, he was likely to accept a son-in-law into the farm, rather than run the risk of losing his daughter's help in the home, if she married and left.

To the sons-in-law, the advantages of 'marrying in' were obvious. Five of the 21 had fathers who were not farmers and therefore had little chance of obtaining land by inheritance from parents; nine of them had other siblings working at home and better placed in the family to inherit their parents' farm; six of them had parents whose farms were too small to support a family without working off; and one had been refused the tenancy of his father's farm by the landlord.

---

652 farmers in England and Wales 76 per cent were trained by parents or relatives, 72 per cent completed their education at the age of 15 or less, and 11 per cent had Farm Institute, College or University training.

Marrying a wife with a farm did not enable these men to begin farming on their own account any earlier than those who married before or at the time of taking over a farm from their own parents (Table 103a), but they were able to marry at a much earlier age (Table 103b) and avoided the risk of remaining single which had to be taken by those who inherited from parents.[1]

Table 103: Succession of married farmers to own or to wife's parents, age of starting to farm and age at marriage

a. Age of starting to farm

Succession to:	Under 30	30–34	35 and over	Total
Own parents	14	10	16	40
Wife's parents	10	3	8	21
Total	24	13	24	61

b. Age at marriage

Succession to:	Under 26	26–30	31 and over	Total
Own parents	8	11	21	40
Wife's parents	12	7	2	21
Total	20	18	23	61

Single sons on small farms who were obliged to support an aged parent, were likely to remain single, for they were not usually an attractive marriage proposition, whether in terms of age, financial position or social status. In contrast, single daughters who had to care for aged parents were in a stronger bargaining position, because of the great demand for local farms from farmers' sons. Thus they were at least likely to obtain the satisfaction of marriage at an early age (Table 104a), even though this often involved sharing a home with the widowed parent of the wife.

The strength of the demand for local farms of any sort is indicated by the preponderance of farms of under 60 acres which had been taken over from the parents of wives (Table 104b). Only in exceptional demographic circumstances was it likely that a large owner-occupied farm would pass out of the control of the male side of the family. There were five cases where larger farms had, in fact, passed to a daughter, and in two of them the farm had passed to the youngest

[1] A third of the farmers who had succeeded their own parents were unmarried at the time of the survey.

daughter, who was also the youngest child in the family. These two had stayed on with ageing parents after other brothers and sisters had married and left home. Their parents had retired in favour of the daughter and son-in-law on their marriage, in one case creating a considerable amount of bitterness on the part of the dispossessed sons, who would have liked to return to the parental farm.

Another of these five larger farms had not passed wholly into the control of the son-in-law at marriage, for his wife's only brother

Table 104: Marrying in, wife's age at marriage and size of farm

a. Wife's age at marriage

	Under 20	21–25	26 and over	Total
Married pair inherited farm from wife's parents	6	11	4	21
Others	29	54	39	122
Total	35	65	43	143

b. Size of farm

	Under 60 acres	Over 60 acres	Total
Married pair inherited farm from wife's parents	16	5	21
Others	62	62	124
Total	78	67	145

remained at home without marrying, and the two men went into partnership. This case was interesting, for this partnership arrangement had an adverse effect on the expectations of the following generation. The couple had only one child (a son) who left home at the age of 21 while still single, having estimated that he had little chance of inheriting the farm and marrying before the age of 40.

The remaining two cases where large farms had passed to daughters, involved 'all daughter' families, where the daughters who had obtained the farms were those who had married at the most opportune time in relation to their parents' ages and state of health. On one of these, the eldest daughter had married a farmer's son and left home when her father was aged 60 and both parents were still in good health. Her younger sisters remained at home and helped to run the farm.[1] After the father had passed his sixty-fifth birthday, one of the daughters married a farmer's son, who, in the local phrase, 'took his father-in-law out'. At the time of the survey, the other two sisters were in their thirties, still unmarried, and supporting their now ageing and ill parents on a smallholding, to which they had retired when the married sister and her husband had taken over the main holding. As the mother said: "They are both engaged to boys from 'over 40-cow' farms, but I don't want them to marry yet." In a case of this nature, the same friction that usually arose between brothers over the possibilities of inheritance was likely to occur between sisters, and the family tensions revolved around marriage possibilities and filial responsibilities, as well as inheritance.

Many of those farmers who had married in had worked away from home before marriage. This was an advantage they shared with those others who had an urge to farm but little chance of obtaining a family holding.[2] It gave them a source of income not dependent on the whims of their father, the size of the family holding, or the needs of their family of origin. In addition, work off the family holding usually involved travelling some distance from home to the source of employment, and often (particularly with farm work) meant 'living in', or living near their work, rather than at home. This gave them a wider spatial and occupational range within which to find a suitable

Table 105: Age at marriage, 'progressives' and other farmers

Age at marriage	'Progressives'*	Other farmers, excluding those with non-farming fathers	Total
Under 26	21	28	49
26–30	13	22	35
Over 30	7	35	42
Total	41	85	126

* Includes those with non-farming fathers and adjusted for those classified in more than one of the three groups: dual-business, self-made men, and married in.

---

[1] Where there were no sons in a family operating a farm too large to be worked by the father alone, one or more of the daughters took on the role of son, or sons. Even on small farms, when there were no sons there was a tendency for the daughters to be much more interested in farm work than those who had brothers to do the farm work.

[2] Fourteen out of 21 of those who had married in, 11 out of 12 of the dual business farmers who had not inherited a family holding and 11 out of 13 of the self-made men.

wife, and provided an opportunity for early marriage, unencumbered by family responsibilities and affiliations (Table 105).

For some, a non-conformist ethic provided the spur to work hard and save hard, without which it was impossible to progress from small beginnings. For others, the circumstances in which they found themselves at, or after, marriage, appeared to trigger off an urgent desire to succeed. It is not possible to say how much the success of these people was due to inherent personal qualities, and how much to environment. But it is not without significance that those who had married in had unfavourable demographic and farming backgrounds, whilst 12 out of the 16 dual-business farmers were eldest sons. Two of the other 'dual-business' farmers had lost their fathers at an early age, and the remaining two were members of large families and had left home before marriage. All the self-made men too, had started out with some unfavourable circumstance or combination of circumstances such as being an eldest son, having to marry because of pre-nuptial conception, father dying early or going bankrupt, father not a farmer or father only possessing a small part-time farm. Patrimony having been denied them, these 'progressives' had made good use of matrimony, thrift, and social position[1] in the course of their successful farming careers.

One incident illustrates the habits of thrift which led to success in the face of odds created by a harsh environment and lack of capital. The farmer in question had started up on a small farm, then moved to another and amalgamated adjacent land as this became available on the death or bankruptcy of the former occupants. When first visited, he and members of his family were completing the harvest of a field of hay which had been badly affected by the weather. It was dry, but some of it was of very poor quality, particularly that which had been lying in hollows or tractor wheelmarks. He agreed to be interviewed but not until the family had finished the field. I offered my assistance to complete the job. The offer was accepted; I was given a hand rake and joined the farmer in combing the stubble for any wisps of hay left by other members of the family, who were loading haycocks onto a tractor trailer. The job was almost completed when the farmer and his family departed for tea, with the request for me to "put these last three haycocks on the trailer and then clean out the hay loader". After tea, the farmer returned, and, surveying with satisfaction the spotless field and the empty hay loader, remarked, "Well, there's something in the old saying after all! Now, what can I do for you Maister?"

[1] Of the 13 self-made men, five are lay preachers, two are rural district councillors and two are prominent in the National Farmers' Union.

A contrast is provided by a dual-business farmer, the eldest son of a full-time farmer. In his early twenties he had married a girl who had worked and lived in town, and who had town-dwelling parents. He described how they had built up a large farming business from very small beginnings in less than 20 years. "I worked for my father until I got married, and for two years or so afterwards. He never paid me or my brothers anything; and, although you could manage when you were single, it wasn't much good for a married man. So we left him and went to a little place of my grandmother's, and started up there with one cow, which was all we could afford. After a few years there, the farm was sold and we had to get out. This farm was the only place available; it was much bigger than we had thought of, a long way from the road, and everything was in poor condition. We came with 10 cows and three young heifers, and were worried at first how we were going to run and stock it. We had to have something to get the milk out to the road, so we bought a Land Rover on hire purchase. We soon found that H.P. was dear money and next time we wanted something we went to the bank. After that I realized I could earn more than £6 for every £100 I borrowed—if I can buy two beasts for £50 apiece, keep them for a few weeks and then sell them for £70 apiece, that's a lot quicker money than you get many other ways. Then everything was in such poor condition, that we just had to 'set to' and fix it ourselves—the landlord wouldn't help. Now I never hesitate to go to the bank if I want any money: they can see my books, and know I'm on the right side." Risk-taking by this farmer, and extreme thrift by the other, had both achieved the same ends, but neither without hard work.

In this area, a farmer was likely to be successful if he started farming, either on a large farm inherited from his parents, or on a farm acquired with capital supplied by parents. But for a man who did not start with these advantages, success required four pre-conditions: a farm to start on; a means of gaining access to sources of capital; knowledge and contacts to enable him to gain control over more land; and a skill at handling whatever farm resources he was able to acquire.

The acquisition of a farm of reasonable size from the parents of wives was not common and, in general, those who started out in this way have not achieved a large farming business. The type of farm available from this source was usually more suited to part-time farming, with the farmer working off full-time and his wife running the holding during the day.[1] This also meant that the potential farmers, to whom this means of acquiring capital and land would

[1] Fourteen out of 21 of these farms were run on this basis.

o

appeal, tended to be those who had a non-farming job. Such farmers were not in a strong position to operate within the local system controlling the supply of land, nor had they the requisite skill to handle more should they acquire it.

Some sons of local part-time farmers, and some sons of those full-time farmers whose holdings were not large enough to employ all or any sons at home, went out to work on farms at a distance from home. If they could acquire a local wife, a farm, and enough capital to start farming, they were in a strong position for climbing the farming ladder. They had kin and friends who were farmers, and these contacts (reinforced by those of their wives) gave them a good chance of adding land to their original holding, or else of being able to find a larger farm, once they had made a successful start.

Some men married farmers' daughters whose fathers were in a position to 'set up' the daughters and sons-in-law in a place of their own.[1] When this occurred, the son-in-law could hardly go wrong if he was a hard worker and skilled at farming, for his wider experience gave him an advantage over neighbours who had never left the local area, yet he had a local network of contacts for support, advice and influence. One of these farmers explained his success on a farm in the poorest part of the area: "A lot of folks round here don't know how to farm: they can't, or won't, realize that the more stock you keep, the more grass you grow; but if you don't put plenty of lime or slag on in the first place, you can't start to build up your stock numbers." This was a heretical view in a parish where low stocking rates and almost complete dependence on the 'corn bag' were the rule.

Other men, not in the fortunate position of having parents or in-laws who could help them to start, took small places and went out to work at whatever job paid the highest wages. By this means they accumulated capital against the time when the chance of a larger farm came along or they could acquire more land adjacent to their existing holding. Their objectives were more likely to be achieved quickly if they had a small family. Those who had a large family either managed to achieve full-time farming status only after their children were of working age and were providing supplementary family income, or never managed to rise above part-time status.[2]

Dual-business farmers have made the most progress from small beginnings. They were brought up to farming and also either inherited

---

[1] As distinct from those who took over the farms of their wives' parents.

[2] Cf. the case study in Ch. VII where the farmer with the large family only managed to achieve full-time farming status towards the end of his farming career.

another trade from their parents, acquired one by chance, or realized the importance of combining another self-employed business with farming. They have had the best of both worlds, in that they started out with local parents (and consequently have an extensive network of connections amongst farmers), and their other businesses give them a means of accumulating capital from non-farm sources. Their movement about the district in furthering their other businesses keeps them well informed on farming matters, and they quickly hear about any particular developments through which stock or land is likely to become available.

Because of their contacts and position as creditors to some members of the community, dual-business farmers often have been able to acquire control over more land, or to expand their other businesses to fit in with the needs of their family developmental cycle as and when it best suited them. Many other farmers have not been so able to control their affairs, for limits to their freedom of action have been set by chance, by demographic circumstances and by economic conditions.

EFFECTS OF CHANCE AND CHANGING ECONOMIC CONDITIONS

Irrespective of their reasons for leaving home, there is a large element of chance involved in the acquisition of farms by farmers' sons if they do not obtain their fathers', those of relatives, or marry wives with farms. Some may wait for years before the type of farm they really want becomes available locally. For example, one farmer's son whose father had a large farm had waited seven years after marriage, hoping that a farm would become vacant near that of his father. He had eventually moved 'down country' when he could see no prospects nearer home. His father remarked: "He wanted badly to branch out on his own, but there was nothing available locally, so I set him up 'down country'. It's left us short of labour but I let him go."

In these circumstances it is not surprising that many couples, rather than cut their ties with an environment where they understood the farming, had many friends and relatives and had an accepted place in society, took whatever farm was available at marriage, in the hope of moving later to one more suited to their requirements. In the past, with a high proportion of tenanted farms, it had been possible for about a third of the farmers to do this,[1] usually spending a relatively short period of under 10 years on their first farm before

---

[1] Thirty-six out of the 42 farmers who had moved from a smaller farm to a bigger farm had tenanted their first farm,

moving to their second, which they would then occupy for a longer period, unless they progressed from it to a third one (Table 106).[1]

Table 106: Period of occupancy of farms by farmers who moved from farm to farm to better themselves

| | Period of occupancy | | | | |
	5 years and less	6–10 years	11–15 years	Over 15 years	Total
First farm	13	21	7	1	42
Present or second farm	9	5	6	22	42

The decrease in tenanted farms which has occurred since 1950[2] had made it much more difficult, either to obtain a reasonable farm initially, or to move from it to one more fitted to meet increasing family requirements or rising ambitions. Parents now have to find not only stock and equipment for non-inheriting sons, but also enough money for a deposit on a farm, where they cannot purchase one outright. Also, if a farmer once starts out on a farm owned by himself or his parents, he must find a willing buyer before he can consider moving to another, whether as owner or tenant.[3] In the better farming parts of the area, this is having the effect of delaying the departure of children from the larger farms, either because no farm of reasonable size is available to rent[4] or because of the unwillingness to start up on a small farm from which they may have difficulty in moving, in view of the shortage of larger farms within the range of their financial resources. There are seven farmers with farms of over 30 cow equivalents in size, who have more than one child in the family; and who have at least one of these children over the age of 30. On six of these farms, two children or more live and work at home and one of the two children is over the age of 30 and still single.

[1] This table understates the position, for it includes all farmers who were in their second or third farms, irrespective of how long they had been farming.

[2] Prior to 1950, 60 per cent of all surveyed farms in the area had been tenanted. By 1960 this had dropped to 31 per cent.

[3] The case has already been cited, in another chapter, of the part-time farmer who had to relinquish the tenancy of a better farm which he had obtained, because he could not dispose of the small one which he owned.

[4] I was told on numerous occasions of a '40-cow-and-over' farm which had been offered for rent by tender, and for which there had been 200 applicants. The successful applicant, in the words of one informant, "had paid such a high rent that he couldn't afford to employ any labour, and was growing thinner every day". The story may have been exaggerated in the telling, but it indicates the extent of local interest in large farms available for rent.

Some full-time farmers in the early stages of their family developmental cycle took the risk of starting up on a small farm only to find that now, as their family demands increase, it is almost impossible either to move to another and bigger farm or to find land available locally which they can add to their current holding. In consequence, they have low farm resources per family member. In the words of one of them, farming a holding of less than 50 acres within sight of his parents' farm: "This is a good little farm, but I could do with more land; and that's very hard to get hold of just round here."

Amalgamation is taking place now faster than in the past.[1] This makes up partially for the reduced chances of farm-to-farm mobility but, inevitably, the land available for amalgamation is either in small parcels, or is of poorer quality and situated in the parts of the area where it is difficult to make a living by farming full-time. Most of those in the better farming area who have managed to acquire more land are not able to make the most effective use of it, because of its distance from their main holding (Table 107). Thus the greater

Table 107: Nearness of amalgamated land to farmers'
main holdings and altitude of main holdings

Amalgamated holdings: situation relative to main holdings	Main holdings: altitude		Total
	900 ft. and below	Over 900 ft.	
All near or contiguous	1	28	29
Not all near or contiguous	10	23	33
Total	11	51	62

availability of land for amalgamation is not solving the problems associated with farms of inadequate size in the full-time farming areas. Furthermore, it may be creating problems for the future in the part-time farming areas by enabling some people to farm full-time there and thus foster a tradition of full-time farming, which could slow down the occupational mobility of the rising generation.

THE COMPLEX INTERRELATIONSHIPS AFFECTNG MOBILITY

The following account of movement between a number of farms over a period of 40 years, illustrates the complex interrelationships between demographic circumstances, chance occurrences and home and work

[1] Over a period of 30 years, there were 34 cases of amalgamation where whole farms were incorporated by farmers into their original holdings. Of these, 29 were amalgamated between 1950 and 1960.

experiences and influences, within which individuals have attempted to operate kinship or friendship networks in order to obtain farms of a size or situation relevant to their particular needs.

An eldest son (Farmer A1) of a self-made Farmer A, worked on farms away from home (see Fig. 1). When he was in his late thirties he married his employer's daughter, after the death of her father. The second son, Farmer A2, married a part-time farmer's daughter, worked on farms for a time and then obtained a small farm but still continued to go out to work. After the death of their mother, who was considerably older than their father, two younger sons and a daughter, Farmers A3, remained single at home with their father. The second brother's wife's uncle, Farmer B, had a large family— all of whom married except the youngest son, Farmer B2. On the death of his father (who was older than the mother) this man remained at home with his mother. Another son, Farmer B1, progressed through his lifetime from a small to a medium-sized part-time farm. All his sons worked on farms in the district, the eldest, Farmer b1, working for Farmer A1 who had no children. On the death of Farmer A, the two single sons and the single sister, Farmers A3, could not retain the tenancy of their father's farm and had to move. Farmer B2, meanwhile, had been left on his own by the death of his mother. A farm (formerly occupied by his brother, B1) became vacant, after having had a number of tenants and owners since the brother—B1—had moved to a better farm. It was nearer to B2's work and to both his brother B1 and another married sister. B2 therefore moved to it. His nephew, b1, who had inherited the farm which B2 and his mother had been occupying, sold it to Farmers A3, and they semi-retired there. A few years later, their eldest brother, Farmer A1, retired to a part of his farm and sold the rest of it to b1, who had worked with him from leaving school. The eldest brother b1 then took his younger brother, b2, into partnership to farm it, and (as both were single) they lived at home with their widowed father B1 and their youngest sister. The various farm moves are indicated in the diagram. It should be noted that the kinship-connection between the two families was through the marriage of a niece of Farmer B to a son of Farmer A; but this couple were not involved at all in the subsequent farm moves. It is unlikely that the moves would have occurred in the way they did, if b1 had not worked for Farmer A1, proving to be a conscientious worker, and if the fortuitous vacancy of a holding suitable for B2 had not arisen after his mother's death. Kinship here provided a very general link between the two families, but chance, demographic circumstances, and economic relationships determined the moves.

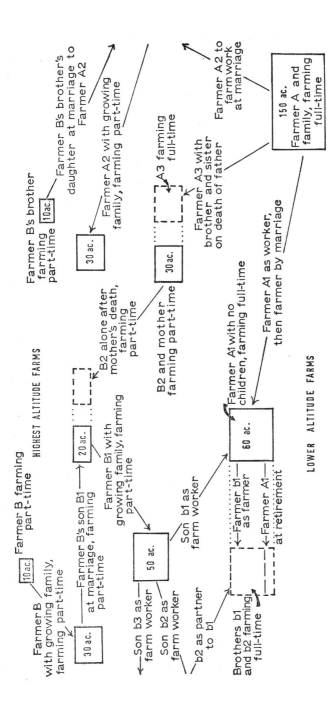

Fig. 1. *Movements from farm to farm over a 40-year period*

It is worth speculating as to the future developments, for an interesting situation has arisen by reason of the early death of the mother of b1 and b2. If the mother had remained alive, the only sister of b1 and b2 (who was 15 at the time of the survey) would probably have achieved her ambition to work in a shop in the local town and would eventually have married in her early twenties and left home. As it is, she is now obliged to stay at home to look after her father and the two single brothers (who farm a separate farm on their own account but live at home). Her brothers, who are around 30, are fast approaching the time when their marriage chances will start to diminish and consequently are anxious to find wives.[1] If one does marry however, it will break up the partnership, for the farm they jointly operate "doesn't give the two of us a fat living; we would be better off on wages; and it wouldn't support two married men and families". If a brother marries before the sister, this is likely to create a brother-sister partnership, one brother moving into the father's house, and the other into that on the farm they are at present farming but not occupying. The sister (in these circumstances) would be likely to go with the unmarried brother, and the father with the married couple. If, on the other hand, the fear of breaking up the partnership, and/or the unavailability of suitable spouses, keeps the brothers single until their sister marries, this again may result in one or both of them remaining single permanently. The sister, with a 'marriage isolate' restricted to the local area (she is likely to be very 'home-bound' catering for the needs of three men all farming), will probably marry a farmer's son who has worked at home, or one who is in non-farm work. In either case, anyone only a few years older than herself is more likely to be looking for a wife and a farm, rather than to have a farm available from parents.[2] If, then, her husband 'marries into' her father's farm, this will leave the two brothers without a housekeeper, and with only one farm available between the two of them. Under these circumstances one may marry and the other stay single (though continuing to live with his brother and sister-in-law); or both will stay single and live together, with a probable deterioration in their living conditions. Unless they can

---

[1] The eldest when discussing marriage remarked: "I've been looking round, but it's not easy you know. If you marry one from the town, or with town ways, she will be wanting a Daimler before you can afford a Ford Popular; and if you marry one of those who has been brought up on a farm, and is working at home on the farm (i.e. the only local women in his peer group likely not to be married already) she will want to be wearing the 'britches' and I couldn't be doing with that."

[2] The area is one of part-time farming. Part-time farmers tend to marry at younger ages than full-time, and therefore, if a suitor is under 30, it is unlikely that his parents will be either dead or ready to retire.

obtain control of enough extra land to make them independent of the father's farm, or unless one of them can himself 'marry a farm', both brothers will only stand a fair chance of marrying and farming on their own account if the daughter marries 'away' within about five years.

In the study area, so far as relations are concerned with incomers or with others with whom they have no close blood ties, the outward semblance of solidarity amongst kin often appears to stem from a need to conceal the internal conflicts within kinship groups. In some families these tensions emerge into open hostility and can result in estrangement between brothers. If this occurs, one brother would not attempt to conceal from an investigator his feelings towards the other. Other conflicts could be less open, rarely verbalized, and frequently never resolved. In the family discussed above, the very fact of co-operation between brothers, and of the acceptance by the daughter of her responsibilities towards her father and brothers, is concealing and postponing action which could resolve the conflicts within the family.

The stereotype of inheritance and marriage amongst farming people is based on a number of assumptions. It assumes that there will always be an heir, that such a person will be willing to inherit, and that other events will not supervene to prevent his taking up the inheritance. It further assumes that (where there are a number of children) the inheritance will be large enough to be divided, and that each will accept his share amicably, marry and depart to a farm of his own, leaving one selected child to inherit the property. This child is then presumed to continue to work for his parents (for nothing), happy in the knowledge that he will ultimately obtain the farm and be able to marry on the death or retirement of his parents. In this area the actual details of succession do not coincide with this stereotype. Lack of available farms at the 'appropriate' time; 'forced-choice' situations occasioned by sudden death, pre-nuptial conception, or action of agencies outside the family; jealousies between siblings; shortage of suitable or willing wives for the older males, and the very limited nature of family resources, all combine to create conditions under which conflict, rather than amity, is likely to prevail.

During the survey, 10 instances were discovered of disputes between brothers and sisters over inheritance, in which a settlement had been effected by a partition of property amongst the disputants. All these cases were amongst the families on full-time farms of medium to large size. There was more to quarrel over, but also more chance of everyone obtaining a share from which they could still make a decent living. If a farmer has only 12 cows, however, and four children to share them amongst, either all members of the family cease to farm and disperse to other occupations or areas; or some disperse whilst one or more of the others remain, with celibacy and isolation as concomitant possibilities to the acceptance of the inheritance. There were a number of small farms where, in the words of one informant, "the two unmarried ones who stayed at home got the lot, the others didn't even get a reminder of their mother".

The divisibility of the inheritance of large farms thus is likely to lead to a wider spatial mobility of some children. This is particularly so where families have been in an area for a number of generations and most of the farms of equivalent size are in the hands of different branches of the same family. As one wife of a larger-business farmer said: "When you get a lot of one family in an area, they tend to get on top of one another, and you get jealousies." The indivisibility of small farms, on the other hand, is a factor likely to lead to the occupational and spatial mobility of children, with an eventual 'dying out' of that particular family because a child inherits who does not marry.

The restrictions on farm-to-farm mobility during the life of individual farmers, which appear to be developing with the change-over from tenancy to owner-occupation, are likely to have different results in different parts of the area. They should result in larger farm businesses for the farmers who continue to farm full-time in those parts where land becomes available for amalgamation because of a changing part-time population and from the 'dying out' or compulsory retirement of small full-time farmers. Unless measures are taken to alleviate distress, however, these economic adjustments will be achieved only at the expense of the misery of single people, widows, widowers, and aged couples, tied to their farms by demo-graphic events in their families of origin, by the circumstances of their upbringing and by economic and social pressures all largely out of their control.

At the other end of the scale, the larger-business farmers will not be able to move as freely between farms in order to fit in with changes in their family developmental cycles and economic conditions. As a result, they will tend to have farming businesses too large for their own labour in the early stage of their family developmental cycle, or too small to provide work and support for all members of the family at a later stage. Particularly if this is associated with any increase in children working at home (married or unmarried),[1] the result could

[1] Because of the shortage of available farms locally and the continued decline in agricultural workers other than farmers' sons.

be subdivision of the larger farms. Further reduction in the employed labour force and an increase in the discrepancy between farm work requirements and the availability of family labour of working age would be likely to have effects on the farmers' sons still at school. Because of their increased participation in the farming operations during school hours, their formal education may suffer and their horizons may be limited to farming. Ultimately, this could increase still further the pressure on available land, forcing up values and rents almost irrespective of the trends in the prosperity of agriculture.

In the absence of government measures to change the course of events, the system will probably achieve a new equilibrium through family limitation and the establishment of a higher threshold of farm business size below which single farmers, barren and deserted couples will be generated.

CHAPTER XI

A SUMMARY OF THE MOBILITY OF
FARM PEOPLE IN THE AREA

THIS study was carried out in an upland farming area which has few local sources of employment other than farming within its boundaries. Population in the area has been declining for over one hundred years, and there is now a low density of population with the people mainly living in scattered farmsteads. The farms are at a disadvantage compared with many others producing the same products; and, on the majority of them, incomes from farming over the decade 1950–60 never rose above the level of agricultural wages.

Almost 80 per cent of the farmers are engaged in dairy farming, the only other type of farming of any importance being cattle rearing. The farms vary in size from a few acres to over 200 acres, but the variation in soil and climatic conditions associated with an altitude range of 700 ft. to 1600 ft. is such as to make measurement of size of business in terms of livestock-carrying capacity more meaningful than in terms of acreage. In these terms 60 per cent of the farms have a business size of less than 15 cow equivalents.

Approximately half the farm families are dependent wholly on the produce of their farms for all the family-earned income. The other half have sources of earned income from other occupations off the farm, undertaken by one or more members of the family living at home. For 81 per cent of the families, farm resources, numbers of people in the household, and off-farm supplementation are reasonably balanced; but for the remaining 19 per cent, farm resources per family member are low, and supplementation by off-farm work is absent or inadequate. Of the full-time farming families, half operate farms of less than 15 cow equivalents, and it is amongst these that most of the families with inadequate resources are to be found. Others with inadequate resources are mainly families in which neither parent works off the property, although one or more of the children do so.

One hundred and forty-five of the farmers are, or have been, married, and 38 per cent of these married families are in the early phase of their family developmental cycle, 46 per cent are in the middle phase, and 16 per cent are in the late phase. More of the 27 unmarried farmers are over than under the age of 45; and only one is under 35 years of age. Most of the unmarried farmers are dependent for a living on the resources of their farm and the majority of them live on small farms, as do the families in the late phase of their family developmental cycle. These latter are widowers, barren couples, and couples all of whose children have left home. Unmarried farmers and 'late phase' married farmers, together with some 'early phase' farmers with large families, make up the bulk of the problem families amongst whom farm resources, numbers in the household and supplementation by work off the farm are not well balanced.

Amongst the 633 family members living on the farms there are 82 females for every 100 males. This difference between the sexes is due mainly to the much greater number of unmarried sons than unmarried daughters, who are of working age but who live at home, and of unmarried male farmers than unmarried female farmers. The difference in the numbers of males and females reflects the wider spatial and occupational mobility of daughters of farmers compared with sons, and provides the key to the mechanism of farming replacement which operates in the area.

The majority of the farmers are sons of farmers (81 per cent), but, as indicated in the foregoing paragraphs, by no means all the farming families consist of the 'ideal family unit' of father, mother and children, which will be able to perpetuate itself on its present, or another, farm. An imperfect biological replacement process, together with out-migration of some farmers and their children, are essential to the continuation of a system whereby the majority of farmers are sons of farmers. Without subdivision of holdings or the creation of new farms from unoccupied land, more than one son per married farmer can become farmers only if some siblings share a farm, some farmers do not marry, some married farmers do not have children, some leave the industry part-way through their career, and some children do not follow their fathers' occupation of farming.

Of the farmers surveyed, 29 per cent are unmarried farmers, childless couples with the wife over the age of 45, or married couples and widowed persons who have no children living at home. In addition, an indeterminate number of current farmers will not complete their active life in farming, or will move to another farm outside the area. The death, retirement or movement of all these people will ultimately provide chances of a farming career in the area for those sons of farmers who will not inherit their father's farm, or who do not 'marry into' a farm, as well as for any potential entrants from outside the industry.

The incidence in the past of celibacy, barrenness, out-movement of farmers and dissociation of children from their parents' farms, will have had an influence on the number of current farmers who have followed relatives on their farms. The higher the incidence, the fewer the current farmers who will have direct familial associations with their farms. In fact, 48 per cent have followed parents or relatives of themselves or their wives on the farm they are occupying at present. Of the married farmers who have followed parents or relatives, two-thirds have followed the farmers' parents or relatives, and one-third have followed those of their wives. The lack of continuity is not due, in any great degree, to people inheriting family farms and then moving to other farms, for only slightly more, 51 per cent, began their farming careers on a family holding. Movements of people away from family holdings have been more or less balanced by movements of others back to family holdings after starting to farm away from them. Thirty per cent of all farmers have moved from one farm to another during their careers, but only a third of these mobile farmers started to farm on a farm previously occupied by a parent or a relative of the farmer or his wife.

It is probable that the proportion of farmers who succeeded relatives in the previous generation was also about a half, for only a quarter of the present farmers, or their wives, have lived on their present holdings since childhood. This concept of a halving of family associations with all farms in each generation is further supported by the fact that only 15 farmers can claim family associations of over 100 years with their current farms.

An estimate of the future position (based on the current occupation and place of abode of children from 66 families where all children are of working age) indicates that 40 out of 203 sons and daughters are likely to take over from parents. This represents 45 per cent of the 89 farms occupied by the 66 families, by 16 unmarried farmers over the age of 45, and by seven childless couples with the wife over 45. Forty-eight per cent of the current occupiers of these 89 farms followed parents or relatives—the same proportion as for all farms.

Half the unmarried daughters work at occupations other than farming, compared with one-third of the sons (although half the married sons and sons-in-law are not engaged in agriculture). Only a quarter of all sons are married, however, compared with two-thirds of the daughters. Married and unmarried daughters not living at home are residentially dispersed over a wider area than are sons.

On all except the smallest farms (and even on these, if the head of the household is dead) the labour requirements of the farm ensure that one or more of the children work at home. Those eldest daughters who are also eldest in the family tend to be employed at home, because they are the first children to come of working age; and daughters from families in which there are no sons may also work on the farms. Usually, however, sons are much more frequently employed at home than daughters.

This difference in employment between sons and daughters accentuates the divisions in outlook between the sexes which develop through childhood and adolescence. From an early age a boy on a full-time farm becomes immersed in farming. His home environment, his play environment, and his contacts inside and outside school are with farming, and with other sons of farmers. He absorbs a knowledge of, and an interest in, farming because of his participation in farm tasks from an early age and because of his close contacts with his father and with neighbouring kin. On family farms, he is likely to stay away from school to help with farm work in busy seasons, and his absences from school may have a detrimental effect on his formal education. A farm-reared girl will participate in the activities of the adult world too—but in the home, rather than on the farm. Often, she will share in her mother's struggles to keep house, frequently with inadequate resources and facilities, and against the farm's competing claims for time and money. To many girls brought up under these circumstances, non-farm work and life is glamorized by knowledge of other ways of life gained at school, by visits to town, by the reminiscences of mothers with experiences of work other than farming, and by their contacts with older sisters who work in other occupations.

On reaching working age, far fewer girls than boys are needed to help at home. Since there are few opportunities for work in the immediate neighbourhood, many girls take work in urban areas or in country districts at a distance from home. This widens their spatial and occupational 'marriage range' as compared with that of their brothers working at home. In addition, marriage for them is not bound up to the same extent with the inheritance of a family holding, or the availability of a local farm, as it is for the sons of farmers who wish to marry and start to farm at the same time. They thus marry at an earlier age than their male peers, and some marry into towns or into other country areas.

A number of demographic and environmental factors have an influence upon which farmers took over farms from their parents. These factors comprise birth position in the family, child's age in relation to parents', the difference in age between parents, family size, chance occurrences such as pre-nuptial conception or the early death of a farmer or his wife, together with the farm size, economic conditions and work histories of a farmer or his parents. For example, very few farmers who were eldest or only sons took over from parents, if their father had been under 25 at their birth; but relatively more youngest or intermediate sons did so in such circumstances—though often at the cost of a late age of succession.

Late age of succession to a parents' farm can result either in the succeeding son remaining unmarried or (if he does marry) in *his* son remaining unmarried. This latter may occur because a man who marries late in this area often marries a woman considerably younger than himself, dies before her, and leaves his son with a widowed mother to support for many years. Eventually the son will succeed to the farm on the death of his mother, but by that time he will be at an age when his chances of marriage are low, because many of his female peers will be married already or will have left the locality.

The circumstances which produced unmarried farmers were associated mainly with the full-time small farms where children and/ or parents had not worked off them. With larger farm businesses it was often possible to make other arrangements for the marriage of a remaining son such as dividing a large farmhouse or giving him a cottage on the farm. Alternatively, some farmers on the larger farms could afford to retire in favour of their sons (or daughters, where there were no sons), or to split their holding to allow a son to marry and start farming before the parents retired.

Daughters were less likely than sons to be left single on small farms after the death of parents. With a wider occupational and spatial mobility, those who worked off the farms were likely to have married and moved away. Furthermore, those who remained at home provided marriage partners, and a means of farming, for sons of non-farmers or part-time farmers who wanted a small farm and a wife to run it whilst they worked off at other employment.

Movement of a son or daughter away from a family holding, or out of farming, was not necessarily a matter of free choice. Pre-nuptial conception could create a situation under which family or social pressure led to the marriage of the couple concerned, irrespective of the availability of a family or non-family holding on which to start farming. Evidence from case histories, and other material, suggests that pre-nuptial conception had been used as a means of forcing parents, either to retire in favour of a son or daughter, or to provide capital and livestock to set them up on another farm.

The net result, for sons, of the competing claims of marriage and inheritance was that a lower proportion of farmers who married under (rather than over) the age of 30 took over their parents' holdings. In addition, a higher proportion of the non-inheriting farmers moved from one farm to another to better themselves; and proportionately more of them have dual businesses or work off their farms. In contrast, the highest proportion of farmers following relatives are those on full-time small farms, or who work full-time on their farms themselves but have some family member working off. These family-earning farmers tend to have low farm resources per family member and a high proportion of them have married down the social scale. Many of the other farmers on small full-time farms have remained unmarried.

Marrying down socially, marrying early but wanting to farm, or wanting (or having) to marry but not being sufficiently well placed in the family to take over a parents' holding, all these tended to create conditions under which movements up and down the 'farming ladder' occurred. A farmer's son who had worked away from home (at farm work or at some other occupation) was able to marry, once he could find a wife and a place to live. He had an occupation for the support of a family and was not tied to his parents' farm by work, close kinship association or duties. If he had been obliged to work off his parents' farm, it was unlikely that he could depend on patrimony as a source of capital for a farm of his own. This left him with the alternatives of matrimony or parsimony. If he sought a farm through matrimony, he was unlikely to become a full-time farmer, for it was usually the farmers on the small farms who were left with a daughter on the farm, and no sons. On such farms there were either no sons or the sons worked off the farm and married or moved away from home. Daughters in these circumstances married at normal ages; the son-in-law joining the household but going out to work to help support the three-generational family. Normally, the daughter and son-in-law would not inherit until both parents had died. By that time, it was unlikely that the son-in-law would be able to acquire the status of a full-time farmer. The demands of a developing family, a greater experience of other work than of farm work, and a pattern of life and standard of living geared to part-time farming (together with owner-occupation) usually ensured that the family did not wish, or were not able, to move to a larger farm which they could operate on a full-time basis.

Part-time farmers thus include full-time farmers' sons who have moved down the farming ladder by marrying a wife with a small farm which is inadequate to support a family unless the husband works off. Often this has meant a loss in social status but a gain in income. Another group of part-timers are also sons of full-time farmers. They inherited small farms and after marriage worked off them to support their family. Subsequently, they had been unable, or unwilling, to climb the ladder back to full-time farming—a move

P

which may have improved their social status, but which was unlikely to help their financial status or their enjoyment of material goods. Part-timers who are on the first rung of the farming ladder are those sons of non-farmers who have married a farmer's daughter with a farm, or are incomers from urban areas whose wives have urban backgrounds too. These incomers have entered farming part-way through their married lives—some with the object of becoming full-time farmers, but most of them using part-time farming as an end in itself.

There is also a group of self-made farmers who are sons either of part-time farmers or of full-time farmers from small farms. They have experience of farm work, gained either at home or, more commonly, on farms at some distance from home. Because of an early marriage, or the unlikelihood of inheriting their parents' holding, they started out on a small farm. Parsimony, often stemming from a non-conformist ethic, together with their having worked off the farm initially at whatever occupation earned the most money, enabled them to accumulate capital for a larger farm. Their membership of the local kinship and friendship networks enabled them to find a farm, within their means, and their experience of farming (in particular the wider knowledge of those who had worked at a distance from home) has enabled them to run it successfully as a full-time business.

The dual-business farmers are also amongst the more prosperous members of the community. Starting usually in a small way, they have built up a trading or service business in conjunction with their farming. Their trading operations provide them with a source of capital from outside the farm, and also with contacts and knowledge which enable them to put that capital to the best use in acquiring land or stock to increase their business size.

These self-made men and dual-business farmers represent approximately 15 per cent of the farmers surveyed and are the ones who have managed, within their own lifetime, to rise in farming or financial status above that of their parents. Much of the movement up and down the 'farming ladder' was a generational movement, however. Sometimes it took three generations before a family which had entered farming at the lowest level achieved full-time farming status for at least some of its descendants. In the process, many members of the various generations moved out of farming. Farmers who are sons of full-time farmers have changed their farming status least compared with their parents, for three-quarters of them are full-time farmers. In contrast, three-quarters of the farmers who are sons of dual-business or part-time farmers are in a different employment grouping from that of their parents.

Some of the immobility of sons of full-time farmers has been due to a proportion of them either inheriting or being set up by parents upon adequate-sized holdings from which there has been no need for them to move. The problem families, however, include many married or unmarried farmers who are trying to follow the full-time tradition of their parents without the necessary resources of land or capital.

Fewer wives of farmers, than their husands, have farming parents; and fewer of them with farming parents had worked at home prior to marriage. Although, for almost three-quarters of the married pairs, both the farmer and his wife were brought up in country areas and are living within five miles of their birthplace, some country-bred husbands are married to wives from urban areas, and a proportion of country-bred wives lived in urban areas prior to marriage.

Assortative mating occurred in about half of all the marriages, with farmers on the larger farms showing the highest degree and the part-time farmers the lowest. Occupational mobility of farmers and wives also took place, and this worked against the stabilizing effect of assortative mating, although its influence was *least* amongst the families on the larger farms and *most* amongst the families on part-time farms. Irrespective of the farmers' current socio-economic status, in over half the married couples either the husband or his wife have work histories which include non-agricultural work. Including employment in farm work for people other than parents, three-quarters of the married pairs had work experiences external to their own homes before marriage. The farmers on the large farms are the only ones to have a lower proportion of wives with non-farming experience. Thus, although a high proportion of farmers and wives (considered separately) are country born, of farming parentage, and have farm work experience only, a considerable intermingling of experiences and backgrounds occurred at marriage. This has affected the mobility of children, who have been influenced by the occupational and spatial dispersion of their parents before marriage, and by that of their parents' kin.

Where both parents had engaged in farm work prior to marriage, a high proportion of sons who are married, and of married daughters' husbands, are farming or working on farms. Fewer are so employed where one or other parent had not worked on farms prior to marriage; and fewer still where both parents had been in other occupations. The same relationships hold for the employment of unmarried daughters, but only where *both* parents had not worked on farms are proportionately fewer unmarried sons employed in agriculture. For those sons who have married and left home whilst their parents are still farming, and for all daughters, the movement out of farming tends to be from those families which are either the newest entrants to it, or are on the lowest rung of the farming ladder.

Those sons who are working on farms away from home are likely to develop into the 'progressives' of the next generation, the future self-made men and dual-business farmers. They represent a 'survival of the fittest' from amongst the newest entrant families, in that they have a desire to farm and have a local kinship and friendship network; but they have a wider experience of farming than have those farmers' sons who work at home on small farms. Furthermore, they are not tied to a family holding, and can thus marry early and have a long married life, independent of home, in which to build up an adequate farming business.

Many of the unmarried sons who work at home on small farms are likely to inherit either, at a late age, holdings of inadequate size, or a tradition of farming but insufficient capital or experience fully to exploit it. These are destined to remain unmarried or to marry and bring up families in near-poverty.

Sons of larger farmers are likely to be faced with difficulties, too. In the past, those not likely to inherit a family holding were able to start farming on their own account on whatever rented holding was available locally at the time they married. They could do this and be reasonably secure in the knowledge that as their family needs increased they would be able to move to another larger rented holding which they could probably stock with their share of the family inheritance. With the large changes towards owner-occupation which have occurred in recent years, there are now far fewer rented holdings available. Consequently, the owner-occupied holdings of reasonable size are tightly held in reserve within particular families, for one or other sons of the kin group. This is having the dual effect of forcing some sons away from the area in search of suitable farms, and of keeping more than one son at home on other farms.

Starting out on a small farm and amalgamating land adjacent to it is an alternative to moving from one farm to another. This process has been occurring more rapidly since the large changes to owner-occupation. Available farms for amalgamation, however, are usually the small poor ones, vacated on the death or retirement of single farmers and barren or deserted couples, or vacated by those part-time farmers who leave the industry. For kinship and locational reasons, such farms are more readily available to the part-time progressives and dual-business farmers, than they are to the sons from the larger farms. Some of these sons may have taken a small farm near to home when they married, only to find now that there is no adjacent land available for amalgamation, and no larger farm to which they can move.

Unless measures by external agencies modify the trends developing, the system of farming replacement appears to be working towards a new equilibrium. This is being achieved by amalgamation of the smallest farms at one end of the scale; by the splitting up of some large farms at the other; by family limitation amongst the full-time farmers and by a raising of the threshold of farm-business size, below which are generated single farmers, late age of marriage couples and couples whose children leave farming.

The effect of these changes will be to increase still further the proportion of full-time farms operated by farmers and their families. These are the farms on which it is most difficult to adjust income to meet changing family needs and farm labour requirements to fit in with the labour available at different stages in the family developmental cycle.

CHAPTER XII

RELEVANCE OF THE STUDY TO THE PROBLEMS OF MOBILITY IN AGRICULTURE

THIS study was confined to a small area deliberately, so that mobility patterns of farm people could be examined in detail and an analysis made of causal agents. It is necessary now to see how the mobility described for this one area compares with that for farm people elsewhere, and whether the way in which mobility operates and is determined in this area applies in other areas and situations.

FAMILY FARMS AND THE CYCLE OF FAMILY DEVELOPMENT

In the study area, almost all the farms are family-operated ones and consequently the family developmental cycle has very important effects. Most of the mobility of land and people consists of compensatory adjustments to a situation where a relatively fixed area of land is associated with a dynamic organism, 'the family', having needs and labour resources which change with the successive stages of the family developmental cycle.

Problems associated with the balancing of family resources and needs will occur wherever family farming is practised, because a cycle of development is common to all families. Sociologists have recognized the influence this cycle has on human activities[1] but, until recently, there has been a tendency in agricultural economics to look upon the family farm as a relatively fixed productive unit, vaguely referred to as 'the farmer and his family' or 'the farmer and his wife'.[2] In fact, the operation of the family developmental cycle, together with the uncertainties of demographic events, ensure that at any one time the families in an area of family farming will vary greatly in composition, numbers, productive ability and needs. Also, over time, a particular family which is associated with a fixed area of land may pass from a period of over-employment to one of under-employment, or vice-versa, merely due to family changes.

[1] See Watson and Susser, *Sociology in Medicine*. Williams, in *Ashworthy*, discusses the effect of the cycle on the efficiency of operation of farms.

[2] As late as 1959 an O.E.C.D. study defined a farm as economically viable when a 'typical' family (two full-time workers) obtain a 'sufficient' income: *The Small Family Farm—A European Problem. Methods for Creating Economically Viable Units*, O.E.C.D. Paris, 1959.

Any business system based on the family will almost inevitably vary in productivity and efficiency over time, if mobility of human and other resources into and out of it does not keep pace with the biological changes occurring.[1] This is the central problem of family farming. In the future, either ways of ameliorating hardships amongst family farmers and measures to increase agricultural efficiency must be devised to fit in with the working of the family developmental cycle, or farming will have to be restructured in such a way that it is no longer dependent upon the family for its operation.

For family farming in this country, or in any other country where the elementary family[2] is the basic unit, situations can be postulated which will vary with the different stages in the cycle of development of the farm family.[3]

Situation 1: Where the farm resources are adequate to support the people living on the farm during the first stage of the cycle of family development.

In this situation, the labour of the farmer and his wife may be sufficient, or not, during the first stage. This will depend on the size of the business unit needed to support the family. Where the labour is adequate for this stage there will be underemployment in the second stage, if children remain working at home and the farmer cannot, or does not, increase his size of business by more intensive operation, addition of more land or movement to a larger holding. Should adjustment occur by reason of all children leaving home, the original size of farm business is likely to become too great for the declining powers and needs of the farmer and his wife in the last stage of the cycle. As a consequence, the farm productivity may fall.

[1] This is not confined to farming. Small shops and family businesses pass through the same cycle. Similar problems to those which arise in family farming probably occur wherever skills or goodwill and property associated with them are passed on from parents to children, under conditions where tradition, or the size of the business, discourages the employment of labour external to the family. The intermarriages between small shopkeepers and farmers, described so graphically by Arensberg in *The Irish Countryman* were all alliances of similar systems which differed only in the productive processes.

[2] The 'elementary family' refers to the farmer, his wife and children. Where 'extended' families operate farms, labour supplies and family needs are more even over time, due to the overlap of the generations. An 'extended family' farm must be proportionately larger than an 'elementary family' farm, if it is to provide adequately for the greater needs of a larger household.

[3] These stages are discussed in Ch. III. The first is where no children are of working age or there are no children. The second is where some children are of working age and living at home. The third is where all children have left home or there have been no children.

The negative correlations between advancing age and progressiveness, productivity, or efficiency, indicated in other studies,[1] can be explained as a natural reaction of farmers to their reducing vigour and reducing needs in the latter stages of the cycle of family development.

Where the labour supply in the early stage of the family developmental cycle is inadequate, there will be an incentive to adopt labour-saving equipment[2] if capital is available. Where capital is in short supply,[3] farmers may rely on child labour.[4] This latter expedient will ensure a supply of labour for the second stage of the cycle, for sons who have worked on the farm from an early age are likely to accept this as their vocation when they leave school.[5] The labour supply

[1] Sheppard, *A Survey amongst Grassland Farmers*. The Social Survey, C.O.I., 1960; H. Falding: *Precept and Practice on North Coast Dairy Farms*. University of Sydney, Department of Agricultural Economics, Research Bulletin No. 2, 1958; Thomas and Richardson, unpublished report on a problem farming area in the Pennines, 1961; Ministry of Agriculture, Fisheries and Food, *The Problem of the Small Farm Business*; Helen C. Abell: *The Exchange of Farming Information*. Canadian Department of Agriculture, August 1953; Ross Parrish: 'Innovation and enterprise in wheat farming', *Review of Marketing and Agricultural Economics*, N.S.W., Vol. XXII, No. 3, Sept. 1954; G. A. Pond, W. W. Wilcox and A. Boss: *Relation of Variations in the Human Factor to Financial Returns in Farming*. University of Minnesota, A.E.S. Bull. 288, June 1932.

[2] Here again correlates between progressiveness and age can be explained in terms of the family developmental cycle.

[3] Heady and others point out that capital is badly needed in the early stages but hard to obtain because of inadequate equity, and they state that labour productivity is high because of its shortage. They also discuss the effects on productivity of farm resources of different stages of the family developmental cycle. See E. O. Heady, W. B. Balk and G. A. Peterson: *Interdependence between the Farm Business and the Farm Household with Implications on Economic Efficiency*. Iowa State College, A.E.S. Research Bulletin 398, June 1953.

[4] H. Krier (Rapporteur): *Rural Manpower and Industrial Development*. O.E.E.C., Paris, August 1961, comments upon the tendency for farm children to be employed at home from an early age and on how this can affect their education.

[5] This point is also made in a number of other studies of farming. See for example Rees, *op. cit.*, Arensberg, *op. cit.*, Chapman, *op. cit.*, and Sheppard, *op. cit.* Lipset and Bendix, *Social Mobility in Industrial Society*, p. 221, make the general point in relation to urban employment: 'The larger the proportion of persons working in a particular kind of job in a city the greater the number of 14-year-old youths who desired to go into that occupation'. P. F. Lazarsfeld, in 'Jugend und Beruf', *Quellen und Studien sur Jugendkunde*, Vol. 8, 1931, p. 13 (quoted in Lipset and Bendix, *op. cit.*), interpreted this as follows: 'The nature of occupational choice is not determined primarily as an individual decision, but rather is the result of external influences. For the occupational impressions offered by daily life are proportional to the actual occupational distribution. The greater the number of metal workers the more frequently will young people hear about the occupation and the greater will they be stimulated to choose it.'

may then be excessive if there is more than one son. Should adjustment then occur by one or more sons leaving home after receiving a strong bias towards farming (possibly at the expense of their schooling) such children are likely to increase the demand for small farms.[1]

Situation 2: Where the farm resources are inadequate for family needs in the early stages of the family developmental cycle.

This may occur where the family has a small farm or where the household is a large one. In these circumstances, if the family remains in farming and obtains no additional land, either a low standard of living will have to be accepted or the farmer will have to supplement his farming with other work. Under both circumstances, children are likely to leave home and the occupation of farming, either to escape the poverty of full-time farming on a small farm, or because, on a part-time farm, they have come under the influence of a home and work environment not dominated by farming.[2]

During the middle stage of the cycle, if the farmer and/or his children work off the farm, the family is likely to be adequately provided for, irrespective of the production from the farm. Later, during the third stage when all children have left home, the farmer and his wife should be able to run the farm themselves, although probably only at a low level of productivity. If the farmer has worked off, pension provisions or savings should enable the couple to live in reasonable comfort. On the other hand, if only the children have worked off and then they leave home, the parents may face difficulties in attempting to gain a living solely from the farm.

When parents have married late or the early death of one parent has occurred, a child may be 'trapped' on a small full-time farm caring for one or both parents. A son in such circumstances would be unlikely to marry and the family association with the farm probably would die with him. A daughter, on the other hand, could be a

---

[1] If capital is not available initially for labour saving equipment, it is unlikely to be available later, at least not in sufficient quantity for sons to be 'set up' on farms of reasonable size.

[2] In England and Wales in 1944 fewer farmers' children from small farms took up farming than from larger ones, the proportions increasing progressively with acreage, see Chapman and others, *Agricultural Information and the Farmer*, p. 51. A similar relationship has been shown for various parts of the United States, see, for example, E. C. Young: *The Movement of Farm Population*. Cornell University, A.E.S. Bull. 426, March 1924, p. 35. Furthermore, farmers who work off their farms are usually on the smaller holdings (*National Farm Survey of England and Wales*, 1946, p. 13, Table 2). It is reasonable to assume, therefore, that the greater occupational mobility of children of part-time farmers will apply to the country as a whole and not only to the area with which this study is concerned.

potential partner for a part-time farmer or for a farmer's son seeking a wife with a small farm.

Situation 3: Where the farm resources are adequate for the farm family at the middle stage of the family developmental cycle and where the business size is sufficiently large to fully employ the farmer and at least one other member of the family apart from the farmer's wife.

This is the ideal family farm envisaged in the O.E.C.D. publication cited previously.[1] It should be clearly realized, however, that where the elementary family is the basic unit for family farming, it is only possible to provide labour from within the family for such an 'ideal' farm for about half the duration of the family developmental cycle. For the 15 or 20 years until one or more sons or daughters come of working age, either the farm will be chronically short of labour, leading inevitably to the employment of the young children, or there must be an adequate supply of farm workers available to fill the gap.[2] Furthermore, a constant supply of family labour from the middle stage onwards is only possible if there are a number of sons who marry successively and leave home, or if one delays marriage and remains at home until his parents retire. Unless the farm is large enough to provide for two families, or unless the parents retire early, such a son is likely to marry late or to remain single. Either of these occurrences may lead to the severance of the family connection with the farm. This is particularly likely to happen if an eldest or only son remains at home to inherit, for, even if the parents married late, the first-born is still likely to be in his thirties when they retire or die.

Because of the reduction in family size which has occurred amongst

---

[1] *The Small Family Farm—A European Problem.*

[2] This point, together with the effect of birth control on family farming, is illustrated well by the case of one of the surveyed farmers. He is the youngest son of a prosperous farmer who had a large family. The eldest son obtained the father's farm; all the other sons were set up on farms of their own and daughters were either set up too, or married into acceptable farming families. By the time the youngest son married, capital was running short and a reasonable farm was not easy to find in the district. Eventually his mother financed him into a sizable local farm which had been neglected and was difficult to operate. His wife, also a youngest child, had received secondary education and had a profession. They postponed having children and she continued in her profession for eight years. Very hard work on the part of the husband, skimping on labour by only employing a youth, and the additional income earned by the wife, have enabled them to develop the farm and at the same time keep up appearances with all their relatives. But postponing a family has meant that it will be 24 years from the time they started a farm before they can expect full-time assistance from a son.

farming families in this country,[1] only a small proportion of farmers will have enough sons to furnish a relatively constant labour supply for the 25 years or so from when the first child comes of working age to the retirement of the farmer.[2] For many of the others with only one son, reliance on family labour will mean either delaying still further the age of marriage or reverting to a system of three-generation households, where overlapping of generations ensures a more continuous supply of labour for operating the farm. But national trends are towards earlier ages of marriage,[3] and multiple generation households are not common.[4] These trends would appear to be paralleled in agriculture.[5]

The discussion of the three situations postulated has indicated that family farming with a fixed area of land per family is not a very efficient method of utilizing resources of either land or labour, or of meeting the changing requirements of the family. Yet family farming has persisted and, in this country and in Europe, it is becoming still more dominant, as farm workers move out of the industry at a faster rate than farmers or members of their families.[6] In these circumstances, measures aimed at increasing the average size of farms (the usual remedy advocated for increasing the efficiency of agriculture and the incomes of farmers) will reduce the total number of farmers but will not decrease the problems of family farming, unless other

[1] For the status group 'Farmers and Farm Managers', the number of live births per married women fell from 4·30 for those married between 1890 and 1899 to 2·31 for those married between 1920 and 1924. This status category, together with the 'Own Account' category, showed the highest percentage fall, see Glass and Grebenik, *The Trend and Pattern of Fertility in Great Britain*, pp. 111–12, Table 41.

[2] If the ages of marriage for such farmers and sons varied between 25 and 30 years and retirement was between 65 and 70, a family of three sons would be required to provide a labour force of father and at least one son for 25 years. On average, this would need a family of six children.

[3] *1951 Census England and Wales*, General Tables, H.M.S.O., London, p. 69, Table 23.

[4] M. Young and P. Wilmott: *Family and Kinship in East London*, London, 1957, Appendix 6, Table 30, p. 211. This suggests that 6 per cent of households were three and four-generation households in Bethnal Green and 12 per cent in Great Britain in 1951.

[5] In my survey, 12 per cent of the households were three-generation households. In Ashworthy farm families there were 3 per cent, and in Llanfihangel and Gosforth 16 per cent. In Ashworthy, farms were relatively poor and many people moved from farm to farm. Mobility was not so marked in the other areas. Wibberley states that there has been a general decline in three-generation households on farms in Europe: G. P. Wibberley; 'The changing structure and function of rural communities' in *Changing Patterns of Rural Organization*, 2nd Congress European Society for Rural Sociology, Bonn, 1961, p. 27.

[6] In Ch. I, p. 5.

compensatory measures are taken. These should be designed to level out the supply of labour required for the operation of family farms throughout the family developmental cycle, to encourage the retention of hired workers for the operation of the larger farms and to ensure that adequate sources of non-farm remuneration are available for members of farming families.

In the absence of official intervention, members of farming communities make their own adjustments to meet the difficulties involved when attempting to balance land resources, family needs and family labour. Three types of adjustment occur in the survey area:

1. Movement of some farmers from farm to farm and of some land between farms;
2. Partial or complete occupational mobility of some farmers and some members of their families;
3. Involuntary demographic wastage.

Similar adjustments are likely to occur in other areas of family farming but the degree to which each type of adjustment occurs will vary with the particular demographic circumstances, and the home and work environments which influence farmers in the areas concerned.

Some general principles governing each of the three types of adjustment are suggested in the following pages and these principles are related to differences and similarities between mobility of farm people in the area of study and elsewhere.

MOVEMENT TO OTHER FARMS AND LAND AMALGAMATION

On the assumption of a relatively fixed total area of farming land, the amount of movement of farmers between farms, and of land between farmers, is governed by:[1]

i The rate at which established farmers die or retire;
ii The rate of movement out of farming by farmers who have not completed their working life;
iii The rate of movement into and out of farming by farmers' sons;
iv The rate of entry into farming of people from other occupations;

[1] I realize that the availability of capital, economic conditions in farming and other industries, and some degree of personal choice, all enter into the mobility decisions of farmers. The intention here, however, is to examine the effects on farm-to-farm movement and land mobility of spatial and occupational mobility of farm people and of demographic wastage from farming families.

v The degree to which children or relatives of farmers succeed parents or relatives on the same farms;

vi The rate of movement into and out of a defined area by farmers and their sons searching for farms.[1]

Farm-to-farm movement is a chain reaction. Opportunity for the reaction to occur is created when a farmer dies or retires without children or relatives taking over the farm, or when a farmer leaves the occupation part-way through his career (or when a farmer leaves any particular area to farm outside it).[2] The reaction ceases when a vacated farm is amalgamated into an existing one, or when a vacated farm is taken up by a new recruit to farming (or by a farmer from another area). The recruit may be a farmer's son who has not farmed on his own account previously, or he may be someone from another occupation. Between the beginning and the end of the reaction a number of farmers may move from one farm to another.

The amount of movement from farm to farm in any given time period will depend on the *length* of each chain reaction and the *frequency* with which new reactions start. The length of the chain is determined by the pressure of new recruits wanting farms and by the demand for land from established farmers wishing to augment their existing holdings. The frequency with which new reactions start depends on the amount of demographic wastage amongst farm families, the amount of movement out of farming (or the district) by established farmers and the degree to which children of farmers do not follow their parents on the same farm.[3]

In theory, there would be economic advantages to be gained from a farming structure in which farmers and land could move freely between farms, and in which the farming population was young,

[1] This may be considerable in some areas but for the country as a whole the rate would not be very appreciable, for it would only apply to farmers and sons emigrating or immigrating in search of farms.

[2] The explanation presented in this and the next paragraph refers to the farming industry as a whole, when read without reference to the phrases in brackets. If these are included, it refers to any defined farming area.

[3] Williams in *Ashworthy* indicates the number of farm changes occurring over certain time periods and he shows how land becomes redistributed between farms over time (Ch. II). He does not distinguish clearly, however, between turnover of farms due to families leaving farming or dying out, and turnover due to farmers moving from farm to farm. He also explains the movement as being a consequence of the attempt by farmers to set up all their sons on farms of their own. This is not an adequate explanation. However much a farmer desires to set up his sons, or they wish to farm, the opportunities to do so only arise when farms become vacant. In any one area and time period this depends on demographic and occupational wastage from farms, and not upon the desires of farmers to set up all their sons on farms.

vigorous, and with experience of other occupational environments. In practice, these ways of achieving greater farming efficiency cannot all operate effectively at the same time for any one area.

Circumstances are most favourable for amalgamation of land when demographic and occupational wastage from farming is high and when there is a low demand for farms from farmers' sons and others. Such conditions, however, slow down movement from farm to farm amongst owner-occupiers, who are only likely to move when they have assured buyers for their current farms at prices which will enable them either to buy and stock larger farms or to semi-retire to smaller ones. Where intake is low and wastage high, replacement will be mainly from within the occupation and the average age of farmers will be high.

Movement from farm to farm will be feasible when inward pressure is high and wastage is high, but demographic and occupational wastage from the larger farms is not likely to be high when economic conditions are favourable enough to encourage farmers' sons and others to compete for farms. Consequently, opportunities for movement from smaller to larger farms, or for new recruits to move into the larger farms, will only occur under such conditions if wastage from small farms is higher than from large ones, thus enabling farmers from the larger farms to vacate their farms by semi-retiring to a smaller property. Alternatively, much of the intake of farmers' sons and others may occur at the bottom end of the farming ladder because of the unavailability of larger farms.

There will be low movement from farm to farm and few opportunities for amalgamation when pressure for farms is high and where wastage is low, since turnover of farms will be low and the demand for farms will keep chain reactions short.

Details of mobility trends in the United States, Britain and Ireland, illustrate the relationships between intake, wastage, farm to farm movement and amalgamation. In the United States, the proportion of farmers' sons taking up farming has probably almost halved between successive generations. Anderson[1] shows that in two New York State counties 31 per cent and 43 per cent of farmers' sons are farmers themselves compared with 50 per cent and 77 per cent of the sons of the grandfathers' generation. This analysis is supported by figures of 30 per cent and 38 per cent for farmers' sons taking up farming around 1950, as quoted by Lipset and Bendix, and by Young's estimate (made in 1920) of about 70 per cent as the proportion engaged in farming of all men brought up on farms in

[1] Anderson, *Transmission of Farming as an Occupation*, p. 16.

New York State.[1] Thus in the United States the pressure of sons entering farming has been progressively reduced. This reduction has been accompanied by a lengthening of the average period of occupation of farms[2] (which provides some indication of a slowing up in movement from farm to farm[3]), by an increased rate of reduction both in the number of farms[4] and in the proportion of people engaged in agriculture,[5] and by an accelerated rate of increase in the average size of farm.[6]

There has not been a similar reduction in the pressure of sons on the farming industry in Britain, judged by the comparatively small

[1] See Lipset and Bendix, *Social Mobility*, p. 21; and Young, *Movement of Farm Population*, p. 16.

[2] Around 1910 the average period of occupancy for free owners was 14 years, that for mortgaged owners 9·2 years, for cash tenants 3·8 years and share renters 2·6 years—quoted by Ashby and Davies, *op. cit.*, p. 11, from *Agricultural Year Book of the United States*, 1923, p. 594. At the 1940 census, owners had occupied their holdings for 17 years, tenants for 6·0 years and share renters for 4·0 years—quoted by J. Ackerman and M. Harris (editors): *Family Farm Policy*, Chicago, 1947, p. 89.

[3] Average lengths of occupation of farms are often used uncritically as a measure of degree of movement from farm to farm. They actually measure rate of turnover of farms which is not the same thing. Occupation lengths are related to the ages at which farmers commence farming and the ages at which they die or retire after a full career in farming; they are affected by the proportion of farmers who do not complete their working life in farming and they also reflect the amount of movement of farmers from one farm to another. Consequently, the amount of movement from farm to farm at different time periods will only be accurately measured by lengths of occupation if the proportion of farmers leaving farming partly through their careers is the same for the different time periods, and if no changes have occurred in the ages of starting to farm and of retiring or dying.

[4] Between 1930 and 1940 the number of farms decreased by 3 per cent, between 1940 and 1950 by 11 per cent and between 1950 and 1959 by 18 per cent—calculated from U.S. Bureau of Census, *Statistical Abstract of United States 1960* (Eighty-first Edition), Washington D.C., 1960, p. 615. Although the number of farms in the United States has been considerably reduced, the tendency has still been towards an increase in the proportion of family-operated farms. See: *Family and Larger-than-Family Farms*, Agricultural Economic Report, No. 4, U.S.D.A. Farm Economics Division, January 1962, conclusions, p. 30.

[5] This was   30·1 per cent in 1920
                 24·8 per cent in 1930
                 23·2 per cent in 1940
                 16·6 per cent in 1950
                 12·0 per cent in 1959
Statistical Abstract U.S. 1960, p. 615.

[6] The average acreage of farms in U.S.A. increased by
                 11 per cent between 1930 and 1940
                 24 per cent between 1940 and 1950
                 17 per cent between 1950 and 1954
Ibid., p. 621.

drop between 1851 and 1951 in the number of relatives working on farms,[1] and by the high percentage of farmers' sons either currently engaged in agriculture or destined for the occupation.[2] In keeping with these trends, there has been virtually no change in the number of farmers in Great Britain,[3] little change in the average size of holdings or the median of acreage distribution[4] comparable with farm-size changes in the United States, and very little change in the average lengths of occupation of farms.[5]

Average national figures may often conceal opposite trends occurring in different sectors of the farming economy. Thus, amalgamation is common in my study area, particularly of the smaller poorer farms, but the proportion of farmers who moved from farm to farm during their careers is lower than in Ashton's survey (30 per cent compared with 43 per cent). On the other hand, Ashton found little evidence of amalgamation, but the pressure of people entering from other occupations was higher and more farmers' sons were likely to take up farming than in my area of study.[6] These findings support the statement made earlier that amalgamation is not compatible with a high intake of farmers under conditions where there is no new land available for development.[7]

---

[1] Bellerby, 'The distribution of manpower in agriculture and industry 1851–1951', *Farm Economist*, Vol. IX, 1958.

[2] From two-thirds to three-quarters of all farmers' sons, Ashton, *op. cit.*, Chapman and others, *op. cit.*, and the present study.

[3] Bellerby, *op. cit.*

[4] D. K. Britton: 'Are holdings becoming larger or smaller?' *The Farm Economist*, Vol. VI, No. 7, 1950, pp. 188–97.

[5] Ashby and Jones, *op. cit.*, pp. 8–11, quote 15–16 years as the average length of occupancy for tenants in England and Wales in 1919. *The National Farm Survey*, p. 33, gives 13·5 years as the average length of occupation for all farmers in England and Wales up to 1941. Ashton, *op. cit.*, p. 153, gives 14·7 for his sample of farmers in Oxfordshire and Warwickshire in 1950 and for my own survey the average length of occupation was 14 years. Even for the 1955 national sample of small farm businesses studied by Ashton and Cracknell, *op. cit.*, p. 12, occupational length was stated to be 15 years.

[6] In Ashton's survey 69 per cent of the farmers were sons of farmers and 73 per cent of farmers' sons were farming or doing farm work. In my survey 81 per cent of farmers were sons of farmers and 63 per cent of farmers' sons were farming or doing farm work.

[7] It is of significance that a successful policy of farm amalgamation is operating in Sweden, where the proportion of farmers' sons entering farming (35 per cent) is lower than in most other European countries. See W. J. Thomas: 'Swedish agricultural policy since the War', *Agricultural Review*, Vol. III, No. 11, April 1958, pp. 36–41.

Amalgamation of existing farms can occur more easily when new land is available because some farmers move from existing farms to new farms and some farmers' sons and some incomers take up new farms. How much amalgamation

The farms which Ashton studied in Oxfordshire and Warwickshire were larger and on much better land than the upland farms with which this study has been concerned. The absence of amalgamation amongst the larger, better farms of Ashton's survey, and amongst the larger farms in this survey, is in line with the changes which have occurred in the number of holdings of different sizes in England and Wales. Over the period 1885 to 1955 only holdings in the 50–100 acre size group have increased in number, those in the 100–300 acre group have decreased least whilst decreases of 31 per cent and 23 per cent respectively have occurred in the number of those holdings of under 20 acres and over 300 acres (Table 108).

Table 108: Percentage change in number of holdings,
England and Wales 1885–1955*

	Size groups of holdings					
Time period	Under 20 acres %	20–50 acres %	50–100 acres %	100–300 acres %	Over 300 acres %	All holdings %
1885–95	−7	+3	+4	+2	−6	−3
1895–1913	−4	+4	+3	+1	−6	−1
1913–21	−7	+4	+4	−1	−11	−3
1921–31	−10	−6	+2	−2	−6	−7
1931–39	−10	−6	−2	−1	0	−6
1939–50	+7	−6	−2	−2	+6	+2
1950–55	0	−3	0	−1	0	−1
1885–1955	−31	−10	+9	−4	−23	−19

* Calculated from *Scale of Enterprise in Farming*, p. 9, Table II.

In terms of the theory of mobility developed in this study, these changes can be explained as follows:

At the bottom end of the scale of farm size, farms have become available by demographic and occupational wastage.[1] These have been amalgamated by neighbouring farmers on similar sized or rather

---

occurs will be influenced by rates of occupational mobility into and out of farming, together with the rate of development of new land. In Western Australia, the rate of development of new land between 1940 and 1960 has facilitated a 14 per cent reduction in the number of holdings of less than 2,000 acres without any appreciable change in the total number of holdings in the State.

[1] Sons of farmers on small farms and son of part-time farmers, who are mainly on small farms, are more likely to leave the occupation than those on larger farms. Moreover, demographic wastage is higher due to celibacy and barrenness.

larger farms, who have thereby been able to continue to farm full-time. As economic conditions have made it less easy to make a living from full-time farming on the smallest farms, so the threshold of farm size below which full-time farming does not give a decent return has risen; and amalgamation has occurred amongst the farms previously operated full-time. Thus, up to 1931, the 20–50 acre group was probably gaining from the under 20 acre group but, from then onwards, the 20–50 acre group began to lose numbers. At the other end of the scale, the 100–300 acre group probably gained numbers at the expense of the over 300 acre group. This probably occurred because of the splitting of larger farms under the pressure of sons wishing to farm, and because of the difficulties of maintaining multiple holdings intact where partible inheritance operated.[1] Again, however, the trend was reversed after 1931, when the over 300 acre group gained numbers and the 100–300 acre group lost numbers (Table 108).

There are three broad groupings of farmers involved in these changes: part-time farmers, family farmers and farmers dependent upon employed labour. Over time, the threshold of farm size separating each of these groups has probably risen with changes in the national and farming economies. The middle group, organized on a family basis, has increased in importance, however, as hired workers have left farming at a much faster rate than family workers,[2] and as the proportion of farms with two or more regular hired men has decreased.[3] In terms of holdings the only size group to have increased in numbers is the 50–100 acre group. Most of the holdings in this group are likely to be family farms when not operated in conjunction with another holding.

Irish statistics show similar trends in the changes in the number of holdings of different sizes, but there the largest decline has been in holdings of under 15 acres, with increases occurring in the 30–50 acre group as well as in the 50–100 acre group.[4]

For Ireland, the changes which have occurred in the number of

[1] Britton, 'Are holdings becoming larger or smaller?' p. 192, suggests that, up to 1933, more land was involved in the partition or dismemberment of holdings of over 160 acres than was involved in the reverse process of amalgamation.

[2] Bellerby, 'Distribution of manpower in agriculture and industry 1851–1951', p. 3.

[3] For details of comparisons between 1851 and 1951 see J. A. Mollett: 'The size of farm staffs in England and Wales in 1851 and 1951', *The Farm Economist*, Vol. VI, No. 6, 1950, pp. 150-3. For the position in 1957 see Hirsch, 'Manpower on British farms', p. 534, Table 6.

[4] *Commission on Emigration and Other Population Problems*, Reports, Dublin, 1954, pp. 43-5, Tables 28 and 29.

farmers operating farms of different sizes can be compared with the changes in the number of holdings of different sizes.[1] As would be expected, the greatest decrease in the number of farmers has been in the small acreage groupings and increases have occurred in all farm size groups over 30 acres. The percentage decrease in the total number of farmers between 1926 and 1947 was 7·3 per cent, while the decrease in the total number of holdings between 1931 and 1949 was 5·1 per cent.

For England and Wales a similar decrease has not occurred in the number of farmers as the number of holdings has decreased. Between 1885 and 1950 the number of holdings decreased by 19 per cent, but between 1891 and 1951 the number of persons describing their occupation as 'farmers' increased by 17 per cent. Thus, although there has been a big decrease in the number of small holdings, some of this decrease has probably helped to maintain an increased population of 'family farmers' on rather more farms of medium size.

There has been a decrease in the number of farmers in Scotland over the period 1891 to 1951.[2] Presumably some of this decrease has contributed towards the increased number of farmers in England and Wales, due to the migration of farmers from Scotland to England.[3] Even if all the reduction in Scottish farmers could be accounted for in this way, which is most unlikely, this would still leave a net internal increase in the number of farmers in England and Wales.[4]

[1] In the *Commission on Emigration and Other Population Problems*, Reports, census figures for *farmers* are broken down by *farm size*, Table 20, p. 34. Elsewhere the distribution of *holdings* by size is presented pp. 43–5.

[2] From figures given by Bellerby in 'The Distribution of Manpower in Agriculture and Industry 1851–1951', p. 3, Table 1, this decrease is 28 per cent. Bellerby's figures do not agree with those given by G. F. Hendry: 'Labour in Scottish Agriculture', *Journal of Agricultural Economics*, Vol. XI, No. 4, January 1956, p. 416, Table 1, also stated to be taken from the Census of Population. Hendry's figure of 52,000 for 'farmers' in Scotland in 1951 is incorrect. The Census figures are: farmers and crofters 39,186, retired farmers and crofters 7,210, sons and daughters of farmers and crofters 5,719. The figure to compare with previous Census figures is that for farmers and crofters 39,186, not 52,115 which is the total of all the above categories.

[3] This occurred from 1880 onwards and was still in progress in 1932 when the problem was studied by E. Lorrain-Smith: *Go East for a Farm*, Agricultural Economics Research Institute, Oxford, 1932.

[4] The number of partnerships has increased in the past 20 years. This would probably increase the number of farmers' sons describing themselves as 'farmers' for census purposes and may help to account for the number of farmers under the age of 25 doubling between 1931 and 1951—from 5,000 to 10,000. The largest increase in numbers and proportion, has been in the age groups 35–44 and 45–54,

PART-TIME FARMING AND RURAL TRADES

One interpretation which may be put on the above figures is that the number of part-time farmers with a full-time other job has decreased, whilst that of the full-time farmers on family farms has increased. This could be due, partly to a new generation of full-time farmers taking over holdings formerly held by part-time farmers, partly to former part-time farmers changing over to full-time farming and partly to farmers with a full-time job reporting themselves as 'farmers' for census purposes.[1]

In numerous studies carried out at different times in the past 20 or 30 years, part-time farmers have been shown as those occupying the smallest holdings.[2] But it is these small holdings which have decreased most in the period under consideration. It is reasonable to expect therefore that the number of part-time farmers occupying such holdings has been affected by the rapid rate of decrease, but that this would not show up in the census figures if those farmers with a full-time job normally reported themselves under that job and not as farmers.

Further support for the contention that there may have been a decline in the number of part-time farmers comes from the reductions which have occurred in the number of rural craftsmen and in non-agricultural rural workers.[3] The blacksmiths, wheelwrights, joiners and many of the country tradesmen have gone, and to the publicans who remain, time spent in renovating their properties in order to attract the car and coach trade is likely to prove more remunerative than time spent on milking cows or rearing fat cattle.

---

in which the increase over the 1891 figures has been 17,000 and 19,000 respectively, or 38 per cent and 39 per cent.

[1] The two age-groups with the largest percentage increases over the 1891 returns were those which would be recruited to farming from 1920 to 1950. From the early 1920s to the mid-1930s, other full-time jobs to supplement farming may well have been difficult to obtain in many farming areas. In that part of the period 1931–51 when conscription was in operation, some recruits to farming may have found it politic to go into full-time farming, or to report themselves as 'farmers' for census purposes.

[2] E. Thomas and C. E. Elms: *The Farms and Estates of Buckinghamshire.* Survey Studies 4, Part 1, Bulletin LI, Agricultural Economics Department, University of Reading, 1938; *National Farm Survey of England and Wales 1946*; Butler, *The Small Farms of Industrial Yorkshire*; Ashton and Cracknell, 'Agricultural holdings and farm business structure in England and Wales', *op. cit.*; and the present study.

[3] This has been well documented by W. M. Williams; *The Country Craftsman*, London, 1958, and by Saville, *Rural Depopulation*.

Conditions favourable to part-time farming exist in some areas where there are industries situated in the countryside, or where urban industrial centres are within easy reach of farming people. Thus, in my study area, 34 per cent of the farmers have other full-time work or have another self-employing business, and in parts of the West Riding of Yorkshire where farms and factories are intermingled, the proportion of part-time farmers is very high.[1] In contrast, part-time farmers comprised 16 per cent of the farmers surveyed by Ashton in Oxfordshire and Warwickshire,[2] where it is reasonable to expect that farms would be further from sources of industrial employment. Part-time farmers in Gosforth were rather more prevalent at 23 per cent[3] than in Ashton's survey. The description of the Gosforth parish given by Williams suggests that this was because the area at that time still retained some of the features of the rural social organization of the previous century.

In general, part-time farming would seem to be concentrated nowadays in those areas within easy reach of urban employment. A rough indication of this can be obtained from the proportion of farmers with another full-time occupation in various counties, as recorded in the National Farm Survey.[4] Thus the counties with 20 per cent or over of farmers with another full-time occupation are concentrated around London, in or round the Black Country, and in the industrial or mining and quarrying counties of Wales.[5] Those counties with less than 10 per cent of farmers with another full-time occupation are the typically agricultural counties such as Cornwall, Norfolk, Lincoln (Holland) and the North Riding of Yorkshire.[6]

[1] Only 55 per cent of the farmers surveyed in Butler, *The Small Farms of Industrial Yorkshire*, were farming full-time.

[2] Ashton, *Social Origins*, calculated from data on p. 136.

[3] Williams, *Gosforth*, calculated from Tables 2 and 3, Appendix II, p. 208.

[4] There is a great need to standardize definitions of the different types of part-time farmer. I use the term to identify farmers with a full-time other job or business. The National Farm Survey follows Thomas and Elms and distinguishes between part-time farmers—those with another business but with farming still their main occupation (viz. 'dual-business' farmers), spare-time farm occupiers with full-time other employment plus a farm, and hobby occupiers. The position is further confused by the use of the term 'part-time farmer' to indicate a farmer who has a farm with less than a stated number of 'man day equivalents' of stock or crop units, irrespective of whether he has a supplementary job or not, see Ashton and Cracknell, *op. cit.*, and P. M. Scola: 'Problems of farm classification', *Journal of Agricultural Economics Society*, Vol. X, No. 1, June 1952.

[5] At the 1951 Census all these counties, with the exception of Shropshire, had less than 1,000 persons employed in Agriculture per 10,000 occupied persons. See Census 1951 Industry Tables, Table A.

[6] At the 1951 Census, all these counties had well over 1,000 persons employed in Agriculture per 10,000 occupied persons. Lincoln (Holland) had the lowest

Without carrying out a detailed analysis of nineteenth-century census enumeration schedules, it is not possible to determine whether the proportion of part-time farmers has decreased or not in different counties. There is, however, adequate evidence of the decrease in rural industries and trades, and of the tendency for those populations in rural areas at a distance from urban development to become more agricultural in nature.[1] The number of such areas is likely to decrease in the future as the continued increase in physical mobility made possible by modern transport results in formerly remote agricultural areas becoming the residential areas for urban workers.[2] The relationship which develops between these people and those engaged in agriculture will be fundamentally different, however, from the interdependence in the economic sphere which occurred in the past between farmers and rural craftsmen and tradesmen.

In the past, farmers' children unable to farm on their own account could enter a variety of trades in the vicinity of home or in the nearest market town. These occupations and farming were mutually dependent for both trade and capital.[3] Money made in retail trading in one generation could be used by the next in agriculture and vice versa.[4] This could operate through an appropriate marriage or through a person with a family background of the one occupation returning to that occupation from the other or setting up a child in

proportion of farmers with another full-time occupation (2 per cent), and the highest number of people engaged in Agriculture (4,007 per 10,000).

[1] Wibberley indicates that many upland areas and some isolated lowland areas are becoming more and more dependent on agriculture; see G. P. Wibberley: 'Some aspects of problem rural areas in Britain', *Geographical Journal*, Vol. CXX, Part 1, 1954, p. 53. For some rural districts in Wales he shows that the primary population increased in importance by up to 15 per cent between 1931 and 1947: see G. P. Wibberley: 'Principles of land planning in relation to rural development', *Journal of the Proceedings Agricultural Economics Society*, June 1949, p. 226. See also Saville, *Rural Depopulation*, and Williams, *The Country Craftsman*.

[2] Wibberley points out that commuting over distances of 50 miles is already commonplace in America and over 20 miles it is becoming common in U.K.; G. P. Wibberley: *Agriculture and Urban Growth*, London, 1959, p. 221. A glimpse of the future is suggested by the German businessman who has a country property in Killarney and flies twice a week from Shannon Airport to attend his business in Hamburg.

[3] As late as 1930 this still applied in parts of rural Ireland, see Arensberg, *The Irish Countryman*.

[4] For example, I know one Scottish family where, over three generations, various members moved between farming and the following trades: weaving, milling, corn 'proving', malting, brewing, distilling, public house ownership, coal and corn buying and selling, selling seed potatoes, and propagating new varieties of potato.

it. It should be noted that the amount of capital required to start up in some of the rural trades or crafts was not as great as that required for farming but often there were greater possibilities of capital accumulation in trade. Consequently, one child could be set up relatively cheaply in a trade which later might bring considerable capital back to farming.

Because of the availability of these other occupations, farm-reared people or those with a family background of farming could remain in the countryside, or very close to it, and maintain their connections with kin and the farming industry, but obtain their livelihood from other activities. Although this is still possible today for some trades and in some areas, the scope for such interchange is much more limited. The 'corn dealer' of today will probably be a representative of a large compound feedingstuffs firm situated at one of the main seaports, and a farmer of any substance will think nothing of driving 30 miles or more to the cattle market of his choice, taking his wife along to do her shopping in the nearest supermarket.

Obviously, interchange of people and capital between agriculture and other occupations still occurs, but probably mainly either at the bottom of the farming scale in farming areas close to industry,[1] or towards the top of the scale, when industrialists and other wealthy men take up farms for a hobby or because they have a child interested in farming.[2] The greater proportion of children from the largest farms who receive grammar or public school education[3] probably results in a greater movement out of farming of these children compared with children from family farms.

In the past, movement into and out of farming could occur not only at the top and bottom of the scale of farm sizes,[4] but also amongst the family-operated farms in the middle. The families on these farms have now lost the opportunity for such movement, as the small family businesses in the market towns and villages have

[1] Such as my survey area and areas similar to those described by Butler in *Small Farms of Industrial Yorkshire*. Butler shows that 38 per cent of the full-time farmers in the study area had previously not been farmers or farmers' sons and that 56 per cent of the part-time farmers were not from farming families (pp. 23 and 38 *op. cit.*).

[2] In the area studied by Ashton, entry from other occupations was most frequent on farms of under 50 acres but there was an appreciably greater entry of non-farmers' sons into farms of 200–300 acres than into farms of 100–200 acres. Ashton, *Social Origin of Farmers*, p. 141.

[3] Chapman and others, *Agricultural Information and the Farmer*, p. 53.

[4] Movement such as occurred for example when miners settled on marginal land in the area of the present survey, or when fortunes made in commerce were invested in land to establish some of the largest and most progressive agricultural estates of the eighteenth and nineteenth centuries.

been replaced by large-scale organizations centred on the large towns. Thus there are now fewer chances for people to operate dual businesses and, of even more importance, children from family farms no longer have available an avenue for first-stage occupational and spatial mobility into businesses associated with farming and carrying an equivalent social status.

If we accept the theses of Ravenstein and Redford,[1] which suggest that migration from the country occurs over short distances and proceeds in waves, the elimination from the villages of most of the small family businesses has made much wider the occupational, spatial and social gap which has to be crossed by offspring from family farms in their movement from farming to urban employment. The alternative occupations available to such children now involve them either in a leap upwards into the professional classes, or in a drop in social status[2] from the ranks of self-employed farmers to that of 'the workers'. But, because of the labour demands of the family farm, few of these children will receive an education adequate to make an upward movement possible. Furthermore, their preoccupation with farming ill prepares them for industrial employment, even assuming that they were willing to accept the decline in status. The increase in the number of holdings in the 'family farm' size groups, referred to in Table 108, supports the idea of proportionately more children in this group remaining in farming now than in the past. Although some of these children will have moved down the farming scale into smaller farms than those of their parents, the evidence of this study suggests that, wherever they have had wholly farming backgrounds, they will have clung to their full-time farming status.

MIGRATION OF PEOPLE FROM AGRICULTURE

Two questions need to be answered in order to sustain the contention made in this chapter that a decrease in local occupational opportunities has been partially responsible for maintaining and even increasing the number of full-time farmers in Britain.[3] The first question is: Why have *farm workers* not been inhibited in their movement out of agriculture by the disappearance of rural occupations closely

---

[1] E. G. Ravenstein: 'The Laws of Migration', *Journal of the Royal Statistical Society*, Vol. XLVIII, June 1885; A. Redford: *Labour Migration in England, 1800–1850*, Manchester, 1926.

[2] A drop in status according to the assessment of family farmers.

[3] The contention is a paradoxical one for it rests on the same argument as that usually advanced to explain rural depopulation. This does not invalidate it, in my opinion, in the same way that the absence of a decline in the number of farmers does not invalidate the depopulation argument.

linked to farming? The second is: Why have farmers and their children in Britain been affected differently from those in other countries by the decline in rural occupations and the large increase in urban occupational opportunity?

On the question of why farm workers move from the land, one major difference between farm workers who move from the land and farmers and their relatives who do so is that a move into the ranks of the 'working class' involves farmers in a loss of status, whereas farm workers gain in status by such a move and they also benefit financially. Wages of farm workers have been lower than those for other occupations and, until recently, in many cases their standards of housing left much to be desired. In addition, the tied cottage system has made them dependent on their employers for a home as well as a job. A move away from agriculture has enabled them to achieve independence in their home lives and at the same time it has given them an increase in wages and a reduction in hours of work.[1] By contrast, a move to another occupation would involve a farmer's son in loss of status and possibly also in loss of heritable property. As long as a son remains in farming he has some hope of obtaining a farm of his own and of achieving the highly regarded status of a self-employed farmer. The farm worker, however, has no property to inherit and very little chance of obtaining a farm of his own.

A further point is concerned with the difference in skills and knowledge required by farmers and farm workers. Most working farmers and their sons possess the same skills as farm workers, but workers do not require to exercise some of the managerial skills and knowledge which are essential to the farmer. Farm management is dependent upon an intimate knowledge of land, natural conditions and people, in a relatively limited area.[2] Much of the knowledge has to be built up over a period of time, a lot of it is not applicable to other areas, and very little of it is of use in another occupation. In comparison, the skills and aptitudes of farm work are usually trans-

[1] Although some of its methods of enquiry were rather naïve, the study by W. G. Cowie and A. K. Giles, *An Enquiry into Reasons for the Drift from the Land*, Selected Papers in Agricultural Economics, University of Bristol, 1957, indicates quite clearly the strength of feeling which still prevails amongst farm workers about the tied cottage system. Recent studies in France and the Netherlands show that the reasons for leaving agriculture are principally economic ones. See the general discussion of this point in Krier, *Rural Manpower and Industrial Development*, Chapter 1.

[2] This does not mean that principles of management cannot be taught and cannot be applied to varied conditions. But most working farmers still learn by experience and not by science. Until such time as technical and economic training is an integral part of the education of most farmers they will continue to be limited in their mobility by the need to learn by experience in a particular locality.

portable within farming[1] and often out of it into other occupations. The farm worker is accustomed to working outside in all weathers, which makes him an ideal railway lengthman, builders' labourer or contractors' drainlayer.[2] In the past it was very easy to step from farm carter to brewers' drayman in the town; both tasks involved a knowledge of horses and a skill with them, and both required an ability to handle heavy weights. Today the farm worker can make the transition from tractor driving and maintenance to bulldozing, lorry driving or garage work. Also, in the past, the girl whom the farm worker married would often have worked in the town in domestic service and thus would have experience of town ways and contacts with people there. Similarly now, the wife of a farm worker will frequently have worked in the nearest town in shop, office or factory.

One factor related to the recruitment of farm workers may be holding farmers' sons on the full-time holdings. Stockmen and shepherds have become increasingly difficult to replace as the older generation of them die or retire. Driving a tractor from 7.30 a.m. to 5.30 p.m. for five and a half days per week is far more attractive to youth than is work with stock which entails rising at 6 a.m. each day to milk cows, feed bullocks or feed pigs. Stock work, too, is a dead-end job for a farm worker, if he does not wish to spend his whole life on the land, whereas the mechanical skills of the farm are highly transportable into other occupations. Consequently, where hired labour cannot be obtained for stock work, reliance has to be placed on the farmer's family and his son is likely to become practised from an early age in a job requiring skills and knowledge useful only in farming.

The farmers and farmers' sons in Britain do not appear to have moved out of agriculture to the same extent as have their counterparts in other countries. Three differences between the agricultural industry in Britain and in many other countries offer an explanation of this.

Firstly, the agricultural skills and knowledge required by farmers in Britain have been more varied than those needed by farmers practising mono-culture or a single type of animal husbandry in those countries where agriculture has been established from virgin land. Pioneer farmers, however, needed to know or to acquire by practice, many more of the skills which were provided by rural

---

[1] Williams, in *Ashworthy*, shows that the farm workers were spatially the most mobile members of the community.

[2] In France, the building trade has been shown to be an important link in the movement of workers from agriculture to industry. See Krier, *Rural Manpower and Industrial Development*, p. 72.

craftsmen in Britain. Thus, a boy growing up on a farm in a new country would not only absorb farming skills, but would also become familiar with the skills necessary for timber clearing, bush carpentry, building construction, metal working and butchery. These would be as much a part of his environmental background as would be the limited skills of a farming system based on one or two products. Consequently, a boy reared under such conditions may well find it easier to move into these ancillary occupations than into another type of farming. This would be particularly likely to occur if the local demand was high for labour in these occupations, as the economy of the country became more differentiated. Furthermore, there was no long tradition of attachment to a particular piece of land, or even to a particular locality, to hold sons, and with other occupational opportunities available to them they were not exclusively dependent on patrimony for either their livelihood or their social position. In Britain, on the other hand, farmers' sons were reared under conditions where division of labour and social differentiation were closely related and also where a long period of attachment to a particular farm or locality conferred social prestige upon a family. Farmers in the new countries had not the same urge to keep sons at home as they had in Britain, where cheap hired labour had always been available for use on family farms in the 15 to 20 years of the family developmental cycle before children became of working age. As a result, there was not the same incentive to organize the operation of the farm on a one-man basis as there was in those countries where hired labour was scarce and expensive. Under the conditions prevailing in the pioneer countries, it was therefore possible to manage without sons if they left home; whereas in Britain it was expedient to prevail upon sons to stay at home and thus save the farmer the expense of hiring labour.

The second difference between agriculture in Britain and many other countries has been, and still is, the low proportion of the actual working population engaged in agriculture and the greater proportion of hired workers in the labour force compared with other countries.

Farmers and members of their families were the main source of industrial labour in those countries where hired farm workers were not numerous, and where the agricultural population was a high proportion of the total population. Thus, if industry was to develop it had to draw its labour force from members of farm families. Whether industry pulled or increases in farming efficiency pushed people out of agriculture, the ones to leave would be farmers' children rather than farmers, except in very adverse farming circumstances. In Britain, even 100 years ago, 80 per cent of the working population were not engaged in agriculture, and three quarters of the people in agriculture were employed workers. Those workers were the people who were least tied to the farming industry by bonds of kinship, property or filial responsibilities, and they had the most to gain financially and socially by leaving.

In any country, the attractive force of alternative employment at a distance from home is likely to diminish once the number of people engaged in agriculture becomes a very small proportion of the whole population. As Lipset and Bendix and Lazarsfeld show,[1] those children most likely to be recruited into any particular industry are those in closest contact with it. Consequently, vacancies which arise in urban employment are most likely to be filled by people already living in these areas. Labour shortage would have to be acute before the demand reached out to the small proportion of the population engaged in agriculture. Even where there was such a demand, the ones likely to hear about vacancies would be those with the most direct contact with people engaged in those industries,[2] or those who lived nearest to them.[3] The kinship and friendship bonds with people in urban areas would probably be stronger amongst farm workers than amongst farmers, because of the previously greater movement away from agriculture of farm workers compared with that of farmers' families.

The above analysis suggests that it will become increasingly difficult to encourage people out of agriculture in Britain as the proportion of people engaged in it falls to an even lower level and as the farming population comes to consist to a larger degree of farmers and their immediate families. A reversal of the conditions tending to hold people to farms would seem to be necessary to effect a change. The evidence presented in this and previous chapters suggests that effective measures would be the provision of training in other occu-

[1] See p. 216, n. 5.

[2] Research by Grange shows that many school leavers hear of jobs through their kinship and friendship networks and that their friends or relatives often speak for them to employers, particularly about apprenticeships; see J. Grange: *A study of school-leavers in a Lancashire town*, unpublished research work, Manchester University, Dept. of Social Anthropology and Sociology, 1962.

[3] Hagerstrand shows that for migration from a rural parish in Sweden over a 100-year period some destinations were preferred to others, even when economic opportunities were equal. He suggests that this occurred because of an accumulation of social contacts with some places and not with others. In support of this he shows that the exchange of telephone calls at present between the parish and other areas is geographically distributed in close conformity to the migration field: T. Hagerstrand: 'A century of migration to and from a rural parish in Sweden' *Rural Migration*, Bonn, 1959, p. 147.

pations for school children, together with the provision of other occupational opportunities within the geographical and social reference area of farm people.

Farmers and children of farmers have moved out of farming to a considerable extent in other countries without necessarily having had prior training and experience of other occupations. This is largely due to the third difference between agriculture in Britain and that of some other countries, namely, that in the past 100 years her farmers have not experienced the economic and natural disasters which have driven people off farms in other countries.[1] Many farmers in the U.S.A., Canada, New Zealand and Australia walked off their farms in the years of depression following the first World War, and at other times because of droughts, dust-bowl formation or unsolved soil deficiencies.[2]

DEMOGRAPHIC WASTAGE FROM AGRICULTURE

Members of farmers' families have left the land in large numbers in countries like Italy and Ireland where farming conditions and population pressures have resulted in extreme poverty. In Ireland some reduction in the number of farms in the smallest size groups has occurred due to demographic wastage.[3] Thus, despite a high birthrate amongst the married sector of the population, there has been a shortage of children to take over the smallest farms on the death or retirement of their previous occupiers. This has resulted from the late ages of marriage of many farm people, from the relatively high proportion of single farmers, and from elderly parents carrying on alone after the migration of their families to other countries in search of work.[4] Numerous studies of Irish rural areas show that the poorer the farming district, the more remote it is from urban development and the fewer the local alternative occupations, the older will the population be and the more this population will consist of 'incomplete families'.[5] This has come about because of the greater rate

[1] Although in previous centuries the enclosures had driven people from the land in Britain.

[2] For example, in 1930 in the U.S.A. two-thirds of the farms recorded as changing ownership did so because of forced sale, mortgage foreclosure or taxation delinquency. Even in 1940 half the farms changing ownership changed for these same reasons. U.S. Bureau of Census, *Statistical Abstract of United States 1960*, p. 615.

[3] See p. 226, n. 4 and 227, n. 1.

[4] *Commission on Emigration and other Population Problems*, pp. 83–8.

[5] Calculations made from data supplied by T. W. Freeman (private communication) show that for various rural surveys in Ireland the proportion of farmers who

of emigration of young people from such areas and particularly of young women.

As birthrates fall in countries like Ireland[1] there will be fewer children available to take over from parents or relatives[2] and the number of farmers will drop unless economic conditions in farming improve relative to industrial conditions in immigrant countries. If the relative economic position of agriculture continues to decline, however, the reduction in the number of farmers amongst the smallest farms still may not be fast enough to result in an increased standard of living for the farmers who remain.

In England and Wales it seems that agricultural conditions have never been poor enough, or supplementation of farming by other occupations has never been scarce enough, for an overall shortage of farmers to occur. The reduction in the number of holdings which has taken place in some areas as 'incomplete families' have died out or people have moved away[3] would appear to have been more than made good by the formation elsewhere of new farms from smaller holdings, under the pressure of farmers' sons and others entering the farming industry.[4] This does not mean that demographic wastage is of negligible proportions in Britain. It occurs for the same reasons as

---

were bachelors, spinsters, and widows with single sons, varied from 54 per cent in the poorest most remote area, to 15 per cent in an area where farming conditions were relatively favourable and where other employment opportunities were available. Mogey reports that for Northern Ireland similar variations occurred in the proportion of married farmers and 'incomplete families' with changes in both the quality of farming and accessibility to industrial employment. See J. W. Mogey: *Rural Life in Northern Ireland*, 1947.

[1] Although the average size of completed families in the 26 counties is double that of Great Britain, there was a decrease of 27 per cent in the average size between 1911 and 1946 and decreases of 30 per cent and over amongst the higher age-of-marriage groups, which were more prevalent in the rural areas. *Commission on Emigration*, pp. 94 and 95.

[2] Where farms are owned and there is a tradition of preserving the family connection with a particular piece of land, as occurs in Ireland, other relatives are brought in to take over farms if there are no direct heirs. The poorer the farm the greater the chance that the family will have no direct heirs and the more difficult it will become to persuade other relatives to take on the farm.

[3] See *Mid Wales Investigation Report*, Cmd. 9631, H.M.S.O. 1955, in which details are given of the number of derelict holdings in the area surveyed and of the approximate length of time since they were abandoned. 782 derelict holdings were counted within the boundaries of 1,404 existing farm units. 258 of the 782 were estimated to have been abandoned prior to 1905 and the others at regular intervals up to 1954. The rate of abandonment worked out at ten or eleven holdings per year.

[4] When the agricultural population is only 4 per cent of the total population, only a very small proportion of the non-agricultural population needs to take up farming to make an appreciable difference to the total intake of farmers.

it does elsewhere.[1] Not all farmers marry and not all those who marry have children. Thus, at the 1951 Census, single farmers amounted to 18·3 per cent of all farmers in England and Wales, and, at the family census of 1946, 17·5 per cent of all farmers' wives who had married between 1920 and 1924 were childless.[2] These figures suggest that, from demographic wastage alone, somewhere around a third of all farms in Britain are likely to become available for people other than the sons or daughters of their occupiers. This is quite apart from those farms which became available because all the children leave home or because the farmer leaves farming before completing his working career. Nevertheless, all this wastage will only contribute to a reduction in the number of farms and an increase in their size, if the number of farmers' sons and others entering farming can be reduced below the number of farmers leaving the industry by death, retirement or occupational wastage.[3] The fall in

[1] Thus, rural migration of both sexes in England and Wales has been greatest from those areas with the lowest population density and with the highest proportion engaged in agriculture. (See Saville, *Rural Depopulation*, Tables IV (*a*), (*b*), (*c*), and (*d*), pp. 49–52.) These areas also have the lowest proportion of females to males and the highest proportion of single males. It is not always easy to see this from straight comparisons of population figures, because of the number of people working in urban areas who now live in rural districts. I have examined the 1951 Census figures for the rural districts in the West Riding of Yorkshire, an area which I know very well. It is clear from these that the rural districts closest to the non-agricultural industries employing males predominantly (mining and steel) have the highest proportion of married men, and that the mainly agricultural districts most remote from industry have the lowest proportion. The proportion of females to males is highest in the dormitory rural areas serving the main towns, and lowest in the remote agricultural areas: Census 1951, *General Tables*, Table 31. The details quoted refer of course to all people living in rural areas, not just to farmers. But it seems that, in areas where large farms predominate, it is farm workers rather than farmers who are affected by demographic wastage. Thus in Eskdalemuir (a parish in one of the border counties where farms are large), all the farmers are married but many of the shepherds remain single with widowed mothers or siblings. The reason for this is precisely the same as that which leads to farmers on small farms remaining single. The shepherd inherits a skill which is often restricted in application to a limited area, his cottage—part payment for the job—is often remote, and the financial and social position is not attractive to the limited number of females in the same social class. See Littlejohn, *Westrigg*. Neville Shute in *A Town Like Alice*, shows that the same demographic forces are at work amongst the Australian stockmen in the outback. In Britain, as in Ireland, it is the remotest areas which have the highest proportion of aged people in the population. See J. O'Connor and G. P. Wibberley: 'Social problems in the development of livestock rearing areas', *Agriculture*, Vol. 59, 1953, p. 564.

[2] Calculated from Tables A.70, p. 33, in Glass and Grebenick, *The Trend and Pattern of Fertility in Great Britian*, Part II, Tables.

[3] In Sweden, where a vigorous policy of land amalgamation is in operation, it

the birthrate in farming families[1] will reduce the total supply of sons and daughters available in the future and will increase the demographic wastage arising from an increased number of 'incomplete' families. The effect on the number of farmers of this reduction in potential supply and this increased wastage could be counteracted, however, by an increase in the proportion of all farmers' children entering the occupation or by more people entering full-time farming from other occupational backgrounds.

has been estimated that for every ten farmers there are only six farmers' sons who are potential farmers. See A. K. Constandse: 'Planning in agricultural regions', *Sociologia Ruralis*, Vol. II, No. 1/2, 1962, p. 96.

[1] See p. 219, n. 1.

CHAPTER XIII

SUBSIDIZING MOBILITY

UNFORTUNATE effects could arise from any trends which may be developing towards an increase in family farms and a decrease in part-time farms. The study reported in previous chapters indicates that other occupational experience in the background of farm parents is a very important influence determining whether children are encouraged to remain in farming and whether they choose to remain. Moreover, the ability and willingness of the farmer or his children to take another job may make a big difference to the standard of living of the family, or may make possible the saving of capital for farm expansion. Even in the area of study, where industrial experience was quite common, farm boys were strongly inclined towards agriculture. How much more eager to farm will they be in areas where alternative occupational opportunities are not available?[1]

The British system of income subsidization by price supports does nothing to discourage sons of farmers from following their fathers' occupation, nor will the price system proposed for the European Economic Community. Furthermore, we are likely to make the situation even worse if we continue to use direct subsidies such as the *Small Farm Scheme*, which discourages movement out of small full-time farms, freezes the size structure of small farms and puts a premium on their price.

The two alternatives seem quite plain. One alternative is to allow agriculture to run down gradually so that, in time, many more farms become marginal, demographic wastage increases, and the pressure of poverty forces small farmers out of the industry partly through their careers. Carried out with sufficient ruthlessness such a policy would undoubtedly achieve its objects of reducing the number of farmers and increasing the size of farming units. But its cost would

---

[1] Maris shows that the 'generation pressure' is greater than unity on farms of over 10 hectares in the sandy soil regions of the Netherlands where other occupational opportunities are limited. The generation pressure is a measure of the relationship between the number of sons waiting for a farm and the number of farms becoming vacant. Where it is greater than unity there will be more sons waiting than farms likely to be available, See A. Maris; 'The family farm and problems of succession and changing manpower', *Problems of Mobility of Agricultural Manpower in Relation to Economic Growth*, E.P.A. Project 7/14–11, O.E.C.D. Paris, July 1962 (restricted).

be measured in terms of wastage of human resources, of misery caused to many through no fault of their own, and wastage of social capital invested in rural areas (apart altogether from the votes lost in marginal seats). In addition, the basic difficulties inherent in family farming will still remain, so that similar problems will arise in the future amongst the reduced number of farmers as changes in technology occur and as standards of living increase amongst the non-farming population. The social and political problems of rural Ireland do not suggest that a policy of neglect is a satisfactory way of reducing a farming population.

The second alternative is to subsidize mobility of farm people rather than to subsidize farming directly. Such a scheme should have the following aims:

1. To reduce the number of farmers' children and other people entering small full-time farms.
2. To increase the opportunities for existing farmers to supplement their farming with other employment.
3. To even out the labour supply available for the operation of family farms throughout the family developmental cycle.
4. To encourage earlier ages for starting to farm, earlier normal retirement ages, and voluntary retirement, irrespective of age, for those least able to operate their farms efficiently.
5. To encourage the voluntary amalgamation of land.

The second alternative should result in a reduction in the number of farmers within one generation, if policy for agriculture was designed to achieve the aims outlined and if such a policy was vigorously implemented.

This chapter will be devoted to a consideration of the measures necessary to achieve these aims.

MAKING OTHER INDUSTRIES ACCESSIBLE TO FARM PEOPLE

This study has shown that children of farmers will leave the industry for other employment, or will accept part-time farming as a way of life, if they have been brought up in an environment which includes some occupational experience not related to farming. Often such an environment occurs in areas where there are small farms on poor land situated near the industrial centres, but, if other work opportunities happen to be available, it can also occur in good farming areas and have similar effects. Thus, in one of the parishes in my area of study where farming conditions were good (by the local standards) most of the farmsteads were situated in or close to the village. In this village a surviving rural craftsman operated a thriving joinery and building business and employed a number of youths whose fathers were full-time farmers. One farmer with a medium-sized farm had two sons who were thus employed. This farmer was a respected member of the farming community and he had family connections with his farm which extended back for over 300 years. In other parishes, with a similar quality of farming land but with no local employment opportunities apart from farming, farmers' sons from much smaller farms were either working at home or on the farms of relatives.[1]

The powerful effect of industrial opportunity on occupational mobility of farming people is shown by the increases in part-time farming and in movement away from farms which have occurred in the areas of good farming surrounding the large industrial centres in Michigan.[2]

In all the surveys which have been discussed, the majority of the farmers originated from places within a few miles of their farms, whether or not their parents had been farmers. Furthermore, most farmers' children who left farming migrated short distances to the nearest alternative occupation. The establishment of industries in close proximity to farming areas, or the provision of adequate transport to industrial employment, would seem to be the first logical step to take, if we wish to increase occupational mobility out of farming and to increase opportunities for part-time farming.

The establishment of industries in rural areas is not a new idea. Numerous commissions and individuals concerned with rural depopulation have made the same recommendation. The vital difference between such recommendations and mine is that, in the past, the concern has been to preserve the *status quo*, whereas I consider that such industrial opportunities, if provided for men, will change the existing pattern. Too often when industries have been established in rural areas with the idea of checking rural depopulation, they have been industries which have mainly employed females. These may

[1] Reimann states that, in some industrial rural communities in the Federal German Republic, social prestige no longer depends on the possession of land, despite the fact that 80 per cent of the families in the communities own land. F. Reimann, in G. P. Wibberley (Rapporteur): 'The changing structure and function of rural communities', *Changing Patterns of Rural Organization*, p. 105.

[2] Beegle and Halsted, *Michigan's Changing Population*, p. 7 and p. 30; Ralph A. Loomis, I. McKee Dean and James J. Bonnen: 'The role of part-time farming in agricultural adjustment in South Michigan', *Quart. Bull. Michigan Agricultural Experimental Station* (East Lansing, Michigan), Vol. 44, May 1962, pp. 644–53; and A. R. Loomis and A. E. Wirth: 'Financial progress on Michigan farms—a contrast between part-time and full-time farming', *ibid.*, pp. 625–43.

well have prevented the migration of some young women, but, in so doing, they may have accentuated the farming difficulties in these areas. By the provision of more wives for farmers' sons who had no other occupational opportunities apart from farming, demographic wastage from small farms would be reduced, the demand for full-time farms would be intensified, and the population living on farms would be increased.

Industry in rural areas will help towards a solution of agricultural underemployment only if it provides employment opportunities for men of all ages. Some industries employing mainly female labour may be necessary to retain an adequate number of young women but, assuming the trend towards earlier marriage continues, such industry could be planned on the basis of providing employment for the 15–20 year age-group of women. On the other hand, industries employing males would need to provide work for the whole working life of at least a part of its working complement, if they were to be used as a means of keeping some men permanently out of full-time farming. Some men would use such industry as a first step to jobs elsewhere, so it would not be necessary to provide jobs for all members of each of the age cohorts amongst the potentially surplus male population on farms.

The first recommendation then is that part of the money at present used for direct agricultural subsidies should be used to subsidize the establishment of male-employing industry and adult vocational re-training centres in or near to areas where it is considered desirable to reduce the number of farms. Alternatively, where it would be difficult or too expensive to establish industry in rural areas, adequate means of transport to work in the nearest centre should be subsidized, again ensuring that provision was made for male labour.[1]

Vocational training schemes for adults in those areas where industry was to be established would only provide for those people already in agriculture and willing to move out of it. For reasons which have already been discussed, farm workers would be the most likely people to take advantage of such schemes. This may not be very desirable for the farming industry. Consequently, further measures would be essential to ensure that potential farmers were encouraged

---

[1] In another context, Wibberley (*Agriculture and Urban Growth*, p. 167) argues that there is a strong case for subsidizing the private transport of individuals living in the remoter rural areas in preference either to expending large sums of money in maintaining costly public transport services, or to establishing industry in areas of low population density. This suggestion is pertinent to my argument and later in this chapter I incorporate the idea in my suggestion for subsidizing part-time farmers.

away from farming rather than that the farming industry was depleted still further of its hired labour force.

The second measure recommended should help to counteract the strong influences towards farming which most farm-reared boys receive, and, at the same time, stimulate a desire for a wider knowledge of farming amongst the farmers' sons who remain in the industry. *This recommended measure is that vocational training for industrial jobs and for agriculture should be provided at secondary modern or comprehensive schools situated in rural areas, and that school holidays should be adjusted to fit in with peak labour requirements on the family farms in the local areas served by the schools.*

The object of providing vocational training for industry in such schools is to present alternative possibilities for employment to children, particularly boys, at the same time as they are absorbing farming knowledge and values.

Extra-curricular and continuation classes may appeal to non-farm rural boys and to farm girls. When there is so much at home to engage the attention of farm boys, however, the chances are not very high of encouraging many away from farming outside school hours or once they have left school. Domestic science and needlework taken during school hours by the girls, because of their applicability to every-day life anywhere, seem to have an effect on the subsequent choice of career, or at least on the desire to follow a career other than farming. The school garden, painting, woodwork, etc., may arouse interest amongst boys, but they do not provide a sufficient preliminary training to counteract the constant training in farming and the farming atmosphere to which the boys are exposed outside school hours. To do this would seem to require more positive preliminary training in engineering, metal work, building construction and the like, during the final years at school.[1]

It would be obviously undesirable, tactically and educationally, to swing the bias in rural schools completely against agriculture. Consequently, vocational courses in other occupations would need to be balanced by an equivalent course in agriculture. Such an agricultural course should be designed to discourage from taking up full-time farms those sons of farmers with inadequate capital, or on small farms. To do this the course would need to emphasize that an adequate living

[1] This problem is not confined to Britain. I recently visited a rural high school situated in a problem farming area of Western Australia where farmers were attempting to gain a living from inadequately sized dairy farms operated under unfavourable physical and economic conditions. The high school possessed 22 typewriters for the vocational training of girls, but had only one wood-working lathe and no metal-working facilities or other equipment for training boys in trades other than agriculture.

could be obtained only if farm sizes were large enough, capital was available in sufficient quantities to take advantage of innovations, and if farmers had technical and economic knowledge to supplement their practical knowledge of agriculture. At the same time, such a course would provide a grounding in the theoretical aspects of agriculture for those farmers' sons who were likely to inherit or be set up on a farm of reasonable size, and it should encourage them to seek further knowledge after they have left school. Properly designed, such a course could also lead those children not able to farm to consider taking further training at a Farm Institute, so that they could take responsible posts on large farms.

Educationalists look with disfavour on 'potato-holidays' and similar concessions to farmers. This is probably because most people unconnected with agriculture do not appreciate the problems of family farming and are unaware of the uneven nature of labour requirements on many farms. When school holidays and peak seasonal requirements for labour on farms do not coincide, the farmers and their children co-operate in defying the school authorities. The demand for family labour at seasonal peaks will increase if the number of farm workers continues to decline. An intensification of the conflicts between farmers and the schools could be a direct result. This educational problem will not be solved by exhortation to farmers on the evils of keeping their children away from school, nor will it be resolved by measures designed to stop the practice. The farmers have little alternative, and the sons are willing accomplices. Consequently, repressive measures are likely to turn fathers and sons still further against education. In all probability, a better education for farmers' children, through greater parental co-operation and a less interrupted schooling, would result from recognition by the educational authorities that the peculiar circumstances of family farming require periodic child-labour. These requirements could be met by the provision of a flexible system of school holidays to fit in with the local needs.

PROVIDING A CAREER SCALE FOR FARMERS' SONS
AND FARM WORKERS

The next measure suggested as a means of retaining an adequate hired labour force in agriculture, despite the provision of other occupational opportunities, is *the encouragement of systems of share and partnership farming between farmers and their children and between farmers and hired workers.*

Such systems should take the form of legal agreements in which certain rights and obligations of both parties were clearly defined and in which was indicated the exact nature of the work and the method of remuneration. For dairy farms the various forms of share-milking agreements used in New Zealand could provide a basis for similar schemes in Britain.[1] Particulars of schemes could be disseminated through advisory channels.

This type of farming arrangement should enable parents partly to relinquish control over decisions and capital to their sons for an interim period, before retirement, and would give sons an increasing share in management and returns.[2] Also, where there was no son in the family, another farmer's son could come in and be in charge of a particular operation, for example the dairy unit. In this way such a son would be self-employed and would not therefore incur the social stigma of being an employed hand, which at the present time is one factor restricting the movement of surplus sons off their parents' farms into employment by others in need of labour.

Another advantage would be that such schemes would provide hired workers with a career scale in at least some systems of livestock farming. Farming apprenticeship schemes, the agricultural vocational training in schools, and perhaps facilities for easy credit, could be associated with these systems for sharing the work and the returns from farming. Minimum qualifications could be specified in the agreements and apprentices could be attached to suitably qualified share-workers. Attracted by career opportunities requiring no capital or through which a suitably qualified share-farmer could obtain easy credit facilities, some farmers' sons might be encouraged to take up this self-employed type of career, rather than attempt to farm a small farm on their own account.

Schemes of this nature may also solve some of the problems facing managers of large farm businesses. As large-scale farming becomes more organized on industrial lines, one big difficulty faced by managers is how to organize operations and enterprises on a relatively large scale, and yet still retain workers who will take a personal interest in the success of the enterprises with which they are concerned. This aspect of labour organization is particularly important with livestock farming, where attention to small detail and acute observation by workers are very essential factors influencing the profitability of

[1] For a description of these and of some of the variants on them used in Britain see J. S. Nalson: *Incentive Payments to Workers in Agriculture*, Department of Agriculture, University of Leeds, 1950, unpublished post-graduate thesis.

[2] Partnership schemes have been devised elsewhere to achieve these objects. See J. B. Cunningham and M. C. M. Case: *Father-Son Farm Business Agreements*, Circular 587, University of Illinois, College of Agriculture, December 1944.

the enterprise. Key workers, paid by results, could be in charge of separate units on a large farm, so that the advantages of units compact enough to be under the supervision of one person could be combined with the advantages of central management of different units.

Share-farming on large farms would only affect a small proportion of the farms in Britain. The system is of equal value to family farmers, however, for it could help to fill the labour gap before sons come of working age. In any area where share-farming was common there would be a supply of share-workers who could move from farm to farm as occasion demanded.[1]

EASING THE LABOUR SITUATION ON FAMILY FARMS

Despite schemes for share-farming, the problem of fluctuating labour supply on family farms would still remain. Although such schemes should retain those hired workers who have farming ambitions, there would still be a greater tendency for workers to leave the land for other opportunities compared with farmers' sons. Consequently, it would be necessary to try and devise means of levelling out the supply of labour on family farms throughout the family developmental cycle. *One way to do this would be to provide more rural housing for members of farming families and to provide retirement grants for farmers at the age of 60.*

These measures should ensure earlier marriage of farmers' sons and earlier transference of farms from parents to children. Before making suggestions as to how the measures could be implemented some explanation is necessary of the way in which earlier marriage

---

[1] An obvious extension of the above ideas would be to establish co-operative farming schemes where individuals specialize within a farming organization large enough to obtain economies of scale. Examples in Britain are the settlements of smallholdings organized on the basis of centralized services which are operated by the Land Settlement Association. Extreme examples of the successful application of co-operative principles to farming in a non-communist country are the various types of co-operative farming settlements in Israel. There 60 per cent of the farming is undertaken in co-operative settlements. These range from *kibbutzim*, with production and consumption on a collective basis, through *moshavim shitufiim*, with production and ownership collective but consumption individual to types of *moshavim* with production, ownership and consumption partly individual and partly collective. *Moshavim* do not appear to solve the problems of succession, scale of operations, and uneven labour supply, which occur on family farms. *Kibbutzim* and *moshavim shitufiim*, however, certainly offer some solutions which appear to be worthy of more study than has been given to them by agricultural economists concerned with the adjustments which can be made to farming in a modern economy.

and earlier retirement would even out the labour supply throughout the family developmental cycle.

The earlier the age at which people marry, the longer the period of time over which successive generations co-exist. Applied to farming, this means that a farmer, marrying at 25 and taking over partial or complete control of his father's farm, will then have the labour services of an active father for the 15 years or so before his own son becomes of working age, assuming that the father had married at the same age. Alternatively, if a farmer's son can marry early, whilst still working at home, his father is less likely to lose his services than if the son has to decide between marriage and leaving home on the

EXAMPLE A

AGE OF MARRIAGE 35 FOR ALL GENERATIONS: NO PARTNERSHIPS OR SHARE-FARMING

Time period in years:	0	10	15	35
Grandfather				
Occurrence	Dies			
Age:	70			
Father				
Occurrence:	Inherits farm and marries			Dies
Age:	35	45	50	70
Son				
Occurrence:	Born	Helps part-time	Starts to work at home	Inherits farm and marries
Age:	0	10	15	35

Notes:
  1. In each generation:
     Period of working for father   = 20 years
     Period of complete control of farm = 35 years
  2. Extra housing is not required
  3. There is a labour gap of 15 years; schooling may be interrupted because of work on the farm and children will tend to leave school at the earliest age possible.

one hand, and remaining at home, but single, on the other. The later the age of marriage, the greater the possibility that a son will not take over the farm until his father retires or dies. Furthermore, the later the age of marriage, the greater the chances of a labour gap occurring between the time a grandfather is no longer active on the farm and the time a grandson comes of working age.

Late marriage amongst farmers inheriting a farm from parents has a number of causes. It is partly a result of a late marriage in the previous generation, partly due to lack of housing on or near farms for two families, and partly due to farms not being large enough to support two families. A policy designed to reduce the number of farmers, and thereby increase the size of farms, would enable two families to live for a time on the income from one farm, and would promote earlier marriage, which in turn would help to even out the labour supply throughout the family developmental cycle.

Two simplified examples (A and B) illustrate the differences between a family farming system with late marriages and one with early marriages and share or partnership arrangements.

There are many permutations which could be made on the two examples by allowing for various demographic occurrences and for personal choice. The examples serve to indicate, however, that early marriage, early retirement, and partnership or share-farming arrangements could provide one solution to the labour problems of family farms in the future and at the same time give an opportunity for farmers to obtain higher education. This is assuming that birthrates continue to fall and schemes are implemented to encourage some sons away from farming so that few farmers will have more than one son available for farm work. The scheme outlined in the second example opposite is dependent both on extra housing being available in the villages or near the farms, and on the willingness of farmers to retire at 60.[1]

Extra housing could come partly from new building in the villages and partly from the renovation of farmhouses which became vacant as farmers die or retire without issue, and the land is taken for amalgamation. *Housing subsidies for building new houses or for renovating*

[1] I realize that this scheme suggests a return to a system similar to the *Altenteil* in Germany and the 'West Room' in Ireland. There are two major differences, however. First, in the future many more farmers will have only one son, who will not therefore be burdened with payments to siblings, as could occur with large families and partible inheritance. Second, I am advocating a separate house, preferably not on the same property; definite stages in the transfer process; and specific rights and obligations for each party at each stage. By these provisions, it should be possible to avoid some of the conflicts which could arise under *Altenteil* or 'West Room' systems.

EXAMPLE B

AGE OF MARRIAGE 25 FOR ALL GENERATIONS: PARTNERSHIP OR SHARE-FARMING ARRANGEMENTS MADE

Time Period in years	0	10	15	20	25
Grandfather Occurrence	Controls management and capital.	Acts as landlord, retires to house in village and helps on farm.		Dies, wife lives on in house in village.	Wife dies.
Age	50	60		70	
Father Occurrence	Marries, takes house in village and works for father on a share basis.	Moves to farm-house, takes control of management on a partner-ship or larger share basis.			Controls management and capital.
Age	25	35	40	45	50
Son Occurrence	Born.		Starts further education or farm training.	Starts work at home.	Marries, takes house in village and works on farm on share basis.
Age	0		15	20	25

Notes:

1. In each generation:
   Period of working for father   =   5 years
   Period of controlling work on share basis   =   10 years
   Period of controlling management on larger share or
       partnership basis   =   15 years
   Period of controlling full management and capital   =   10 years
   Period of helping son and acting as landlord   =   10 years
2. The son can either begin full-time farm work at 15 or carry on with further education until he is 20. If he continues his education to 20 there will be a labour gap of five years to be bridged by hired labour.
3. The farmhouse plus an additional house in the village or nearby provide for the requirements of the three generations.

old ones could be paid to registered housing societies controlled by members of the local farming community.[1] For example, in the area I studied there are a number of Friendly Societies of the sickness-benefit type. Some of these have considerable funds which probably would be better used for housing subsidization than for their original purpose, now largely made obsolete by National Health Insurance. In order to meet the needs and assist the process of change, preference for houses controlled by such societies would have to be given to:

  a. Parents retiring in favour of children.
  b. Children marrying and the son or son-in-law working on the parents' farm.
  c. Farmers retiring or leaving the occupation of farming, but who were willing to give up land to a neighbour for amalgamation.

The local control suggested would ensure that the scheme was used for the benefit of local people and not exploited by incomers looking for cheap housing. However democratic the form of the organization set up, if it had the approval of the local people from the start and it persisted for a number of years, it would be almost sure to come under the control of the local kinship and friendship networks, within which it could best serve its objects.

Retirement grants for farmers from the age of 60 would encourage farmers to retire early in favour of their children. Such grants could also be used to encourage the early retirement of single people, sibling pairs and married couples with no children available or willing to take over their farms. The payment of a retirement grant could be made conditional upon the recipient retiring in favour of a relative or upon him agreeing to the land being amalgamated with an adjoining farm. A farm business size could be fixed below which an an early retirement grant would be paid only if the farmer gave his farm up for amalgamation or for operation by a part-time farmer. Above the fixed size of farm business the grant would be payable under the following circumstances:

  a. If the farmer retired in favour either of one of his children or of a near relative.
  b. If the farmer agreed to sell or rent his property to a potential young farmer with qualifications obtained either through an

---

[1] There are provisions already whereby local authorities can give loans to approved housing societies for building houses for rental to members of the societies.

approved apprenticeship course or through a course of higher agricultural education.

c. If the farmer agreed to sell his property for amalgamation with an adjacent farm.

Retirement grants could be paid for a maximum of two people thus providing for married couples or sibling pairs as well as for single people living alone, widows and widowers. The age of eligibility could be brought below 60 in cases of obvious incapacity to operate a farm for health or financial reasons.

The retirement grants could be of two types, serving two distinct purposes. The first could be a lump sum payable when the farmer retired at the age of 60. This would provide a capital sum which could be used, if desired, as a deposit on a house for retirement. The second could be a weekly sum paid until the person concerned reached the age of 65 and was eligible for the state pension.

Retirement grants used as suggested above could help to improve the labour supply on family farms, speed up the transference of control on family farms adequate in size to support two families, and encourage farmers on small full-time farms to give up their land for amalgamation into adjacent farms.

ENCOURAGING AMALGAMATION AND PART-TIME FARMING

The process of amalgamation of land could be encouraged further by the *payment of amalgamation grants* to people willing to give up their farms. These grants could be based on the assessed value, with vacant possession, of the whole farm or, alternatively, of the land and buildings minus the farmhouse, which could be retained by the person giving up the land, if he wished to live there in retirement. Limiting the maximum size of any one land transaction to less than 100 acres would ensure that land was amalgamated from amongst those holdings where it was most difficult to make a living from full-time farming.

Often there would not be a neighbouring farmer able or willing to amalgamate a holding from which a farmer was willing to retire if he obtained an amalgamation grant. In such circumstances, the sale of the holding could be made to the Crown at the market price. The Crown would be then able to rent the land either to a neighbouring farmer as accommodation land or as a part-time unit to someone willing to take a full-time job off the property. The land would be thus held in reserve until it was practicable to amalgamate it permanently with another farm. Alternatively, the Crown could exercise an option to buy farms for afforestation in those areas where forests offered a more lucrative use for the land.[1]

As indicated in the previous paragraph, part-time farms interspersed with full-time farms would increase the flexibility with which land transfer could take place. In addition, working off improves the income position of farmers on small farms and helps to encourage their children to leave farming. *Part-time farming grants could be paid* as a yearly lump sum per farm, conditional upon the farmer or one male member of the resident family working off the farm at a non-agricultural job[2] and on a full-time basis. Upper and lower limits would need to be fixed for the family income received from off-farm employment and for acreages or man-equivalents of work for the farms on which the subsidy would be paid. When the farmer or other family member ceased to work off the farm, the yearly part-time subsidy would cease but the farmer would be free to apply for retirement or amalgamation grants.

In order to encourage elderly farmers to apply for the retirement or amalgamation grants, no subsidy would be paid for part-time farming if the farmer was 60 years of age or over. Furthermore, this subsidy would be payable to the one family for five years only. This should be an adequate period for a family to become accustomed to the idea of part-time farming, for sons to become aware of the alternatives to farming as a career and for the idea of working-off to become socially acceptable amongst communities formerly made up of full-time farmers. Undue traffic in part-time farms for the sake of the subsidy could be prevented by attaching to the payment of the subsidy a condition that the Crown would have the option to purchase if the. farm was offered for sale to anyone other than a child or next-of-kin during the five-year period, or for a specified time thereafter.

[1] In Northern Ireland, the government is subsidizing the purchase of marginal and sub-marginal land for planting to forests. Those former owner-occupiers who wish to remain in the area are being resettled as forestry workers: *Monthly Agricultural Report*, Northern Ireland Ministry of Agriculture, Vol. 33, No. 5, Sept. 1958, p. 130 and Vol. 34, No. 1, May 1959, p. 4. Treloar has developed a useful method for assessing the relative returns from agriculture and forestry in different locations over a period of 40 years. See D. W. Treloar and I. G. Morison: *Economic Comparisons of Forestry and Agriculture*, Agricultural Economics Research Report, No. 3, Institute of Agriculture, University of Western Australia, 1962.

[2] Farm work is specifically excluded from this recommendation in order to avoid abuses of the subsidy which could arise amongst friends or relatives, whereby members of a group arranged to work for each other so that all could draw the subsidy.

ORGANIZING AND FINANCING MOBILITY SUBSIDIES

All the above recommendations would involve considerable organization, supervision and financial provision. The organization and supervision could be undertaken by a Marginal Farm and Mobility Commission, somewhat on the lines of the Crofting Commission, but with much more power invested in it. The Commission need not normally control directly the transfer of land between farms, although when occasion demanded it could exert an option to buy for redistribution land which came up for sale in the ordinary way. It could achieve much without any legal coercive powers if it were staffed at the district level by people with knowledge of local conditions, and in whom the community had confidence. Such people could achieve the objects of the Commission by operating the subsidies most suitable for particular areas; by making recommendations as to the siting of industry, the provision of transport and the choice of vocational courses; and by collecting regular sample statistics on the demography of the farm people and their mobility. These local statistics could provide the necessary data from which could be formulated, and adjusted, plans for subsidies, industries and training schemes best suited to the requirements of the area.

The finance for all this could come from part of the present subsidy provision for agriculture, but it is obviously impossible to say what would be the annual cost of such a scheme. This would depend on the amount of each individual subsidy payment and on the response of farmers to the scheme. Nevertheless, the following calculations are presented in order to show that considerable incentives could be offered and yet prove less costly to the nation than the present subsidies given to agriculture.

Incentive	Approximate annual cost in £ million	Basis of calculation
Vocational courses in secondary modern and other schools in rural areas. Salaries of extra teachers	6	a. Approximately 57,000 boys in each of the age groups 13, 14, 15 years in rural areas outside conurbations in 1951 Census. b. One teacher per 30 boys teaching 3 classes. c. Provision for one teacher of agriculture and one of other occupations.

Incentive	*Approximate annual cost in £ million*	*Basis of calculation*
		d. Teachers' salary per year £1,500.
Retirement grant for all farmers at the age of 60	10·5	a. All farmers take up subsidy. b. Approximately 52,500 farmers between 55 and 65—1951 Census. Say 5,250 retiring at age 60 each year. c. £1,000 lump sum at retirement and £200 per year for 5 years; amount paid per farmer retiring—£2,000.
Housing subsidy	3·5	a. One-third of the cost up to maximum of £700. b. All farmers retiring at 60 and all taking the grant. c. 5,250 retiring each year.
Part-time grants	10	a. 26,400 farmers on holdings under 275 man-days per year in size, with no other source of income or with a part-time job only (Ashton and Cracknell, *op. cit.*). b. 74,000 holdings of size 275–600 man-days per year (*ibid.*). c. One person from each of the above holdings goes out to work in order to obtain the subsidy. d. Subsidy of £100 per year per farm.
Amalgamation grant	4·5	a. 7,500,000 acres in farms of below 100 acres in size. b. A reduction in acreage of 2 per cent per year on farms of below 100 acres. c. £30 per acre subsidy (maximum figure) on sale of land for amalgamation.

Total grants　　—　　£34·5 million

In addition to the costs outlined, there would be the capital cost of subsidizing the establishment in rural areas of the necessary industries for, say, 100,000 men, or there would be the annual cost of subsidizing transport from rural areas to the centres of industrial employment. The latter would be the cheaper alternative. At £1 per week for all men concerned with the part-time grant, the cost would amount to £5 million. There would also be the cost of capital equipment and extra classrooms for the vocational training in schools and in industrial centres. The housing subsidies and amalgamation grants would reduce over time, for the houses, once built, would serve more than one generation and the number of farms under 100 acres would progressively reduce over the years.

Subsidies of the type outlined would need to be periodically reviewed, for rapid technological and economic changes may make it imperative to adjust both the bases on which the subsidies are assessed and the objects for which they are designed. Thus future conditions may make it desirable to reduce drastically the numbers of full-time family farms by providing mobility incentives which will lead to a large proportion of farms becoming either part-time farms, at the bottom end of the scale of farm size, or large farm businesses, providing careers for farmers' sons as managers and skilled workers in charge of production units. Alternatively, if we continue to place a high social value on 'the family farm', we may have to encourage 'contract farming' as a means of adjusting farm business size to meet changes in the labour supply and needs of the family at different stages of the family developmental cycle. Acceptance of this way of financing, operating and managing farm enterprises will involve, however, drastic changes in the capital structure of farming and in the education, social organization and independent status of farmers.

When considering all these recommendations it should be clearly realized that the problems of inadequately sized farms can never be solved completely, they can only be ameliorated. There will always be problem families at various stages in the process of demographic and occupational wastage. These people will occupy farms which were adequate full-time ones in the previous generation but not in their own. Furthermore, there will always be people willing to make personal sacrifices in order to achieve the goal of full-time farming. The measures outlined in this chapter should help the problem families, whilst at the same time providing opportunities for those who wish to progress by their own efforts from small beginnings to the status of full-time farmer.

In these final chapters I have used the insights obtained from my intensive study and, from unco-ordinated other material, I have tried to build up a picture of the changes in spatial and occupational mobility which have occurred, or which may be occurring, in the

s

farming industry of Britain. I have had to make what I consider are little more than intelligent guesses about past and future trends because, unfortunately, there are no adequate national statistics on the mobility of farm people in Britain and many other countries. We know how many agricultural holdings there are, but we do not know how many people farm them, or how many supplement farming with other work. We do not know the amount of movement from farm to farm or of land between farmers. We do not know the rates of egress of farmers and their children from farming or the rates of inward movement of farmers' children and of people from other occupations. We have very little knowledge of the demographic trends amongst farm people, trends which will affect the supply of farms and farmers in the future. All such knowledge is essential, however, if we seriously wish to obtain national and international data from which plans can be formulated for adjusting the structure of the farming industry to meet the efficiency demands which will be made upon it in the future. This study has indicated to me some of the ways in which mobility problems could be alleviated in agriculture in one small part of Britain and I have ventured to suggest ways in which the general problem could be alleviated. I believe that national studies of a similar nature would not only give insights into many of the problems of mobility in agriculture, but would also provide the statistical data necessary for their solution.

APPENDIX 1

METHOD OF STUDY

Overall approach

The approach to the mobility of farm people, as presented in chapters II to X, was developed mainly as a result of field observations. Originally, attempts were made to set up a theoretical framework within which mobility could be studied and tested by observation. It became clear, however, that much more factual data than was available from the literature was required before hypotheses could be made about the nature and character of the factors influencing the mobility of farm people. Eventually an empirical approach was adopted, out of which it was hoped to discover certain causal relationships which would be illuminating in themselves and which would lead to further hypotheses about the nature of the problem.

An area was chosen where considerable farming problems existed, where part-time and full-time farming occurred, and where there was a range in farm size, but where one type of farming predominated. Farmers were visited with workers who were carrying out economic investigations of farming in the area and other visits were made to influential farmers, planning officials and members of various farming organizations. Local officials of the Rural District Council were contacted whilst I was preparing a list of farmers for sampling purposes, and later I visited those farmers in each parish who acted as electoral returning officers. The views of all these people were obtained on the problems of the area and on the movement of farm people into and out of it.

The information gained, supplemented by available survey data on the economics of farming in the area, was examined in the light of sociological methods used in studies of social mobility in urban communities. From this examination a rough outline was developed of questions which needed to be asked in the survey. A trial questionnaire was drawn up and tested out on a farmer who was accustomed to answering survey questions. The questionnaire was then modified and used in a pilot survey of five farmers chosen at random. The final questionnaire was drawn up after considering the replies and difficulties encountered in the pilot survey. A copy of this questionnaire will be found in Appendix 5, and details of methods adopted in the study are given later in this Appendix.

The information obtained by means of the questionnaire falls into three categories:

1. Physical and economic information about the farms and about any other farms which the farmers had previously occupied.
2. Social and demographic information about all family members on the farms, children who had left home, parents and siblings of farmers and their wives, and about former occupiers of the farms.
3. Information about the mobility of all family members, children who had left home, parents, siblings and former occupiers.

At each interview, some information was obtained in an informal manner, in addition to the answers to the questionnaire. Later on, when decisions had to be made upon methods of analysis and on how to write up the material, this additional information was invaluable and so was the knowledge built up from other informal contacts made while working in the area. For example, the decision to relate mobility to socio-economic groupings (Chapters V to VIII) was taken as a result of observations of the importance of these groupings in the life of the people in the area. A conversation overheard in a public house crystallized the importance of pre-nuptial conception as an influence on mobility. I first realized the important role played by dual-business farmers in changing the structure of farms when I was listening to a farmer's reminiscences about his grandmother, who had sold groceries and animal feeding stuffs, and had acquired numerous parcels of land from her neighbours.

Choice of area

The aim of the study was to examine the mobility of farm people under conditions where farm businesses were economically at a disadvantage compared with other industries and compared with farms in agricultural districts with more favourable natural conditions. At the same time, it was desired to study the effect on mobility of variations in farm business size for farms with basically the same type of farming. The area chosen met these requirements. In addition, it was small enough and sufficiently differentiated from adjacent areas for one person to view it as a whole and become familiar with its main socio-economic features. It had a further advantage in that some parishes within it had been intensively studied previously during the course of an investigation into the farming problems of the area. This meant that there was some material available on the number of farmers and their children together with considerable information about the economics of farm businesses there.

Investigational methods

The bulk of the economic, demographic and mobility information was obtained by means of a questionnaire filled in during the course of a personal interview with the farmer and, wherever possible, his wife. After each interview, as complete an account as possible was recorded of all that had occurred and been said during the unstructured part of the interview. Similar records were kept of conversations, incidents and observations occurring throughout the period of contact with the area. Further mobility information about married sons and daughters was obtained by a postal questionnaire and follow-up visits.

Supplementary information on occupational and residential choices of school-leavers was obtained by a questionnaire to children in the final two years at the secondary modern school serving the area. Information was obtained from school records on educational attainment of 'farm' and 'non-farm' boys and girls.

Official records of births, marriages and deaths were examined to check some of the demographic data obtained in the main survey.

Sampling methods

Information was required about the farmers themselves, the members of their families and the farm businesses they controlled. Details of all properties rated as 'Agricultural' were obtained from the valuation list for the Rural District in which the parishes to be surveyed were situated. The Electoral Lists provided the names and addresses of adults living in the parishes. Matching up the two gave a list of families living on properties rated as 'Agricultural' in each parish. This list was then checked with the electoral returning officer for each parish. As a result of this check, a few names were added of people farming properties over five acres, but not listed as agricultural, and a few were subtracted of people on properties listed as agricultural, but who were not farming the land or who had less than five acres. Multiple holdings were located by means of the local checking, supplemented by information from the valuation lists. The final list obtained was thus one of farm families living at their farm-business address and identified by the name of the head of the family. This list of 372 families was numbered consecutively and a 50 per cent sample drawn, using tables of random numbers. The first five families drawn were used to test out the proposed questionnaire form, which was modified before being used for the main enquiry.

Including the five families in the pilot survey, who were revisited,

172 completed interviews were obtained out of 186 families visited, a response rate of 92·9 per cent. The 14 unsuccessful interviews were made up as follows:

Families living in the house but not farming the land	5
Holding less than five acres	2
Insufficient information obtained	3
Not contacted (wife had just died)	1
Refused	3
Total	14

Four of the five families who lived in the farmhouse but did not farm the land still owned the land.

The size of the sample to be drawn was determined by three considerations:

1. The time available for interviewing.
2. The desire to obtain as much information as possible about the interrelationships between farm families in the area, consistent with 1.
3. The need to include in the sample an adequate number of married children and single children of working age so that analyses could be made of their occupational and residential mobility compared with that of their parents and compared with their parents' economic and social situations.

It was estimated that about 15 completed interviews could be obtained per week. With three months available for the main survey this meant that a 50 per cent random sample was possible. It was further estimated (from previous data about the area) that this would give adequate numbers of children and would at the same time provide some information about most of the families in the area, for information would be obtained from each sample family about parents, siblings and children who were living in the area, but who were not necessarily included in the sample.

Interviewing procedure and collection of general information

Whilst the plan for the study was being formulated, visits were made to farms in the chosen area with field workers from the Agricultural Economics Department of the University of Manchester. These contacts were then extended by visits to local leaders of the farming community and by attendance at markets and farmers' meetings in the area. Later, the electoral returning officers in each parish were visited. Consequently, by the time I was ready to carry out the main sample survey, I had built up a considerable knowledge of the area and its people. Furthermore, numerous people scattered throughout the area knew of me and had some idea of why I was working there.

The five farmers visited in the course of the pilot survey were not notified in advance of my visit. As a result, I had difficulty with some of them in explaining 'on the doorstep' why I was there. To overcome this difficulty a circular letter was devised for use in the main survey. In this the purpose of the survey was briefly stated, how the particular farmer had been chosen was explained and his co-operation was requested. These letters were sent out in batches to all the sample farmers in each parish about a week before survey work began in that parish. They thus served as an introduction when the interviewing visit was made. If the farmer himself was available at the first visit, the interview was carried out immediately, or, if he preferred it, a more suitable time was arranged with him.

The approach adopted at the interview was determined by the attitude of the farmer and his family and by the circumstances of the interviewing situation. Usually, general farming topics were discussed at first and the conversation gradually brought round to the point of the survey. The questionnaire was filled in next and, finally, an unstructured discussion developed on mobility and on any other topics the farm family brought up. The majority of the interviews took from one and a half to two hours to complete, although a three to four hour period spent at one farm was quite common. The shortest interview took half an hour and the longest took one and a half days.

The postal survey was carried out four months after the main survey. This was undertaken to obtain additional information on the residence, occupation and farming background of the spouses of married children. The response rate was 60 per cent. Follow-up visits were made to obtain the remaining 40 per cent of the replies. No farmer refused to give this information.

The questionnaire on occupational and residential choices of school-leavers was supplied to the headmaster of the local secondary modern school. There was no indication on it of where it had originated and it was filled in by the pupils, under the supervision of the head, during the course of ordinary lessons given by him to each of the classes concerned. The completed questionnaires, which were not edited by the school staff, were collected from the headmaster and analysed by me.

Processing and analysis of data

The information from the questionnaire forms was processed and entered up in columns in a ledger-type book, all related data being entered on the same page. For variables, the exact value was entered in one column and an adjacent column was left for the code. For both variables and attributes rough classifications or distributions were carried out as the material was extracted from the original forms. Codes for each variable or attribute were decided upon after consideration of its rough classification and those of related data. These codes were then entered in the appropriate columns in the ledgers.

When the headings for the columns had been entered originally, a number of blanks had been left. Extra classifications suggested by the handling of the data were entered in these blank columns as the extraction and processing of information proceeded. For example, comparison of 'size of farm' with 'numbers working off the property' resulted in a further classification—'farm-business size per household member'.

The coded information from the ledgers was punched on to 80 column Hollerith cards, five sets of cards being used. Set I contained all the general information about the farms and the social, economic, demographic and mobility information about the farmer. Set II had information about inter- and intra-generational movement between farms and about land amalgamations, together with relevant information required for cross-classifications about the farms and the farmer. This information was repeated from Set I cards. Set III contained information about the farmer's wife plus relevant cross-classification material about the farmer and the farms. Sets IV and V contained information about the single and married children plus cross-classification material about the farmer, the farms and the farmer's wife.

Primary classifications of the material were carried out from all five sets of cards. These primary classifications were used to formulate chapter outlines in conjunction with the general information obtained during the course of the study and the unstructured information obtained at each interview. Secondary cross-classifications of the coded material were made as required during the writing of the first draft of each chapter. The ledgers were a source of additional information for case studies and for any cross-classifications which were considered desirable for particular purposes in any chapter, but which could not be obtained from manipulation of the Hollerith cards.

APPENDIX 2

MEASUREMENT OF SIZE OF BUSINESS
AND INTENSITY OF OPERATION

FARMERS were asked how many acres they had of 'crops and grass' and of 'rough grazing'. Their interpretation of 'rough grazing' varied according to the standards on farms around them and according to what use they thought the information was going to be put. Thus a farmer on the lower land was likely to consider as 'rough grazing' a pasture containing a lot of rushes or poor grasses. A farmer living half a mile up the hill (all of whose pasture was equivalent to the previous man's 'rough grazing') would only apply the term to moorland or to land reverting to moor. If either thought, however, that their eligibility for a Marginal Lands grant, the Small Farm Scheme, or a Hill Farming Subsidy, would be influenced by calling a particular piece of land 'rough grazing', 'hill land' or 'pasture', they were likely to call it that, irrespective of its productive capacity.

When measuring size of farm in acres, the conventional way to allow for rough grazing is to calculate an 'adjusted acreage' figure, using some arbitrary scale of equivalence. Alternatively, classical rent theory may be assumed and land productivity measured in terms of rental value. For example, Wynne and Wright in the economic section of *The Small Farms of Industrial Yorkshire*, University of Leeds, October 1958, state:

> The 48 costed farms averaged 38½ acres in size but of this an average of seven acres was rough grazing equivalent to 'little more than' two acres of improved pasture. Thus the average farm size was about 33½ adjusted acres.

Because of the different interpretations of what constituted rough grazing, no attempt was made in the present study to measure size of farm by a combination of acres of 'crops and grass' plus 'adjusted acres' of rough grazing. Rent could not be used either, for 69 per cent of the farms were partly or wholly owner-occupied. For descriptive purposes total acres on the farm were used.

No direct financial data were obtained from farmers. The main reason for this was the feeling that to seek it might have resulted in some people refusing to co-operate and in others terminating the interviews before mobility and social data could be obtained. This

265

could have seriously affected the representative nature of the sample. Moreover, there was considerable information available already about the economy of farms in the area from continuous and periodic economic survey work carried out from the University of Manchester. From the previous economic work, it was known that most of the farms in the area were dairy farms and that the number of dairy cows gave a reasonable indication of the size of the farm business. A 'cow equivalent' figure was therefore adopted as an indication of absolute business size, irrespective of the size of the farm in acres.

All dairy farms were put into size of business groups according to the number of dairy cows they had plus a 'cow equivalent' figure for any breeding ewes kept, based on 1 ewe $= \frac{4}{25}$ cow equivalents. Farms not dairying had a cow equivalent figure calculated according to the number of mature cattle kept and based on 2-year cattle $= \frac{4}{5}$ cow equivalents, 1 beef or nurse-cow $= 1$ cow equivalent, plus breeding ewes as previously stated. The cow equivalent figures were based on livestock equivalent figures quoted in the Farm Management Handbook, Ministry of Agriculture, Fisheries and Food. The cow equivalent figure was not considered to be as reliable an indication of size of business for the non-dairying farms as for the dairy farms. However, most of the non-dairying farms were in both the 'under 15 cow equivalent' group and the 'under 60 acre' group, the two smallest size groups, so it was felt that the measure was sufficiently reliable for comparative purposes.

As explained in Appendix 1, the size groupings were decided upon after consideration of the distribution of each measure relative to the other measures and to other data, for example, whether the farmer worked off the farm or not. The lowest limit for size of business, under 15 cow equivalents, was chosen as being below the level at which it would be possible to make more than a labourer's wage from milk production alone.

With no financial data to give an indication of intensity of operation of the farms, a physical measure was needed. Acres per cow, often used in cost studies, was not considered appropriate because of the wide variation in the quality of the land. In the early interviews it was noted that when giving details of the acreages of their farms farmers usually gave the total acreage, then the acres of mowing grass and finally the acres of pasture. They would then have to think, or shrewdly decide, how many acres of the pasture was rough grazing. The one figure clear in their minds was the precise acreage of grass they mowed each year. The area had a long winter, there was a negligible amount of land cultivated, and bought hay was expensive. But dairying predominated, and, consequently, the amount of land capable of producing a hay crop was a most important determinant of the number of cows which could be kept. Hence the importance of the area of mowing grass in the minds of the farmers and the lavish attention given to the meadows compared with that given to the rest of the farm. 'Acres of mowing grass' gave a fair indication of the productive land resources available and number of cows, or 'cow equivalents', measured the size of business. Where sheep were kept in appreciable numbers they were run mainly on rough grazing and consequently their numbers were not considered to be influenced by the acres of mowing grass available. The measure of intensity of operation decided upon was 'acres of mowing grass' divided by 'number of cows' (or 'cattle-cow equivalents' on non-dairying farms).

SOME DEMOGRAPHIC FEATURES OF THE FARM FAMILIES COMPARED WITH FIGURES FROM NATIONAL AND OTHER SURVEYS

TABLE 1

SEX AND MARITAL STATUS OF FARMERS

Sex and marital status	Farmers in England and Wales, 1951[1]	All farmers in survey 1960	Full-time and dual business farmers in 1960[2]	Farmers in survey plus certain other family members 1960[3]
	%	%	%	%
Women	6·7	4·7	5·4	10·0
Single people (including women)	18·8	15·7	17·9	17·0
Widowed and divorced people (including women)	6·7	4·1	4·6	7·0
Married people (including married women designated as 'farmers')	74·5	80·2	77·5	76·0

[1] Includes managers, calculated from Census 1951 Occupation Tables.

[2] The Census probably does not include those part-time farmers reporting their other occupation but not reporting as 'farmers'. For this reason the figures for the full-time and dual-business farmers in the survey may be more comparable with those of the Census.

[3] The particulars for the farmers surveyed refer to one person on each farm, either the one who was stated to be the farmer, or to the senior partner. The Census includes all people stating themselves to be farmers. Some of these may be wives where the farm is owned or operated jointly, some may be sons or other kin in partnership and some may be sons or daughters taking the designation of their parents. Where it was known that wives shared the decision-

TABLE 2

AGES OF FARMERS COMPARED WITH NATIONAL
AND OTHER SURVEY MATERIAL

Age of farmer	This survey, 1960		Oxfordshire and Warwickshire survey, 1950[1]		England and Wales survey, 1944[2]	Census, England and Wales[3]	
	No.	%	No.	%	%	1931 %	1951 %
Under 35	16	9·3	16	10·9	18	16·5	17·9
35–44	49	28·5	27	18·4	49	22·2	23·2
45–54	42	24·4	41	27·9		24·6	26·2
55–64	44	25·6	30	20·4	32	21·8	19·8
65 and over	21	12·2	33	22·4		14·9	12·9
Total	172	100·0	147	100·0	99	100·0	100·0

[1] J. Ashton: *The Recruitment of Farmers in England and Wales.* Unpublished thesis, University of Oxford, June 1955. Calculated from Table 23, p. 117.

[2] D. Chapman: *Agricultural Information and the Farmer.* Wartime Social Survey New Series. No. 38, H.M.S.O., 1944.

[3] Occupation Tables, Census 1931 and Census, 1951.

making or ownership of farms, or that sons were in partnership, or that a child carried out the functions of farmer but a parent was still nominally the farmer, or that siblings were in partnership, these have been added to the 172 farmers and the proportions of singles, marrieds etc., recalculated to give the figures in the final column.

TABLE 3

AGE DIFFERENCE BETWEEN FARMERS AND WIVES

| Age difference between husband and wife | All farmers in this survey who had been married, 1960[1] % | Marriages of farmers' daughters in Llanfihangel, 1890–1940[2] % | Marriages of farmers in Gosforth, 1900–50[3] % | Farmers in a rural area of Devon[4] | |
				1851 %	1960 %
Wives older than husbands	20·0	16·7	19·0	16·8	6·5
Husbands and wives the same age	6·9	12·5	10·8	14·2	21·0
Husbands 1–3 years older than wives	31·0	22·7	32·4	23·1	25·8
Husbands 4–7 years older than wives	22·8	26·1	24·5	25·1	12·9
Husbands 8 or more years older than wives	19·3	22·0	13·5	20·8	25·8
Not known	—	—	—	—	8·0
Total	100·0	100·0	100·2	100·0	100·0

[1] Includes widowers and widows.
[2] A. D. Rees: *Life in a Welsh Countryside*, Cardiff, 1951, p. 179.
[3] W. M. Williams: *The Sociology of an English Village, Gosforth*, London, 1956, p. 49.
[4] W. M. Williams: *A West Country Village, Ashworthy*, London, 1963.

TABLE 4

TYPE OF HOUSEHOLD

Type of household	This Survey 1960		Bethnal Green survey, 1955[1]	Great Britain 1951[1]	Gos-forth[2]	Llanfi-hangel[3]	Farmers in 'Ash-worthy'[4]	
	No.	%	%	%	%	%	No.	%
1. Person on own	12	7	7	3	0	6	4	5
2. Married couple on own	23	14	17	14			19	26
3. Unmarried or widowed siblings	7	4	1	1	9	6	3	4
4. Other one generation	2	1	1	1				
Total one generation	44	26	26	19			26	35
5. Parents with unmarried children	101	59	62	60			43	57
6. Parents with unmarried children plus unmarried siblings of parents	2	1	2	1			2⎱	
7. Other two generations	3	2	4	8			1⎰	4
Total two generation	106	62	68	69			46	61
8. Parents with married child and/or other children	19	11						
9. Married couple and children with parents' siblings	2	1						
Total three generation	21	12	6	12	16	16	3	4
Total all generations	171	100	100	100			75	100

[1] M. Young and P. Wilmott, *Family and Kinship in East London*, London, 1957, p. 211, Table 30.
[2] W. M. Williams, *Sociology of an English Village*, calculated from information p. 52.
[3] A. D. Rees, *Life in a Welsh Countryside*, calculated from information p. 70.
[4] W. M. Williams, *Ashworthy*, calculated from Table 3, Appendix 3.

APPENDIX 4

CALCULATION OF 'EXPECTED' PROPORTIONS OF MALE AND FEMALE CHILDREN IN COMPLETED FAMILIES

THE number of children in each family was known. The range was from 0 to 11. The expected number of families with 0 to 11 males in them was calculated using the binomial expansion with $p = q = \frac{1}{2}$. This is set out in Table 1. From this it was then possible to work out for each 'size of family' group the number of only boy families, only girl families, etc. When these were added up they gave the 'expected' number of families, see Table 2. This expected number was then compared with the actual number of families in these categories using a χ^2 test as set out in Table 13, Chapter III.

TABLE 1

EXPECTED NUMBER OF MALES IN FAMILIES OF DIFFERENT SIZES

Size of family	Actual Number of completed families	Expected number of families with 0 to 11 male children											
		0	1	2	3	4	5	6	7	8	9	10	11
0	7	—											
1	13	6·5	6·5										
2	22	5·5	11·0	5·5									
3	12	1·5	4·5	4·5	1·5								
4	10	0·625	2·5	3·75	2·5	0·625							
5	6	0·1875	0·9375	1·875	1·875	0·9375	0·1875						
6	5	0·0781	0·4687	1·1719	1·5625	1·1719	0·4687	0·0781					
7	2	0·0156	0·1092	0·3276	0·546	0·546	0·3276	0·1092	0·0156				
8	3	0·0117	0·0937	0·3281	0·6562	0·8203	0·6562	0·3281	0·0937	0·0117			
9	1	0·0020	0·0176	0·0703	0·1641	0·2461	0·2461	0·1641	0·0703	0·0176	0·0020		
10	0	—	—	—	—	—	—	—	—	—	—	—	
11	1	0·0005	0·0054	0·0269	0·0806	0·1611	0·2256	0·2256	0·1611	0·0806	0·0269	0·0054	0·0005
Total	75	14·4204	26·1321	17·5498	8·8844	4·5079	2·1117	0·9051	0·3407	0·1099	0·0289	0·0054	0·0005

TABLE 2
EXPECTED NUMBER OF FAMILIES WITH DIFFERENT SEX PROPORTIONS

Size of family	Actual Number of completed families	Only boy	Only girl	Only boys	Only girls	More boys than girls	Same number of boys as girls	More girls than boys
1	13	6·5	6·5	—	—	—	—	—
2	22	—	—	5·5	5·5	—	11·0	—
3	12	—	—	1·5	1·5	4·5	—	4·5
4	10	—	—	0·6250	0·6250	2·5	3·75	2·5
5	6	—	—	0·1875	0·1875	0·9375	—	0·9375
						1·8750		1·8750
6	5	—	—	0·0781	0·0781	0·4687	1·5625	0·4687
						1·1719		1·1719
7	2	—	—	0·0156	0·0156	0·1092	—	0·1092
						0·3276		0·3276
						0·5460		0·5460
8	3	—	—	0·0117	0·0117	0·0937	0·8203	0·0937
						0·3281		0·3281
						0·6562		0·6562
9	1	—	—	0·0020	0·0020	0·0176	—	0·0176
						0·0703		0·0703
						0·1641		0·1641
						0·2461		0·2461
10	0	—	—	—	—	—	—	—
11	1	—	—	0·0005	0·0005	0·0054	—	0·0054
						0·0209		0·0269
						0·0806		0·0806
						0·1611		0·1611
						0·2256		0·2256
Total	75	6·5000	6·5000	7·9204	7·9204	14·5116	17·1328	14·5116

THE MAIN SURVEY QUESTIONNAIRE

Farm details

Obtained for current farm or farms and for any previous farms)

1 Name
2 Parish
3 County
4 Soil type
5 Altitude
6 Situation

7 Acreage:
    a. Total
    b. Crops and grass
    c. Rough grazing
    d. Mowing grass
8 Type of farming
9 Main sale product(s)
10 If dairying, number of dairy cows in
    milk and dry
11 If not dairying, number and type of
    other stock

12 Do you employ any paid labour apart
    from members of your family?
13 If yes, how many?
14 Do any members of your family, or
    other relatives, work on the farm?
15 If yes, who?   1
    (name and   2
    precise   3
    relationship) 4

16 Do you have another job besides
    farming?
17 If yes, *a.* Description
          b. How many hours per week
             worked at it?

18 On what date did you first occupy this
    farm?
19 Are you owner or tenant at present?

20 Have you changed from owner to
       tenant or vice versa during your
       occupation of this farm?
    If yes, date of change
21 Name of landlord when tenanted
22 For previous farms:
    Date of leaving

Farm movement details

(Obtained for current farm or farms and for any previous farms)

1 *a.* Who farmed this farm before you?
       (Full name)
   b. What happened to him?
   c. Present address
   d. Present occupation
2 Was this person related to you in any
     way?
3 If yes, precise relationship
4 Do you know for how long he farmed it?
5 Do you know who farmed it before
     him?
6 *a.* If yes, full name
   b. Present address
   c. Present occupation
   OR
   d. Last known address
   e. Last known occupation
7 Was this person related to you in any
     way?
8 If yes, precise relationship
9 Do you know for how long he farmed it?
10 If last two occupiers have been
       relatives:
    To your knowledge, how long has this
    farm been in your/your wife's family?
11 Do you farm any other farm besides
       this one?
12 Did you farm another farm or farms
       before this?
13 *a.* Have you
        (i) Added to
        (ii) Given up
        land on this farm since you
            came here?

b. Have you
   (i) Added to
   (ii) Given up
land on any other farm you farm?
c. Did you
   (i) Add to
   (ii) Give up
land on any farm you previously
   farmed

If yes to 11 or 12, obtain Farm details, and
Farm Movement details.

Question 13.
If yes to *a, b* or *c,* enter by each item the
acreage gained or lost.

Family Details A

Farm Code No...........

	Farmer	*Wife*	*Previous spouse*

1 Surname or maiden name
2 Christian name
3 Place of birth (full address)
4 Date of birth
5 Age commenced work
6 Marital status
7 If married, date of marriage
8 *a.* Married before
  b. If yes, date of previous marriage
  c. Date of end of previous marriage
9 *a.* Occupation before marriage
  b. Residence before marriage
10 *a.* Residence before commenced
     farming
  b. Occupation before commenced
     farming
11 Alive or dead now
12 If dead, date of death
13 No. of children born alive⎱ M
   in family of origin ⎰ F
14 Family position in family of origin
  a. In all family
  b. In own sex
15 *a.* Father alive or dead
  b. If dead, date of death
  c. Age now or at death

16 *a.* Mother alive or dead
   b. If dead, date of death
   c. Age now or at death
17 Father's occupation now or at death
18 Father's residence now or at death
19 Father's occupation when subject
    commenced farming
20 Father's residence when subject
    commenced farming

Family Details B

	Children	Farmer's Sibs†	Wife's Sibs†	Previous Spouse's Sibs†
Name and Relationship				
Date of Birth				
Place of Birth				
If dead, date of death				
Present or last address				
Age commenced work				
Present or last occupation				
Marital Status				
If Married, date of marriage				
Secondary Education or not				

†Whether working at home
or on farm when brother or
sister commenced farming

APPENDIX 6

STATISTICAL TESTS

Table number or page reference	Test result	Level of significance	Remarks
CHAPTER 2			
p. 23, para. 2	$\chi^2 = 30\cdot82$	0·01	Measured by proportion of rough grazing.
p. 23, line 15	$\chi^2 = 39\cdot12$	0·01	More rough grazing on peat soils.
p. 24, line 7	$\chi^2 = 71\cdot88$	0·01	Test on '1,100 and under' and '1,101 and over'.
Table 1	$\chi^2 = 16\cdot53$	0·01	
Table 2:			
(a) Type of farming	$\chi^2 = 24\cdot04$	0·01	Test on 'high' or 'other' intensity for 'cattle rearing' or 'other' farms.
(b) Size of business	$\chi^2 = 27\cdot59$	0·01	
Table 3	$\chi^2 = 12\cdot38$	0·05	
Table 4:			
(a) Altitude	$\chi^2 = 19\cdot31$	0·01	
(b) Soil type	$\chi^2 = 13\cdot03$	0·01	
Table 6	$\chi^2 = 11\cdot05$	0·01	Test on 'wholly owned' or 'other' for 'under 15 c.e.' or 'others'.
Table 7:			
(a) Altitude	$\chi^2 = 18\cdot41$	0·01	Test on '1,100 and under' and '1,101 and over'.
(b) Size of business	$\chi^2 = 25\cdot09$	0·01	
CHAPTER 3			
Table 9	$\chi^2 = 7\cdot84$	0·05	Age groups '45–54' and '55–64' combined for test.
p. 41, line 3	$\chi^2 = 6\cdot08$	0·05	Null hypothesis: no. of males = no. of females.
Table 11	$\chi^2 = 16\cdot05$	0·05	Null hypothesis: no. of males = no. of females in each age group.
p. 41, line 11	$\chi^2 = 38\cdot44$	0·01	Null hypothesis: same proportion of single females of working age are farmers as for single males. Corrected for continuity.

Table number or page reference	Test result	Level of significance	Remarks
p. 42, lines 1, 2	$\chi^2 = 1.00$	N.S.	Null hypothesis: no difference in numbers of male and female children.
p. 42, line 3	$\chi^2 = 1.00$	N.S.	Null hypothesis: same proportion of male and female children are under and over 30.
Table 12	$\chi^2 = 10.57$	0.05	
p. 45, line 9	$\chi^2 = 44.86$	0.01	
Table 14:			
(a) Age 25 and under	$\chi^2 = 34.51$	0.01	
(b) Age 26–30	$\chi^2 = 7.90$	0.01	
(c) Age over 30	$\chi^2 = 4.88$	0.05	
Table 15	$\chi^2 = 15.40$	0.01	
p. 47, line 18	$\chi^2 = 30.85$	0.01	
p. 48, para. 2	$\chi^2 = 8.80$	0.10	
Table 17	$\chi^2 = 29.15$	0.01	Test on 'dairying' or 'not-dairying' for 'low land resources' or 'others'.
p. 49, lines 5–8	$\chi^2 = 0.22$	N.S.	
p. 49, lines 9, 10	$\chi^2 = 35.95$	0.01	'Medium' and 'high' c.e.'s per household member combined for test.
Table 18	$\chi^2 = 20.15$	0.01	
Table 19	$\chi^2 = 14.56$	0.01	
Table 20	$\chi^2 = 35.77$	0.01	
p. 51, lines 1–3	$\chi^2 = 32.76$	0.01	
p. 51, lines 15, 16	$\chi^2 = 45.56$	0.01	
Table 21	$\chi^2 = 5.14$	0.05	
Table 22	$\chi^2 = 45.93$	0.01	
p. 55, line 19	$\chi^2 = 3.49$	0.10	
Table 23	$\chi^2 = 3.24$	0.10	
Table 24	$\chi^2 = 7.10$	0.01	
p. 56, para. 2	$\chi^2 = 4.16$	0.05	
Table 25	$\chi^2 = 5.98$	0.05	Corrected for continuity.
Table 26	$\chi^2 = 9.02$	0.05	
Table 27			
Household size	$\chi^2 = 27.21$	0.01	
Farm size	$\chi^2 = 4.07$	0.05	
Farmer type	$\chi^2 = 3.52$	0.10	
Living conditions	$\chi^2 = 13.11$	0.01	Test on 'single' or 'married' for 'good' or 'other' living conditions.

Table number or page reference	Test result	Level of significance	Remarks
CHAPTER 4			
Table 28	$\chi^2 = 16.88$	0.01	Test on movement from non-family-connected farms or from family-connected farms. Corrected for continuity.
p. 67, lines 3–5:			
(a)	$\chi^2 = 6.54$	0.05	Tests of tables on which the statement is based but tables not presented in text.
(b)	$\chi^2 = 9.05$	0.10	
(c)	$\chi^2 = 4.10$	0.05	
(d)	$\chi^2 = 19.38$	0.01	
Table 33:			
(a) single and married farmers compared	$\chi^2 = 3.58$	0.10	Test on whether living over or under 2½ miles from birthplace.
(b) Farmers and wives compared	$\chi^2 = 5.33$	0.05	Test on whether living over or under 5 miles from birthplace.
p. 71, lines 20, 21 p. 72, line 1:			
(a) Farmers	$\chi^2 = 11.43$	0.01	Movement to work compared with residential movement.
(b) Farmers' wives	$\chi^2 = 4.88$	0.05	
Table 34	$\chi^2 = 4.09$	0.05	Test on 'single' or 'married' farmers who had moved 'in or out' of the area or 'not moved'.
Table 35	$\chi^2 = 4.58$	0.05	Test on 'single' or 'married' farmers who had worked 'over 2½ miles away' or 'under 2½ miles only'.
p. 73, lines 1, 2	$\chi^2 = 4.26$	0.05	
Table 37:			
(a) Farmers	$\chi^2 = 69.09$	0.01	Test on movement uphill of those whose parents lived elsewhere compared with those whose parents lived in the area.
(b) Farmers' wives	$\chi^2 = 30.93$	0.01	
p. 76, lines 8, 9	$\chi^2 = 3.61$	0.10	Test on change in altitude of single or married farmers. Corrected for continuity.
p. 77, lines 2, 3	$\chi^2 = 4.64$	0.10	Test on changes in altitude of farmers or wives.
p. 78, line 15	$\chi^2 = 7.50$	0.01	
p. 78, line 16	$\chi^2 = 7.80$	0.05	
p. 78, lines 18–21	$\chi^2 = 7.04$	0.01	

Table number or page reference	Test result	Level of significance	Remarks
p. 78, lines 34, 35	$\chi^2 = 12 \cdot 62$	0·01	Married male and female children compared.
p. 80, lines 16, 17	$\chi^2 = 66 \cdot 33$	0·01	All single children and all married children compared.
p. 81, footnote 1	S.E. $= 0 \cdot 038$ Diff. $= 0 \cdot 12$	0·01	
p. 84, lines 12, 13	S.E. $= 0 \cdot 044$ Diff. $= 0 \cdot 19$	0·01	More daughters working off the farms than mothers had done.
p. 84, lines 26, 27	$\chi^2 = 0 \cdot 08$	N.S.	Data from Table 46.
Table 47	$\chi^2 = 5 \cdot 43$	0·05	Single sons and single daughters doing farm or other work.
Tables 46 and 47	$\chi^2 = 4 \cdot 67$	0·05	Single and married sons doing farm or other work.
CHAPTER 5			
p. 90, lines 15–17	$\chi^2 = 3 \cdot 94$	0·05	'Larger-business' farmers compared with 'other' farmers.
p. 91, line 20	$\chi^2 = 25 \cdot 56$	0·01	'Other-work' farmers compared with 'other farmers'.
p. 91, lines 22–4	$\chi^2 = 2 \cdot 34$	N.S.	'Other-work' farmers compared with 'other' farmers for all those whose fathers were farmers.
p. 91, lines 28–31	$\chi^2 = 3 \cdot 56$	0·10	Based on table not presented in text.
Table 49	$\chi^2 = 4 \cdot 16$	0·05	'upward' and 'downward' social mobility compared.
Table 50	$\chi^2 = 16 \cdot 05$	0·01	
Table 51	$\chi^2 = 4 \cdot 56$	0·05	'Family-earning' farmers compared with 'other full-time' farmers.
Table 52	$\chi^2 = 37 \cdot 75$	0·01	
CHAPTER 6			
p. 102, lines 4, 5	$\chi^2 = 11 \cdot 68$	0·01	Based on table not presented in text.
Table 53	$\chi^2 = 25 \cdot 96$	0·01	
p. 105, lines 11–16	$\chi^2 = 4 \cdot 11$	0·05	'Full-time' and 'dual business' farmers starting on medium farms increased their business size proportionately more than did 'family-earning' and 'other-work' farmers starting on small farms. Corrected for continuity.

Table number or page reference	Test result	Level of significance	Remarks
p. 105, lines 23, 24	$\chi^2 = 3.82$	0.10	'Full-time' and 'dual-business' farmers who had changed farms had increased their business size proportionately more than had 'family-earning and other-work' farmers who changed farms. Corrected for continuity.
p. 105, lines 25, 26 and p. 106, line 1	$\chi^2 = 13.64$	0.01	Moving farms had been a more effective way of increasing business size for those who started on small farms than had amalgamation.
p. 108, lines 14–16	$\chi^2 = 10.04$	0.01	
p. 109, lines 20–22	$\chi^2 = 6.59$	0.05	
p. 109, lines 23–24	$\chi^2 = 4.13$	0.05	
p. 109, lines 24, 25	$\chi^2 = 10.66$	0.05	Increase in proportion of incomers with increase in altitude.
p. 109, line 25	$\chi^2 = 20.15$	0.01	Higher proportion of incomers work off farms.
Table 57	$\chi^2 = 55.54$	0.01	Test of numbers on which percentages based.
Table 58	$\chi^2 = 11.05$	0.01	
Table 59	$\chi^2 = 9.80$	0.05	Test of numbers on which percentages based.
Table 60A	$\chi^2 = 16.29$	0.01	Tenants and owner-occupiers compared.
Table 60B	$\chi^2 = 27.12$	0.01	'Other' reasons and 'death or retirement' as reasons for leaving farms.
Table 60B	$\chi^2 = 9.24$	0.01	'Tenants leaving multiple-change farms', and 'other farmers' compared on whether reason for leaving was to move to another farm or not. Both tests of 60B based on numbers from which percentages calculated.
p. 115, lines 9, 10	$\chi^2 = 2.97$	0.10	'Locals' and 'incomers' compared on occupation lengths of '10 years and under' or '11–20 years'.

Table number or page reference	Test result	Level of significance	Remarks
p. 115, lines 11, 12	$\chi^2 = 8 \cdot 40$	0·05	
p. 115, lines 41, 42	$\chi^2 = 4 \cdot 84$	0·05	Corrected for continuity.
p. 116, lines 6–8	$\chi^2 = 2 \cdot 72$	0·10	
Table 61	$\chi^2 = 18 \cdot 28$	0·01	
Table 62	$\chi^2 = 11 \cdot 42$	0·01	Married 'other work' and 'dual-business' farmers compared with all other married farmers.
CHAPTER 7			
p. 120, lines 9–14	$\chi^2 = 6 \cdot 35$	0·05	Higher proportion full-time farmers took over farm of full-time farming parents than part-time farmers took over farm of part-time farming parents.
Table 64	$\chi^2 = 28 \cdot 43$	0·01	Test on 'full-time farming fathers' and 'other farming fathers' and whether the farmer had worked at home or not.
Table 65	$\chi^2 = 13 \cdot 57$	0·01	
p. 126, lines 4–6	$\chi^2 = 8 \cdot 67$	0·05	Based on table not presented in text.
Table 66	$\chi^2 = 13 \cdot 37$	0·01	
p. 127, lines 12–18	$\chi^2 = 9 \cdot 49$	0·01	
Table 67	$\chi^2 = 6 \cdot 23$	0·05	Corrected for continuity.
Table 68B	$\chi^2 = 22 \cdot 10$	0·01	
p. 131, lines 21–25	$\chi^2 = 12 \cdot 63$	0·01	
p. 131, lines 33–35	$\chi^2 = 7 \cdot 01$	0·01	Based on table not presented in text.
p. 131, lines 36–38	$\chi^2 = 16 \cdot 37$	0·01	Based on table not presented in text.
p. 131, line 39 and p. 133, lines 1–5	$\chi^2 = 3 \cdot 85$	0·05	'Large-business' and 'dual-business' farmers compared with other farmers.
CHAPTER 8			
p. 136, para. 3	$\chi^2 = 19 \cdot 82$	0·01	Higher proportion sons work at home on full-time farms.
p. 138, lines 24–6	$\chi^2 = 8 \cdot 43$	0·01	
p. 138, lines 34–6	$\chi^2 = 8 \cdot 60$	0·01	Hypothesis that daughters of 'other' farmers had taken professional and office jobs in different proportions to daughters of 'full-time' and 'dual-business' farmers.

Table number or page reference	Test result	Level of significance	Remarks
p. 140, lines 19–24	$\chi^2 = 16 \cdot 14$	0·01	
Table 71	$\chi^2 = 8 \cdot 24$	0·01 ⎫	'Family-earning' and 'other-work' farmers compared with 'dual-business' and 'other full-time' farmers. Corrected for continuity.
Table 72	$\chi^2 = 23 \cdot 45$	0·01 ⎬	
Table 73	$\chi^2 = 5 \cdot 95$	0·05	Corrected for continuity.
Table 74	$\chi^2 = 10 \cdot 10$	0·01	
Table 75	$\chi^2 = 20 \cdot 54$	0·01	Corrected for continuity.
Table 76	$\chi^2 = 16 \cdot 90$	0·01	Corrected for continuity.
p. 142, lines 14–16	$\chi^2 = 28 \cdot 02$	0·01	Null hypothesis: same proportion of husbands of married daughters as of married sons employed in agriculture now. (For sons and daughters who did not work at home prior to marriage.)
Table 77	Critical ratio 1·724, degrees of freedom = 62	0·10	Test for differences in average family sizes between, 'family-earning farmers' and 'dual-business', 'small-business' and 'larger business' farmers.
CHAPTER 9			
Table 80	$\chi^2 = 4 \cdot 67$	0·05	Corrected for continuity.
Table 81	$\chi^2 = 7 \cdot 84$	0·05	
Table 82A	$\chi^2 = 8 \cdot 63$	0·01	
Table 82B	$\chi^2 = 8 \cdot 01$	0·05	
Table 83A	$\chi^2 = 0 \cdot 85$	N.S.	Hypothesis: greater proportion of sons working off the farm from families of five and over than from families of four or less.
Table 83B	$\chi^2 = 8 \cdot 76$	0·05	
p. 162, lines 7, 8	$\chi^2 = 6 \cdot 08$	0·05	
Table 84	$\chi^2 = 24 \cdot 63$	0·01	Single farmers and farmers with a wife nine years or more younger than themselves more often succeeded to farms at late ages than did married farmers with wives of other ages.
Table 85	$\chi^2 = 3 \cdot 16$	0·10	
Table 86	$\chi^2 = 11 \cdot 48$	0·01	
Table 88	$\chi^2 = 6 \cdot 70$	0·01	Corrected for continuity.

Table number or page reference	Test result	Level of significance	Remarks
Table 89	$\chi^2 = 7\cdot52$	0·01	
Table 90	$\chi^2 = 15\cdot42$	0·01	Test on whether commenced farming some time after marriage or whether commenced at or before marriage.
Table 91	$\chi^2 = 11\cdot30$	0·01	
Table 92	$\chi^2 = 0\cdot52$	N.S.	
Table 94	$\chi^2 = 12\cdot04$	0·01	
CHAPTER 10			
p. 176, lines 24–7	$\chi^2 = 0\cdot71$	N.S.	
p. 178, para. 2	$\chi^2 = 12\cdot96$	0·01	Smaller proportion farm boys than farm girls in 'A' classes.
p. 178, para. 2	$\chi^2 = 3\cdot99$	0·05	Smaller proportion non-farm boys than non-farm girls in 'A' classes.
Table 96	$\chi^2 = 22\cdot68$	0·01	Test on whether expect to do farm work or other work (boys and girls). Corrected for continuity.
Table 97	$\chi^2 = 18\cdot34$	0·01	Test on whether would like to live in town or country. (Boys and girls.)
Table 98B	$\chi^2 = 12\cdot42$	0·01 ⎫	One or both parents employed in other work compared with both employed in farm work. Corrected for continuity.
Table 99A	$\chi^2 = 8\cdot24$	0·01 ⎭	
Table 99B	$\chi^2 = 2\cdot27$	N.S.	One or both parents employed in farm work compared with both employed in other work.
p. 186, lines 8–10	$\chi^2 = 6\cdot16$	0·05	
Table 100B	$\chi^2 = 5\cdot99$	0·05	
Table 101	$\chi^2 = 5\cdot21$	0·05	Corrected for continuity.
Table 102	$\chi^2 = 4\cdot61$	0·05	
Table 103A	$\chi^2 = 1\cdot22$	N.S.	
Table 103B	$\chi^2 = 12\cdot62$	0·01	
Table 104B	$\chi^2 = 4\cdot94$	0·05	
Table 105	$\chi^2 = 7\cdot62$	0·05	
p. 192, lines 11, 12	$\chi^2 = 13\cdot27$	0·01	Higher proportion dual business farmers were eldest sons.
Table 106	$\chi^2 = 67\cdot26$	0·01	Periods of occupation of second farms tend to be longer than periods of occupation of first farms.
Table 107	$\chi^2 = 5\cdot91$	0·05	Corrected for continuity.

BIBLIOGRAPHY

ABELL, HELEN C. *The Exchange of Farming Information*, Canadian Department of Agriculture, August 1953.

ACKERMAN, J., and M. HARRIS (editors) *Family Farm Policy*, University of Chicago Press, Chicago, 1947.

ALLEN, O. E. 'Some causes of the disparity between farm and non-farm income per head—a comment', *The Farm Economist*, Vol. VII, Nos. 9 and 10, 1954.

ANDERSON, W. A. *The Transmission of Farming as an Occupation*, Cornell University, A.E.S., Bull. 768, Ithaca, New York, October 1941.

ARENSBERG, C. D. *The Irish Countryman*, Peter Smith, Gloucester, Mass., 1935.

ASHBY, A. W. 'The farmer in business', *Journal Proc. Agricultural Economics Society*, Vol. X, No. 2, February 1953.

ASHBY, A. W., and J. LLEFELYS DAVIES 'The agricultural ladder and the age of farmers', *Welsh Journal of Agriculture*, Vol. 6, 1930.

ASHBY, A. W., and J. MORGAN JONES 'The social origin of Welsh farmers', *Welsh Journal of Agriculture*, Vol. 2, 1926.

ASHTON, J. *The Social Origin of Farmers*, Agricultural Research Institute, Oxford, 1950, unpublished B.Litt. thesis.

ASHTON, J., and B. E. CRACKNELL 'Agricultural holdings and farm business structure in England and Wales', *Journal Agricultural Economics Society*, Vol. XIV, No. 4, July 1961.

BARNES, J. A. 'Class and committees in a Norwegian island parish', *Human Relations*, Vol. VII, No. 1, February 1954.

BEEGLE, J. A., and D. HALSTEAD *Michigan's Changing Population*, Special Bulletin 415, Michigan State University, 1957.

BEHAN, DOMINIC *Teems of Times and Happy Returns*, Heinemann, London, 1961.

BELLERBY, J. R. 'Some causes of the disparity between farm and non-farm income per head', *The Farm Economist*, Vol. VII, No. 8, 1954.

—— *Agriculture and Industry Relative Income*, McMillan, London, 1956.

—— 'The distribution of manpower in agriculture and industry 1851–1951', *The Farm Economist*, Vol. IX, No. 1, 1958.

BRITTON, D. K. 'Are holdings becoming larger or smaller?', *The Farm Economist*, Vol. VI, No. 7, 1950.

—— 'Agriculture in the European Economic Community', *Journal of Agricultural Economics*, Vol. XIII, No. 2, 1958.

BROOM, L., F. LANCASTER JONES, and J. ZUBRZYCKI *Five Measures of Social Rank in Australia* (A preliminary report). Paper to Sixth World Congress of Sociology, Evian, 1966.

BUTLER, J. B. *The Small Farms of Industrial Yorkshire*, Part 2, University of Leeds, Economics Section, Department of Agriculture, October 1958.

CAMBELL, K. O. 'Rural population movements in relation to economic development', *Tenth International Conference of Agricultural Economists*. Proceedings, Oxford University Press, London, 1960.

CARPENTER, E. M. 'The Small Farmer', *Journal of Agricultural Economics*, Vol. XIII, No. 1, June 1958.

CHAPMAN, D., and others *Agricultural Information and the Farmer*, The Social Survey, Central Office of Information, London, May 1944.

CLARK, COLIN *The Conditions of Economic Progress*, McMillan & Co., London, 1940.

CONSTANDSE, A. K. 'Planning in agricultural regions', *Sociologia Ruralis*, Vol. II, No. 1/2, 1962.

COWIE, W. G., and A. K. GILES *An Enquiry into Reasons for the Drift from the Land*, Selected Papers in Agricultural Economics, University of Bristol, 1957.

CUNNINGHAM, J. B., and M. C. M. CASE *Father-son Farm Business Agreements*, Circular 587, University of Illinois, College of Agriculture, December 1944.

DAVIS, ALLISON 'Personality and social mobility', *The School Review*, Vol. 65, 1957.

DENNIS, M. A. Private communications, Agricultural Land Service.

FALDING, H. *Precept and Practice on North Coast Dairy Farms*, University of Sydney, Department of Agricultural Economics, Research Bull. No. 2, 1958.

FLETCHER, T. W. 'Lancashire livestock farming during the Great Depression', *Agricultural History Review*, Vol. IX, Part 1, 1961.

—— 'The Great Depression of English Agriculture 1873–1896', *The Economic History Review*, Second Series, Vol. XXII, No. 3, 1961.

FRANKENBURG, R. *Village on the Border*, Cohen and West, London, 1957.

—— *Communities in Britain*, Penguin, Harmondsworth, 1966.

FREEMAN, T. W. Private communication, Manchester University.

FURNESS, G. W. *The Economics of Small Farms in the North West of England*, unpublished M.Sc. thesis, University of Leeds, 1959.

GALBRAITH, J. K. 'Inequality in agriculture. Problem and programme', First Morrison Memorial Lecture, Guelph, 1956.

GALLOWAY, R. E. *Part-Time Farming in Eastern Kentucky*, Bull. 646, Kentucky, A.E.S., June 1956.

GLASS, D. V. (editor) *Social Mobility in Britain*, Routledge and Kegan Paul, London, 1954.

GLASS, D. V., and E. GREBENIK *The Trend and Pattern of Fertility in Great Britain*, Papers of the Royal Commission on Population, Vol. VI, Part 1. H.M.S.O., London, 1954.

—— *The Trend and Pattern of Fertility in Great Britain*, Part II, Tables, Papers of the Royal Commission on Population, Vol. VI, H.M.S.O., London, 1954.

GRANGE, J. *A study of school-leavers in a Lancashire town*, unpublished research, Manchester University, Department of Social Anthropology and Sociology, 1962.

HAGERSTRAND, T. 'A century of migration to and from a rural parish in Sweden', *Rural Migration*, Report of First Congress of European Society for Rural Sociology, Bonn, 1959.

HEADY, E. O. 'Progress in adjusting agriculture to economic change', *Journal of Farm Economics*, Vol. XXXIX, No. 5, December 1957.

HEADY, E. O., W. B. BALK and G. A. PETERSON *Interdependence between the Farm Business and the Farm Household with Implications on Economic Efficiency*, Iowa State College, A.E.S. Research Bull. 398, June 1953.

HENDRY, G. F. 'Labour in Scottish agriculture', *Journal of Agricultural Economics*, Vol. XI, No. 4, January 1956.

HIRSCH, G. P. 'Manpower on British farms', *Changing Patterns of Rural Organization*, Second Congress European Society for Rural Sociology, Oslo, 1961.

JOHNSON, GLEN 'Some basic problems for economists and statisticians arising from U.S. agricultural policies', *Paper to Manchester Statistical Society*, 11 November 1959.

KRIER, H. (Rapporteur) *Rural Manpower and Industrial Development*, O.E.E.C., Paris, August 1961.

KUHNEN, F. 'Die Vertreitung Nicht landwirtschaftlicher Einkünfte bei landbewirtschaftenden Familien in der Bundesrepublick Deutschland', *Changing Patterns of Rural Organization*, Second Congress European Society for Rural Sociology, Oslo, 1961.

KUZNETS, SIMON 'Quantitative aspects of the economic growth of nations. Industrial distribution of national product and labour force', *Economic Development and Cultural Change*, Vol. 5, No. 4, July 1957, Supplement.

LAZARSFELD, P. F. 'Jugend und Beruf', *Quellen und Studien sur Jugendkunde*, Vol. 8, G. Fischer, Jena, 1931.

LEWIS, W. A. 'Economic development with unlimited supplies of labour', *Manchester School of Economic and Social Studies*, Vol. XXII, No. 2, May 1954.

LIJFERING, J. H. W. 'Changes in rural occupational structure and labour organization', *Changing Patterns of Rural Organization*. Second Congress of European Society for Rural Sociology, Oslo, 1961.

LIPSET, S. M., and R. BENDIX *Social Mobility in Industrial Society*, Heinemann, London, 1959.

LITTLEJOHN, J. *Westrigg*, Routledge and Kegan Paul, London, 1964.

LOOMIS, RALPH A., DEAN I. McKEE and JAMES T. BONNEN 'The role of part-time farming in agricultural adjustment in South Michigan', *Quart. Bull. Michigan Agricultural Experimental Station* (East Lansing, Michigan), Vol. 44, May 1962.

LOOMIS, RALPH A., and M. E. WIRTH 'Financial progress on Michigan farms—a contrast between part-time and full-time farming', *Quart. Bull. Michigan Agricultural Experimental Station* (East Lansing, Michigan), Vol. 44, May 1962.

U

LORRAIN-SMITH, E. *Go East for a Farm*, Agricultural Economics Research Institute, Oxford, 1932.

MARIS, A. 'The efflux of labour from agriculture in Europe', *Rural Migration*, Report of First Congress of European Society for Rural Sociology, Bonn, 1959.

——— 'The family farm and problems of succession and changing manpower', *Problems of Mobility of Agricultural Manpower in Relation to Economic Growth*. E.P.A. Project 7/14–11, O.E.C.D., Paris, July 1962 (Restricted).

MARIS, A., and M. A. J. VAN DE SANDT 'Trends in the changing occupational structure of rural areas with special reference to manpower on farms', *Changing Patterns of Rural Organizations*, Second Congress European Society for Rural Sociology, Oslo, 1961.

MARKS, M. Unpublished paper, Department of Agricultural Economics, Manchester University, 1961.

MOGEY, J. W. *Rural Life in Northern Ireland*, Oxford University Press, London, 1947.

MOLLETT, J. A. 'The size of farm staffs in England and Wales in 1851 and 1951', *The Farm Economist*, Vol. VI, No. 6, 1950.

NALSON, J. S. *Incentive Payments to Workers in Agriculture*, unpublished post-graduate thesis, Department of Agriculture, University of Leeds, 1950.

O'CONNOR, J., and G. P. WIBBERLEY 'Social problems in the development of livestock rearing areas', *Agriculture*, Vol. 59, 1953.

PARRISH, ROSS 'Innovation and enterprise in wheat farming', *Review of Marketing and Agricultural Economics*, N.S.W., Vol. XXII, No. 3, Sept. 1954.

POND, G. A., W. W. WILCOX and A. BOSS *Relation of Variations in the Human Factor to Financial Returns in Farming*, University of Minnesota, A.E.S. Bull. 288, June 1932.

RAVENSTEIN, E. G. 'The laws of migration', *Journal of the Royal Statistical Society*, Vol. XLVIII, June 1885.

REDFORD, A. *Labour Migration in England, 1800–1850*, Manchester University Press, Manchester, 1926.

REES, A. D. *Life in a Welsh Countryside*, University of Wales Press, Cardiff, 1951.

REIMANN, F. 'The Changing Structure and Function of Rural Communities' (G. P. Wibberley, rapporteur), *Changing Patterns of Rural Organization*, Second Congress European Society for Rural Sociology, Oslo, 1961.

SAVILLE, J. *Rural Depopulation in England and Wales 1851 to 1951*, Routledge and Kegan Paul, London, 1957.

SCHULTZ, T. W. 'The role of government in promoting economic growth', *The State of the Social Sciences*, University of Chicago Press, Chicago, 1956.

——— *The Economic Organization of Agriculture*, McGraw Hill, New York, 1953.

SCOLA, P. M. 'Problems of farm classification', *Journal of Agricultural Economics Society*, Vol. X, No. 1, June 1952.

SHEPPARD, D. *A Survey Amongst Grassland Farmers*, The Social Survey, C.O.I., London, 1960.

SHUTE, NEVILLE *A Town Like Alice*, Heinemann, London, 1950.

SMITH LOUIS, P. F. 'Studies in a declining population', *Rural Migration*, Report of First Congress of European Society for Rural Sociology, Bonn, 1959.

THOMAS, E., and C. E. ELMS, *The Farms and Estates of Buckinghamshire*, Survey Studies 4, Part 1, Bulletin LI, Agricultural Economics Department, University of Reading, 1938.

THOMAS, W. J. 'Swedish agricultural policy since the War', *Agricultural Review*, Vol. III, No. 11, April 1958.

—— 'Post-war agricultural policy in the United Kingdom'. *Paper to Manchester Statistical Society*, 10 December 1958.

THOMAS, W. J., and W. RICHARDSON Unpublished report on a problem farming area in the Pennines, Manchester University, Department of Agricultural Economics, 1961.

TRELOAR, D. W., and I. G. MORISON *Economic Comparisons of Forestry and Agriculture*. Agricultural Economics Research Report No. 3, Institute of Agriculture, University of Western Australia, 1962.

WARLEY, T. K. 'On keeping up with the non-farming Joneses', *Farm Management Notes*, Nos. 23 and 24, University of Nottingham, Department of Agricultural Economics, 1960.

WATSON, W. *Tribal Cohesion in a Money Economy*, Manchester University Press, Manchester, 1958.

WATSON, W., and M. SUSSER *Sociology in Medicine*, Oxford University Press, London, 1963.

WIBBERLEY, G. P. 'Principles of land planning in relation to rural development', *Journal of the Proceedings Agricultural Economics Society*, Vol. VIII, No. 3, June 1949.

—— *Agriculture and Urban Growth*, Michael Joseph, London, 1959.

—— 'Some aspects of problem rural areas in Britain', *Geographic Journal*, Vol. CXX, part 1, 1954.

—— 'The changing structure and function of rural communities,' *Changing Patterns of Rural Organization*, Second Congress European Society for Rural Sociology, Oslo, 1961.

WILLIAMS, W. M. *The Sociology of an English Village, Gosforth*, Routledge and Kegan Paul, London, 1956.

—— *The Country Craftsman*, Routledge and Kegan Paul, London, 1958.

—— *A West Country Village: Ashworthy, Family Kinship and Land*, Routledge and Kegan Paul, 1963.

WYNNE, A. J., and E. WRIGHT *The Small Farms of Industrial Yorkshire*, Part 3, University of Leeds, Economics Section, Department of Agriculture, October 1958.

YOUNG, E. C. *The Movement of Farm Population*, Cornell University, A.E.S. Bull. 426, Ithaca, New York, March 1924.

YOUNG, M., and P. WILMOTT *Family and Kinship in East London*, Routledge and Kegan Paul, London, 1957.

Agricultural Year Book of the United States, 1923.

An Economic Survey of Agriculture in the Eastern Counties of England, 1932. University of Cambridge, Farm Economics Branch Report No. 22.

Census 1951 England and Wales, General Tables, H.M.S.O., London.

Census 1951 England and Wales Industry Tables, Table A, H.M.S.O., London.

Commission on Emigration and Other Population Problems, Reports, Dublin, 1954.

Family and Larger-than-Family Farms, Agricultural Economic Report No. 4, U.S.D.A. Farm Economics Division, January 1962.

Mid Wales Investigation Report, Cmd. 9631, H.M.S.O., London, 1955.

Monthly Agricultural Report, Northern Ireland Ministry of Agriculture, Vol. 33, No. 5, September 1958 and Vol. 34, No. 1, May 1959.

National Farm Survey of England and Wales, Summary report, H.M.S.O., London, 1946.

Scale of Enterprise in Farming, National Resources (Technical) Sub-Committee, H.M.S.O., London, 1961.

Social Implications of the 1947 Scottish Mental Survey, University of London Press, 1953.

Statistical Abstract of United States 1960, U.S. Bureau of Census, Washington, D.C., 1960 (Eighty-first Edition).

The Problem of the Small Farm Business, Ministry of Agriculture, Fisheries and Food, December 1956. Limited circulation.

The Small Family Farm—A European Problem, Methods for Creating Economically Viable Units, O.E.C.D., Paris, 1959.

The Trend of Scottish Intelligence, University of London Press, 1949.

INDEX

293